Two Forks, Two Spoons

The Legendary Love Story
of Mr. & Mrs. Wonderful

Copyright © 2025 by Deborah Cross Antoine

All rights reserved.

No part of this publication may be reproduced, distributed, or transmitted in any form or by any means, including photocopying, recording, or other electronic or mechanical methods, without the prior written permission of the publisher, except as permitted by U.S. copyright law. For permission requests, contact Deborah Cross Antoine at twoforkstwospoons@gmail.com.

ISBN: 979-8-9919061-2-8 (Color Paperback)

First color paperback edition 2025

TwoForksTwoSpoons.com

This book was written in loving memory of all who have come before us, and is dedicated to all the children, grandchildren, great-grandchildren, and future generations to descend from the loving lineage of Irving and Alzada Cross.

Table of Contents

FOREWORD 7

PART I | The Crazy Crosses of Little Neck Island

Part I Introduction	13	Nana Susan	53
Alzada + Irving	15	Grandpa & Grandma Cross	57
Wedding Surprise	17	Big Mamie	61
Small Houses, Big Families ...	19	Dadisms	63
Domestic Partnership	25	Going to Butler	67
Crossketeer Roll Call	29	The Cross Family Singers	71
Anything Motorized	33	Haves & Have Nots	73
Anything That Floats	37	Tighty-Whities	77
Olympic Trials	39	Marooned Motorcycle Rescue ...	79
Rope Tows & Rapids	43	Thanksgiving with the Crosses ...	81
An Accidental Career	45	Christmas with the Crosses	87
Don't Tell Your Mother	47	Crazy-Wonderful Crosses	93

PART II | Alzada's Weird but Wonderful Childhood

Part II Introduction	97	Alzada's Solo Debut	149
Conflagration	99	The World's Fair	153
Alzada's Mother Susan	103	The Boarder	155
Alzada's Father Louis	109	Lipstick	157
Alzada's Brother Frank	119	You Can Call Me Albatross	161
Alzada's Brother William	123	Class of 1944	165
The Family Business	127	Secret Smokers	169
Island Park	129	Alzada's BFF Betty	171
Banana Curls	133	Letters Home	175
The Prim & Proper Giffords ...	137	A Broken Engagement	179
The Fun & Fearless Weavers ...	145		

PART III | Irving's Not So Wonderful Childhood

Part III Introduction	183	Irving's Sister Irene	205
Irving's Boyhood	187	Irving's Sister Joan	209
Irving's Father Cecil	189	Private Cross	215
Irving's Mother Alice	195	Irving's Uncle Red	219

PART IV | Alzada the Wonderful's Ancestors

Part IV Introduction 225	Bristol Counties 253
Nonconformists 227	The Parents of Alzada the Great 259
The Mayflower 231	Alzada the Great 261
Giving Thanks 235	A Brutal Outrage 263
The Gifford Line 239	The Children of Alzada the Great 267
The Weaver Line 241	Ebb & Flow 271
The Coggeshall Connection 245	Spindles & Spinsters 275
The Brailey Line 249	

PART V | Irving the Wonderful's Ancestors

Part V Introduction 283	The Specters of Angelina 325
Workshop of the World 287	A Gathering of Spirits 331
The Parents of Angelina the Great 291	A Trip to England 335
Angelina the Great 295	Irving's Irish Ancestors 339
The Parents of Thomas the Great . . . 299	Reverend Cross 343
Graduate of the Cotton Mills 303	Following Footsteps 349
The Progressive Crosses of Rishton 307	Nettie the Great 355
The Spiritualist Crosses of Rishton 313	Death is Nothing at All 359
The Crosses Cross the Atlantic 319	

PART VI | The Happily Ever After

Part VI Introduction 365	September 11th 395
Irving's Affirmations 367	Mr. Wonderful 401
Grandpa & Grammy Wonderful . . . 371	Father's Day 405
A Wonderful Retirement 375	L'Chaim! 407
Sir, You're Having a Heart Attack . . 383	The Golden Years 411
1994 387	Lasts & Firsts 417
Fifty Wonderful Years 391	

PART VII | A Wonderful Legacy

Part VII Introduction 423	Dave the Musician 443
Steve the Storyteller 427	Brian the Brain 447
Deborah the Executive 431	Dana the Individualist 451
Pam the Nurturer 439	The Ancestral Symphony 455

AFTERWORD 457   **INDEX** 461

Foreword

MY FAMILY LOVES a good story, especially the ones featuring us, so I think it best to begin with a short and sweet version of the tale that started it all:

Once upon a time, there was a wonderful young couple who had only two forks, two spoons, and one another. They raised six wonderful children in their cozy little house, which was always bursting with laughter and love, and, of course, they all lived happily ever after.

The love story of my parents, Irving and Alzada Cross, reads like a fairytale because that is precisely what it was – a magical, beautiful, daydreamy kind of love that most people can only wish for, let alone sustain for a lifetime. When they were married on February 17, 1950, in Fall River, Massachusetts, all Irving and Alzada owned was a quirky little serving set made up of mismatched amusement park prizes, including two forks and two spoons. And that was enough.

My five siblings and I were beyond fortunate, and our parents showered us with an abundance of love, enriching our lives with the rare currencies of unconditional acceptance, trust, encouragement, and support. Their legendary love has proved to be a kind of generational wealth, a legacy that lives on in their many adoring descendants, extended family, friends, neighbors, colleagues, and even strangers just lucky enough to have met Irving and Alzada. To this day they are known to us all as Mr. & Mrs. Wonderful.

Despite their own not-so-wonderful childhoods, Irving and Alzada already had what mattered most when they first met – a profound love for each other and the shared dream of creating a big, happy family. And that's exactly what they did.

Irving passed away on Father's Day in 2008, just hours after he and Alzada met their twin great-grandchildren, Leila and Meriem. We felt this loss profoundly, but his physical departure became the spark that ignited my curiosity and inspired me to write this family memoir.

In mourning my father, I yearned to know more about what shaped his life and my mother's. I regretted not asking him more questions while he was alive, and my interest in knowing more about both sides of my family history became a passion.

Who are we? Who came before us? What were they like? How did they live? Who did they love, and who loved them?

When my siblings and I were growing up, the focus was always on the here and now; we certainly didn't worry about the future, and we heard very few details about the past. It was just all about us, the craziness of a big, happy, always busy family, and the shared adventures – mostly funny and offbeat – that defined our lives.

But I had questions, and I needed answers, and the more answers I got, the more questions I had. With just names and dates to go on, I had naively first imagined my ancestors, particularly the women, as quaint, bland, passive caricatures living simple lives in old-timey dresses.

Instead, I unearthed painful buried secrets and tapped a well of tears for all those who died unloved, before their time, or miserable, for one tragic reason or another. I never expected to find so much anguish pulsing through the roots and branches of my family tree, just as I would have never imagined myself attending a séance to attempt communication with my long-gone great-grandmothers.

I felt connected to these people I had never met. They were a part of me, and as I dug deeper into the past, I realized that the lives and experiences of all the people that came before us have brought us to where we are today.

My genealogical journey started with DNA kits from *Ancestry.com* and *23 and Me*, gifted to me by my daughter Rebekah, and quickly developed into detailed research and documentation efforts spanning thousands of historical records and two continents.

My everyday obligations, which included executive positions in the non-profit world and a busy personal life as wife, mother, daughter, and friend, often took precedence over the progression of my passion project.

On November 7, 2022, my mother Alzada passed away at the age of ninety-six in our little family home in Swansea, Massachusetts, where she'd lived for more than sixty years, fourteen of which she spent without the love of her life. The loss of my father inspired me to start writing this book, and it was the loss of my mother that moved me to finish it.

Mom and Dad are buried together under an oak tree in Mount Hope Cemetery in Swansea, and it's been sixteen years since I started penning this memoir.

I'm now retired – sort of – and enjoying time with my wonderful husband, Clarel, our children, and our grandchildren, and while I know there will always be more to discover, this book is a celebration of those who came before us, with hopes that it will scatter blossoms on the paths of all those who follow.

– Deborah Cross Antoine

PART I

The Crazy Crosses of Little Neck Island

1949 – 1970s

Crazy Cross Family Tree

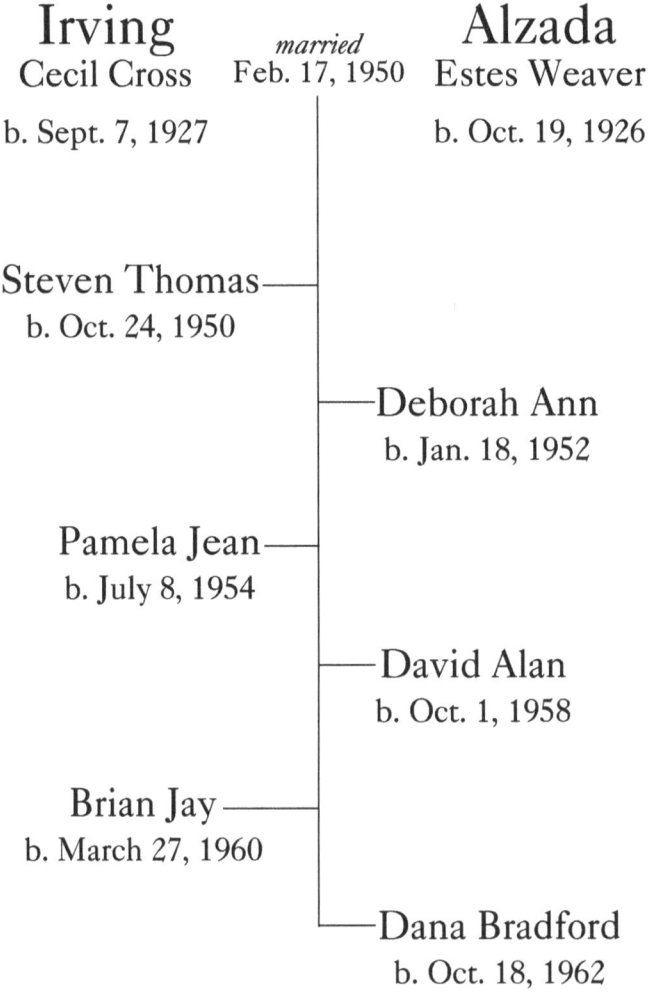

The Crazy Crosses of Little Neck Island

I GREW UP on Little Neck Island, a tiny New England hamlet located in the coastal town of Swansea, Massachusetts, where there were no strangers because everyone knew everyone.

Back then, neighbors affectionately referred to our rambunctious family of eight as the "Crazy Crosses" because we lived every minute of every day in the moment, a carefree and loving lifestyle in which having fun together was the essential ingredient.

My vivid memories of those days have always been a guiding light for my adult life, and I believe the same is true for all my siblings. Although nothing is ever truly perfect, my childhood was as close to idyllic as possible. We might have been challenged financially, but we had the necessities, and my family is proof positive that money doesn't cultivate happiness.

The family our parents created was intentional – never mind our oldest brother Steven's October (early) arrival after their February wedding; it was all a direct result of their own not-so-happy childhoods and the damaged or distant relationships they'd witnessed or been a part of. When Alzada met Irving, they were both longing for a happy family of their own, and it was only a matter of time.

Alzada and Irving.

Alzada + Irving

Alzada and Irving were attracted to each other at first sight.

It was 1949, and Alzada, age twenty-three, was working the soda fountain at a corner drugstore in Fall River. From behind the counter, she could watch everyone coming and going from the store, and one day, a very attractive young man caught her eye.

He was tall, slim, and elegant-looking, and Alzada, instantly smitten, noticed right away that he had an appealing kind of hip action while playing pinball with his friends. Pinball gave him an appetite, and the pretty girl behind the counter – a classic beauty with an easy smile – was even sweeter than the sodas she served.

Alzada always gave him a little extra ice cream each time he came in, embellishing the recipe, concocting extra-special sodas just for him – and pretending not to hear when he bragged to his friends that the cute fountain girl gave him drinks for free. (Alzada was paying for his ice cream sodas!)

The handsome fella with the sweet tooth and swiveling hips was one Irving Cecil Cross, and he had a lot going for him: at twenty-two, he was the youngest licensed electrician in town, and doing well by the looks of his brand new bright yellow 1949 Willys-Overland Jeepster.

Boy, is that something, Alzada said to herself.

But there was something more than just his good looks, sharp wit, and magnetic personality, and Alzada recognized it very early in their blossoming relationship; it was the essence of Irving's generous and genuine spirit – his kindness. If a friend needed money, Irving would lend it to him, and he would even let friends borrow his precious Jeepster.

For their first date, Irving picked up Alzada in his newly shined car. He wore a stylish, well-made suit and showcased his impeccable manners at the fancy restaurant he took her to, and their first date became the happiest day of both their lives, with happier days yet to come.

Shortly thereafter, she found out his snappy suit was rented, and his Jeepster was repossessed, so Irving had to settle for a broken-down Ford truck and ten-cent beers when planning their dates. Expensive restaurants were no longer within their reach, but they never had been – and none of that mattered.

Alzada had fallen in love with a man who valued relationships and people more than money and possessions, and she was always proud to be seen with Irving. He was the man she had always imagined falling in love with and she was the woman he was hoping for – they were made for each other.

On that first date, Irving truly swept Alzada off her feet – but on their wedding day, he got swept off his.

Wedding Surprise

Once, when asked how Irving popped the question, Alzada said with a laugh, "I'm not sure he asked me – I think it just…happened."

Irving and Alzada became Mr. and Mrs. Cross on February 17, 1950, a freezing cold Friday, and their small, simple wedding ceremony was held in the modest parlor of the parish house of the Fall River First Baptist Church. Alzada's oldest brother, Frank, was Irving's best man, and Frank's wife Betty, Alzada's best friend, was her matron of honor.

Within seconds of being officially pronounced man and wife, still standing hand in hand at the altar, Alzada's overwhelming happiness vanished in a cloud of confusion and disbelief as Irving was wrenched away from her.

"It felt like there were people pulling our hands apart. Who would do such a thing to a newly married couple?" Alzada recalled. "And then I looked, and it was Irving – he had passed out!"

Irving was just about to fall on the floor when 5'2" Frank – a whole foot shorter than 6'2" Irving – caught him. Best man, indeed!

The little wedding party got the woozy newlywed into a chair, and as he came to, Irving said, "OK, finish it."

When everyone told him he was already married, he looked down at his hand, saw the ring, very calmly said, "Oh," and then escorted his new wife home to their new apartment. From swooning to honeymooning!

A photo of the complete Crazy Crosses taken Easter morning 1964 in Swansea. From left to right are Pamela, Dana, Mom, Dad, David, Brian, Steven, and, yours truly, Deborah.

A still from a home movie of our family home on Little Neck Island in Swansea, Massachusetts.

Small Houses, Big Families

Unbeknownst to Alzada at the time of their wedding, Irving had lost his job that morning, and just three days earlier they'd rented their new apartment on Durfee Street in Fall River. No wonder he fainted.

This would be the first of many times early in their marriage when they would put down two-weeks' rent with no idea how they'd scrape together enough for the next two weeks; but Alzada and Irving never felt deprived because there was so much joy and love in their house from the beginning, so much activity and laughter.

And, while it is left to legend as to whether they knew it for certain on their wedding day, Alzada was already pregnant and quickly grew tired of climbing up three flights of stairs to their apartment.

The young couple soon moved in with Irving's parents and his much younger sister Joanie in Swansea, unaware that the little house on Little Neck Island would later become their home for a lifetime. The 1949 deed to the house was actually already in Irving's and his mother Alice's names – a once-unfathomable purchase made possible by the G.I. bill upon Irving's discharge from the army in 1947.

It was while living here that Irving and Alzada had their first child, Steven Thomas Cross, in October 1950, but this first stay was brief. As an electrician by trade, Irving had to go where the work was, so their small-but-growing family moved around a lot in the beginning.

He was on a job in Connecticut when Alzada gave birth to their second child – me, Deborah Ann Cross – in January 1952, and we all moved in with Mom's mother, my Nana Susan, in Fall River, while Dad found us a place to live in Connecticut.

Almost as soon as the Connecticut job ended and we'd moved back to Fall River again, Dad found his next job in Trenton, New Jersey, where, about as soon as he landed, all the other workers went on strike. Dad was feeling lonely and had time on his hands, so he called Mom and asked her to come down with the me and Steve for a visit.

"Oh, Irving, I wish I could," she said to him, but it would be too difficult to travel with two babies.

Nana Susan overheard and offered to babysit, and without letting Dad in on her plans, Mom took an early morning train down to Trenton to surprise him. She caught a cab to the rooming house where he was living, and sure enough, his car – unlocked – was parked outside. She got in the passenger seat and waited, because strike or no strike, Dad still had to report to work every day.

"His face when he came out and saw me in that car was like sunshine at midnight! He hugged me tightly, like we were newlyweds," Mom recalled. "We went to Atlantic City and stayed in this rickety old hotel with paper-thin walls and rented a bicycle built for two on the boardwalk. It was just – what a great time!"

This little surprise visit had turned into a romantic, whirlwind mini-honeymoon, but, it wasn't long before Dad found a place for us all to live, and Mom boarded that New Jersey-bound train again, this time with two children in tow and much more luggage.

"Steve was a very active little boy who just wanted to run up and down the aisle on the train, while Deb threw up for 160 miles," Mom said, laughing. "So, I moved to New Jersey with two babies! I felt like, where he goes, I go. Wherever his work takes him, then that's where I'll be."

In August of 1953, Grandpa and Grandma Cross reverted legal ownership of the Swansea house back to Dad, but continued to live there until 1958, when our growing family made the permanent move back home.

At top left is my baby picture, and at top right are Dad and Steve. At bottom left is Mom with Steve and me, and at bottom right are toddler Pamela and five-year-old me (on the swing) at Nana's house.

At top left is Dave in 1960, and at right, baby Brian in 1960. On the bottom, bath time for our three youngest brothers – Dana, Dave, and Brian

In July of 1954, our sister Pamela Jean arrived, followed by David Alan in 1958, Brian Jay in 1960, and finally, Dana Bradford in 1962. The Cross Family "forever home" (which is still Cross-owned) was small for our big family – just 936 square feet – but it was all we needed.

"We had six kids and only one bathroom!" Mom once marveled. "But I never pushed Irving that we needed a bigger house. We stayed in the house that we could afford. It's a small house, but to us, it didn't feel small."

Mom was used to big families in small houses. There were only two bedrooms and two beds in her family home at 733 New Boston Road in Fall River – one bed her two older brothers shared, and the other bed she shared with both of her parents, sleeping between them for as long as she could remember.

After Mom's father Louis died in 1944, her brother Frank and his wife Betty moved in, followed by her brother Joe with his wife Johanna and their young daughter, Joan, and by 1950, she was living with her mother, two brothers, two sisters-in-law, three nieces, and one nephew in a two-bedroom house. Mom, who never slept alone, continued sharing a bed with her mother until she married Irving and moved out.

When my siblings and I were growing up, sharing beds was both a necessity and a fun family activity. I shared a bed with my sister Pam in our small upstairs bedroom until I left for college – on cold nights we used a hairdryer to heat the sheets – and on weekend mornings, all of us kids would pile into bed with our parents, where we would laugh and make plans for the day or just snuggle up together.

There was always plenty of room, and their little house on Little Neck Island was a home of their very own where Mom and Dad could raise a big, happy family their own way.

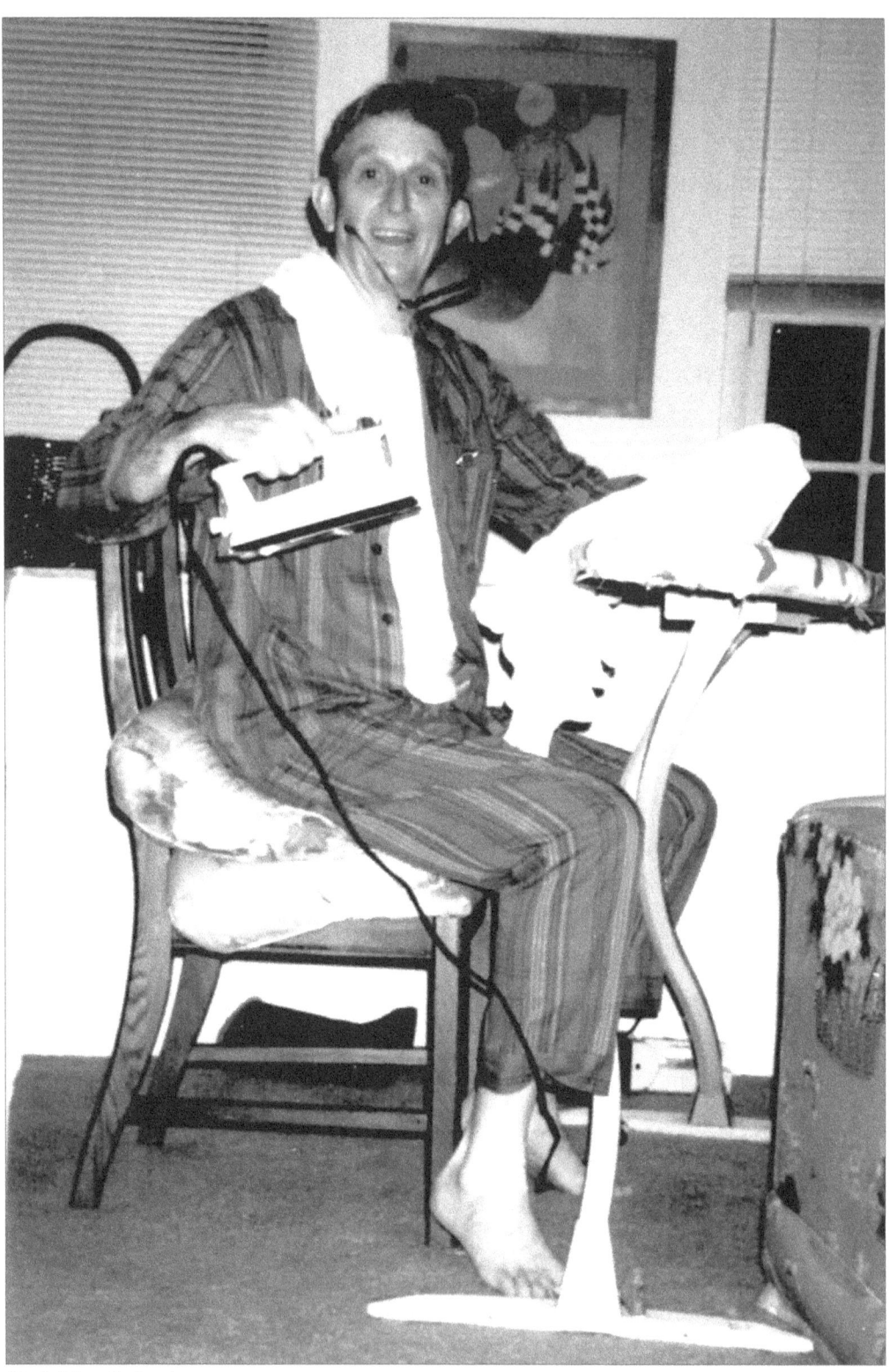

Dad doing the ironing.

Domestic Partnership

I believe one reason my parents prevailed as a couple was because they lived "married life" their own way.

Words like "traditional" and "normal" rarely applied to us "crazy" Crosses, and it had been that way from the start. With both effortless instinct and intentional effort, our parents' marriage was both a passionate love affair and a steadfast domestic partnership.

In the stereotypical 1950s marriage model, and as per every TV sitcom of the era, the husband was the breadwinner who left the house and went to work, and the wife was the homemaker who stayed and cared for the whole family. They were two separate people in two separate spheres trying to maintain very distinct gender roles and social norms. This was not the case in the Cross house.

Dad was never out of work for long, and eventually Mom started working full-time, but they both made ample time for each of us, for all of us, and for each other. Mom handled most of the household chores, but Dad always handled two of the most daunting in a household of eight (sometimes with pets, including a whole family of Saint Bernards at one point) – the vacuuming and the laundry. I do wonder if it was because he got to operate electric machinery while he did it, but it doesn't matter why he pitched in, only that he did.

Sometimes Dad would joke with Mom about being the family laundryman – "Alzada, you know that big white square thing down in the basement? That's a washing machine!"

One time, Mom gave vacuuming a go. She lugged it out and looked it over, but finally she had to ask Dad – "How on earth do you turn this on?"

Many years later, Mom recalled, "For the life of me I couldn't figure out how to do the vacuum cleaning. That's because Irving would always do it, and I never once asked. When the children were babies, I would never say, 'Gee Irving, would you mind holding him a little bit while I do this?' He did things on his own. I did not demand them. He was very good about doing things to help out, no matter how much he was working."

Of course, practically every day of their married life, Dad asked Mom if she realized just how lucky she was to be married to him. A true statement, but also a teasing way to say how lucky *he* was to be married to *her*. Once, Dad's older sister Irene complained to Mom about her newly retired husband, saying that he was hanging around in the kitchen and getting in her way, and Mom told her, "You know, anything my husband wants to do, I don't care what he does!" She just let him be himself, and the same was true for us kids.

Excluding laundry and vacuuming, my mother had many fine "domestic" skills, chief among them sewing. The most notable outfits were made in the late nights leading up to Easter Sunday, but she sewed everything for my sister Pam and me – dresses, capes, and coats, all with fabrics made and purchased in Fall River, including my prom dresses!

"I would make things for the boys, I would make gowns – Deb was never ashamed that her mother had made her gown," Mom recalled. "They were all just real good kids."

Mom's devotion to creating clothes for us made an impression on me, and I vividly remember painstakingly making my first daughter Jessica's Christmas outfit, complete with a white eyelet pinafore.

Mom also made all of her and Dad's square dancing costumes.

"We loved to square dance! We went to a lot of places, like down the Cape and conventions and stuff like that. The club was called Four Hands Round and Tom Daly was the caller. We had a Halloween dance, and I had to make costumes for us. I made him the Jolly Green Giant and

Mom and Dad, ready to go square dancing in custom outfits made by Mom. And at bottom right, me and my first daughter Jessica, wearing the Christmas outfit I made for her.

I was Mrs. Butterworth. We had wonderful times. At one of the meetings I made him a Playboy Bunny!"

Dad always used to talk about what spectacular legs he had. He would say, "You know, I have the best-looking legs – and I mean of all the women!"

While Mom had competition for "best legs" in the relationship, it was always a pairing of equals, even if society (or Tom Daly) was calling the moves. Bow to your partner, *do-si-do*!

Dad at the beach – get a load of those gams!

Crossketeer Roll Call

Like the Musketeers of the Dumas novel, all six Crossketeers were born and bound into an adventurous and inseparable kinship – "*All for one and one for all.*"

Steven Thomas Cross | b. October 14, 1950

The Storyteller

Steve, the first child, was born fun-loving and curious, bounding with energy and lusting for adventure, with a talent as big as his passion for telling stories.

Deborah Ann Cross | b. January 18, 1952

The Executive

I was the second bundle of joy, and while I liked having fun, I was always the responsible, studious, hard-working one, a high achiever that kept my "crazy" side concealed – mostly.

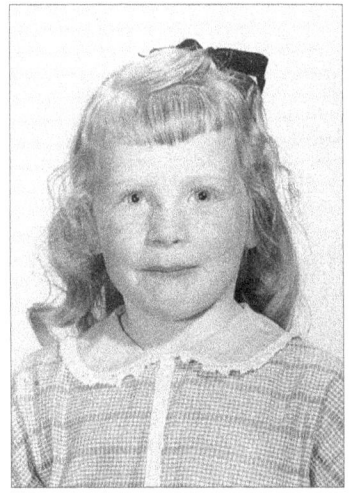

Pamela Jean Cross | b. July 8, 1954

The Nurturer

Pam was born with a natural gift for nurturing and has always been a caring and loving soul, first playing nurse as a child, and then becoming one for fifty years.

David Alan Cross | b. October 1, 1958

The Musician

A heartbreakingly handsome boy born with strawberry blond hair, "Davey Boy," as Dad called him, was gifted with an innate love and aptitude for music and performance.

Brian Jay Cross | b. March 27, 1960

The Brain

If you switch the vowels around in the name "Brian" you get the word "Brain" – and what a perfect fit for the uber smart fifth child, whose keen mathematical mind and knack for trivia, puzzles, and games is matched only by his remarkable patience and enthusiasm.

Dana Bradford Cross | b. October 18, 1962

The Individualist

Dana, the baby of the bunch, has always been inquisitive, free-spirited, and adventurous, a precarious combination of personality traits for this do-it-yourself engineer.

Clockwise from bottom left – Dave, Pam, me, Steve, Dad, Mom, Brian, and Dana (in utero).

All of the above are frames from our home movies. From top to bottom, our Volkswagen bus on one of our family trips to New Hampshire; go-karting with Dad; and David (left) and Dana (driver seat).

Anything Motorized

Our family activities always had a bit of a wild twist to them – like setting up racecourses in parking lots so we could zip around in all sorts of wheeled contraptions, weaving and dodging like daredevils at breakneck speed. We even had our very own dirt racetrack in our backyard, at the center of which was a huge weeping willow tree.

For most families, the state of our backyard would have been an embarrassment – torn up by tire tracks and cluttered with boats, tents, bikes, and paraphernalia – but to us it was a wonderland.

Our youngest brother Dana likes to say that by the time he was old enough to notice, our house had already earned the reputation of being "the fun house" in the neighborhood and among all our friends. But it wasn't just a fun house, it was a cozy escape – and a sanctuary for some.

As Dana recalls, there were kids from families going through divorce or other troubles, and they came to our house to find a little peace and a whole lot of fun. While the adults in the neighborhood might not have been thrilled with our less than pristine backyard, all the kids loved our minibike and go-kart track – and they adored our parents!

Nowadays, laws across most of the United States require both adults and children to wear helmets on motorcycles, but back then, even six-year-old Dana was allowed to drive go-karts or hop on a motorbike helmet-free. Luckily, the independent and adventurously hard-headed Dana has always had a hard skull to match.

Seat belts were also different back then, and I vividly remember one family trip to Cape Cod when Dad, momentarily distracted by a pretty girl in a miniskirt, stomped on the brakes, sending Dana, who was sitting on Mom's lap, flying forward into the windshield – he was, miraculously, unhurt.

Our trusty Volkswagen bus was the go-to family ride, but at one time we also owned as many as six used cars and a few motorcycles. Sounds like fun, for sure, but the challenge was always finding one with enough gas to go anywhere.

On summer weekends, all eight of us would pile into our VW bus for camping trips. We still laugh about the countless hours we spent in the White Mountains on the Kancamagus Highway – though we always called it "Kangamangus" – where we would stop for nature hikes across streams and up mountains.

Once in a while we would find indoor accommodations, always at bargain prices, and I'll never forget one roadside cottage already occupied by a bunch of bats. We were scared out of our wits and dove under the sheets while Dad bravely chased them out.

Most of the time we pitched a second-hand tent in public campgrounds for a few dollars a night. One night, during a torrential downpour, our tent started leaking, so we huddled in the middle in our damp sleeping bags. The wind howled, the rain lashed at the tent, and then, with a dramatic flop, the center tent pole gave out, collapsing the whole thing on top of us. My younger brothers, soaked and scared, cried as we bolted for the safety of our VW bus.

Even perfect parents can't control the weather, but ours never tried to be perfect, and they didn't expect us to be perfect either. A classic example occurred one winter day when I drove the VW bus to college.

After dropping off a friend at her dorm, I couldn't get back into the bus because the door had frozen shut. Thinking I was locked out and unsure what to do, I cut a hole in the fabric roof. Not my brightest moment, but Dad never said so (at least not to my face).

Dad cherished his cars, but he never got upset when something happened to them. Once, my longtime sweetheart Bobby picked me up from college in a car Dad had loaned him – an uninsured car. We were headed home to Swansea and getting a very early start, and Bobby dozed off at the wheel. The car rolled over onto its side, grinding off the passenger door handles and spraying glass everywhere. We crawled out of the wreckage, and with rescue vehicles on the way, I started gathering up the scattered laundry, carefully collecting and concealing my lingerie first.

When we reached the hospital at the crack of dawn, I called Dad to break the news with a tentative "By the way…" and a full confession. True to form, he was surprised and concerned, but not angry – the important thing was we were OK.

We were a family of fun-having, risk-taking thrill-seekers, but we all knew we had to at least try to be smart about it – don't hurt anyone, don't hurt yourself, and be respectful.

Steve said he conclusively realized our parents were unique when he once spotted Dad out riding his motorcycle in the snowy open fields near our house (he had put chains on the tires to keep it under control). And then, Steve saw an even crazier sight – both Mom and Dad on the motorcycle, with Mom facing backwards and holding onto a rope that was towing a toboggan loaded up with our three ecstatic little brothers!

A trio of photos taken one day when Dad and Mom took Steve to the pond to play.

Anything That Floats

A sailboat, a canoe, a surfboard, anything that floats – if it was free and somewhat functional, Dad would bring it home and fix it up. He had a knack for finding used sports equipment or spare car parts, and occasionally he would return with other surprises – like ten pounds of cherries, which we had no problem consuming. He would also make pancakes for the entire neighborhood using an electric skillet, also probably second-hand, on our picnic table out back.

Little Neck Island was technically a little peninsula – also called a neck – that curved south into the Lees River, giving us unregulated water access right by our house, a perk we never took for granted. Nowadays you can safely eat the fish and shellfish you catch in the river, which I just recently did with my brother Brian, but it wasn't always that way.

Back in the sixties there was a textile finishing company upriver that would dump their dye waste into the water, which would float downstream and stain our clothes when we played in the river. One day, Dad had all of us put on light-colored bathing suits, and he took pictures of us before and after playing in the water. The photos captured the effects of the dyes, which stained our suits, and Dad gave the evidence to the offending company and the town selectmen. Thanks to these efforts, the laws and practices changed, the water cleared up, and the ecosystem recovered. We were all very proud of that, and it taught us an early lesson about engagement and activism.

But not all of Dad's aquatic adventures were successful. Mom vividly recalled watching from shore as he took his new (used) sailboat upriver, confidently attempting to maneuver under a low bridge. The mast bent so much it nearly snapped.

Steve eventually got his own beat-up old motorboat. One day, he accidentally ran it aground on our little beach front, putting a big hole in its hull. Dad's only complaint – "Did you have to do that while your mother was watching?"

One time, Dad came home with a surfboard from one of his buddies, thinking it would be great for me to learn how to surf, so off we went to Horseneck Beach to catch some waves. The board was so large and so heavy that my adolescent frame could barely carry it into the water – but I had skis that were too long, a bike that was too small, and roller skates that were too wide, so I was game! Things got easier in the water, and on an early try, I made it up onto the board, caught a wave, and lo and behold – I was actually surfing – Gidget, eat your heart out! But then, the board and I were thrown into the air, and as we both came back down, the board hit me right in the hip. WIPE OUT!

The "anything that floats tradition" is alive and well to this day, carried on through my brothers Dana and Brian, and my nephew Allan, with any number of boats, canoes or other inflatables on the Lees River.

Anyone who visits is most welcome to go out for a spin – and always an adventure! Just ask my husband Clarel, one of our most recent passengers / victims. I took the wheel that day and, channeling my inner Crazy Cross, I gleefully zipped through the water – with Clarel shouting "Stop!" the whole way.

While our nautical know-how has improved over the years, through all our missteps and mistakes, whether by land or by sea, our parents' faith in us never wavered – and their total trust and unconditional love often led us to experiences we might have otherwise missed, turning every challenge into a new opportunity.

Olympic Trials

On Saturday, June 15, 1968, the Cross kids took the local track and field scene by storm, and this legendary day of sporting glory will live forever in family memory. It was the Jaycees' annual meet at Maplewood Park in Fall River, and Dad decided that five of us would grace the event with our athletic prowess, all except Dana, who was too young to compete.

We had no training or conditioning, just a Dad (and Mom) who believed we didn't need any of that to at least give it a try. We were just a bunch of kids with lots of energy, and who needs experience when you have heaping doses of natural talent and all that parental encouragement?

Not only did we all win medals, but we also snagged a headline in the *Fall River Herald News* – *"Cross Family Steals Show in Jaycees Meet."* This was a big deal! Steve broke records in both the 220-yard dash and the discus throw. Dave won three footraces *and* the broad jump *and* took second in the baseball throw, scoring the highest overall point total of any athlete that day. And that's not all – Brian won three medals, Pam dominated the prep division, and I took first in both the 100 and 220-yard dashes in the intermediate division – and I'm still pretty speedy on the tennis court.

The article also gave Mom and Dad a shout out, applauding them for sprinting from one end of the park to the other to watch us all compete in as many events as possible. Even our trusty Volkswagen bus made a cameo in the background of the newspaper photo!

And that's how the Cross family turned a city track meet into our own personal Olympic trials, instilling in us the idea that we could do anything – and have fun doing it!

Cross Family Steals Show in Jaycees Meet

By FRED R. DOLAN

Steve Cross, Case High athlete set two records in Jaycees' annual track and field meet, Saturday at Maplewood Park, but had to share the spotlight with other members of his family—four to be exact.

Steve had firsts in the senior division 100, 220 and 440-yard dashes and discus, and also copped a third in the shotput. His effort in the 220 "has to rank with the finest of the season," according to meet director Jim Wilcox, former Morton coach and now assistant track mentor at Portsmouth Priory.

Runs Away

Cross ran away from the rest of the field with an excellent 23.9 clocking and a new meet mark. Steve established the other record in the discus with a heave of 130 feet, 9½ inches. Wilcox said this "was not Steve's best, but was commendable considering the poor conditions under which he threw."

Steve totaled 22 points, but it was second best to brother David. This youngster showed himself to be a performer well able to carry on his older brother's name as he won the 60, 100 and 220-yard dashes and the broad jump and finished second in the baseball throw in pee wee division for the day's high total of 23 points.

Debby Double Winner

Not to be outdone, Brian Cross had a second and two thirds in the pee wee division and sisters Debby and Pamela also added to the family points. Debby won both the 100 and 220 in the intermediate division, and Pam had two firsts and a second in the prep division.

Wilcox was pleased with the large number of girls who competed. He gave full credit for this to Steve Cross, "who went out and sold the meet to his sisters and some of their friends." With five of their children in competition, Mr. and Mrs. Irving C. Cross did some running of their own to various areas of the park checking on the progress of their offspring.

The article from the Fall River Herald News on Monday, June 17, 1968, detailing our legendary day as community track stars. On the next page, the results of the meet and a photo of Dave that ran with the article (note our VW bus to the left of Dave's face).

Pee Wee Division
Boys
60-yard dash—won by Dave Cross; second Don Flynn; third Brian Cross; time 10.8.

100-yard dash—D. Cross, B. Cross, Don Flynn; time 14.9.

220-yard dash — D. Cross; Flynn, B. Cross; 37.3.

Broad jump—D. Cross, Mike Costa, Brian Cabral; 11 feet, 1 inch.

High jump — Mike Venancio, Russell Boulay, Eric Crofton; 3 ft., 2 in.

Baseball throw—Mike Stukus, D. Cross, Don Petrin; 159 feet.

Prep Division
Boys
100-yard dash — Paul Reed, Tom Gastall. 14.8.

220-yard dash—Gastall, Reed, 34 seconds.

440-yard dash — Reed, Gastall, Wayne Almeida.

880-yard run — Reed, Almeida, Gastall. 3:04.

Broad jump — Reed, Almeida. 10 ft. 4¾ in.

High jump — Almeida, Gastall, (tie). 3 ft. 6 in.

Girls
100-yard dash — Debby Foley, Pamela Cross, Cathy Sullivan. 14.2.

220-yard dash — Pamela Cross, Debby Foley, Elaine DeCambra. 32 sec.

Broad jump —Pamela Cross, Debby Foley, Cathy Sullivan. 10 ft., 8 in.

Baseball throw — Elaine DeCambra, Pamela Cross, Debby Foley. 100 ft.

Intermediate Division
Girls
100-yard dash—Debby Cross, Caron Layson. 14.

220-yard dash—Debby Cross, Caron Layson. 35.

Senior Division
100-yard dash — Steve Cross, Ken Day, Al Livingston. 11.2.

220-yard dash — Cross, Warren Goff, Day. 23.

440-yard dash — Cross. 57.1.

880-yard run—Kaylor. 2:14.2.

Mile—Mike Kolbelecki. 5:34.

Discus — Cross, Day. 130' 9½ in.

Shotput — Brian Palmer, Day, Cross. 41 ft. 11½ in.

Brian, Mom, Dad, Dana, and Dave on the one and only family vacation that Mom tried to ski.

Rope Tows & Rapids

While Dad was the mastermind behind our family escapades, Mom was the often reluctant but almost always willing participant / victim. Consider the first – and last – time she attempted to ski.

During the 1960s, one of our budget-friendly getaways was King Pine, a cozy ski house in Madison, New Hampshire. Skiing cost just four dollars a day, and with low-priced lodging and all-you-can-eat meals that catered to our ravenous appetites, especially Steve's bacon habit, it was the perfect spot for our large family.

While Dad and us kids had mastered the chairlift, beginners like Mom had to be taken up the hill with the rope tow, a long looped rope powered by a motor; you just grab onto it and let it drag you up to the top. All of us urged her on – "C'mon, Mom, just try it!"

Determined, Mom grabbed the rope tow tight. She struggled with the jerky momentum at first, but then she seemed to get the hang of it, and she was getting there…when about halfway up the slope…her skis crossed, and down she went! She was flat on her back, her arms and legs splayed out like a snow angel, but the rope tow didn't stop, and all the skiers behind her tripped and tumbled over in a spectacular domino effect.

We tried to help, but honestly, it was just too hilarious. I still laugh out loud when I think about it. Mom didn't think it was funny at all, and decided then and there that she would never ski again.

Fast forward to when the Cross clan, all adults, were invited by my first husband, Robert, on a whitewater rafting trip in Colorado. Envision Mom on the raft enjoying the gorgeous scenery, soaking in the sunshine and fresh air, blissfully unaware of the chaos about to ensue.

The moment we hit the first rapids, she was launched out of the raft like a cannonball, taking the poor guy sitting next to her along for the ride. She floated downstream for what felt like an eternity before finally reaching the shore, where she emerged boiling mad that not one of us, not even Dad, had jumped in to save her. To be fair, jumping out of the raft at that speed to attempt a rescue would have been a disaster!

Mom also gave tennis a try, but during a doubles match with Steve as her partner, she made the rookie mistake of turning around to look at him as he was serving. *Wham!* The ball smacked her square in the chest, and Steve, the ever-helpful coach, told her it was dangerous to turn around like that. So, she obediently turned back around, only for his second serve to nail her right in the back of the head.

Turns out, like skiing and whitewater rafting, tennis was not for her, but she sure gave us some unforgettable memories and a whole lot of laughs along the way.

Our whitewater rafting expedition. Mom, wearing a pink bandanna, is seated right of center in the photograph above, which was taken moments before she bounced out of the raft. That's Dad at the very front (far right), and behind him are Bob and me (wearing a white hat). My brothers Brian, David, and Dana are the three at the back end of the raft, and at the very back is our rafting guide.

An Accidental Career

Mom might not have been a natural-born athlete, but what she lacked in physical prowess, she more than made up for in guts and adventurous spirit. She was never afraid to try new things, and she always had the courage to do what needed to be done – and what she wanted to do.

When Mom and Dad tied the knot in 1950, she stopped working professionally, and for fourteen years her full-time job was raising six kids. But then, just as she was approaching forty, she "accidentally" stumbled into a whole new career at Raytheon, the industrial and military electronics giant headquartered in Massachusetts.

Mom was no stranger to hard work. In 1944, fresh out of Durfee High School, she dove straight into the workforce, cranking out gas tanks for the war effort at the Firestone Tire & Rubber Company. Her schedule was rough – two weeks of day shifts followed by two weeks of night shifts – with just enough sleep to keep her human and, somehow, still managing an active social life (and a few dates).

Soon after, she went to work at the real estate office of Pierre Ouelette, and just a few years later, she was working two jobs – one as a salesclerk in the R.A. Wilcox stationery store, and the other behind the soda fountain at the corner drugstore – where she met Dad.

"I had always talked about work," Mom recalled. "Irving worked as an electrician on construction, and he could be laid off at any time if the job came to an end, and we could not afford to go on unemployment because we wouldn't be able to survive with the kids. I asked him if it would be helpful for me to work, and he always said no. He didn't want me to work."

When I was about twelve, Mom spotted an ad in the paper for an evening shift at Raytheon and talked it over with Dad, who, thinking it was a long shot, gave it the green light – and she got it! And just like that, Mom had embarked on her new career, and she cheerfully worked second shift from 4:30 p.m. to 11 p.m. as a mechanical assembler for twenty years.

During the day, she was still Supermom, tackling housework and keeping us all in line, and my sister and I helped a lot. I enjoyed making supper for everyone when I got home from school, and Pam liked to tidy up. It was easy, and we were constantly rewarded by Dad, who would shower us with compliments. In particular, he loved my pineapple upside down cake, even though it was made from a mix and canned pineapple.

Of course, when Mom was at work, Dad was in charge at home, which may or may not have led to other "accidental" incidents.

Mom on one of our many family camping trips.

Don't Tell Your Mother

We loved when Dad was in charge of us, not only because he let us do almost anything we could think of, but because he was often the one giving us exciting new ideas we would have never thought up ourselves!

"Don't tell your mother," he'd whisper with a mischievous grin, right before or after we'd done something that would have sent Mom into a tizzy, whether it was one of his brilliant schemes or one of ours.

Like the time Dad took nine-year-old me out on a sailboat in the middle of Lake Sebago, which is more than thirteen miles long, making it the second largest lake in Maine. It was like venturing into the ocean, with big waves and no land in sight, and in maneuvering the wind, our boat turned over! Dad and I emerged from the water, and his first words were, "Sweetheart, swim over there to retrieve my glasses," which I did, and eventually, "Don't tell your mother," which I didn't!

Sometimes, however, Mom ended up the unintended victim of our mischief – like the time she got home from work one night, only to slip and slide her way across the kitchen floor, which we kids had decided to "wax" with butter earlier that evening. Dad just sat there, casually reading the newspaper, as if it were just another ordinary evening in the Cross house.

"I never have a problem with these kids!" Dad would declare whenever our antics came to light.

"Oh, Irving!" Mom would reply, her tone ranging from a weary sigh to an exasperated shout, depending on the severity of the shenanigans. To her credit, Mom was the voice of reason in the room, but she also wanted us to have fun exploring life's adventures. She trusted Dad, but sometimes that trust came with a heavy dose of "Are you sure about this, Irving?"

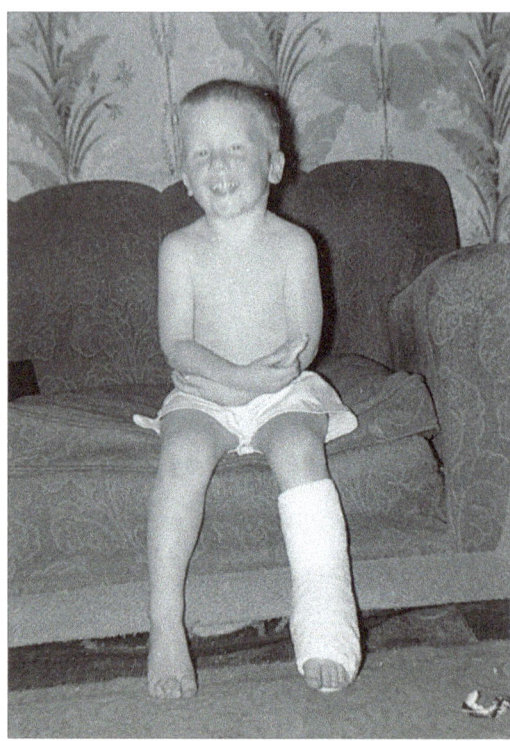

At top left, Mom at the kitchen table with Dave and Brian in her lap, and at top right, Dave with a cast on his leg. Below, Dave on the left and Brian on the right, both balancing on my feet in our Swansea living room in the summer of 1968.

Like the time Dad put chains on his motorcycle tires and pulled us around on snow skis; we had already successfully tested this method with the toboggan. Again, Mom objected at first – "Oh, Irving!" – but ultimately climbed aboard and held the tow rope.

And then there was the time Dad wanted to take me on a multi-mile swim at the Swansea Dam when I was ten. Mom wondered if it would be too much but, in I went, feeling totally safe with Dad by my side. He had me relax and float when I got tired, encouraging me all the way.

There were many other eccentric escapades orchestrated by our father, sometimes with Mom's blessing, but we would NEVER tell her if something went awry – like when ten-year-old Brian flipped a go-kart he was driving, scraping his head and breaking his glasses.

Some things could only be discussed in the "Cone of Silence" – the transparent dome-like device from the 1960's sitcom *Get Smart*, used to create an environment of complete secrecy – but over time, we developed a system for when it was safe to let Mom in on our secrets.

Some tales needed to mellow for a couple of weeks or months, while others required years before they were safe to share.

Take, for example, the day I finally admitted to my truant teenage joyride – a decade after it happened. I was fifteen, feeling invincible, and decided that skipping school to borrow Dad's motorcycle was a brilliant idea. My friend and partner-in-crime, Nancy, eagerly hopped on the back, and off we roared to Cape Cod for a day of sun and sand. The rush of freedom was exhilarating, but there was no rush to tell Mom.

Then there was Brian's infamous garage incident. On an otherwise ordinary day, Brian managed to steer a car straight through a neighbor's garage, crashing in through one side and out the other, like some kind of low-budget action movie stunt. This one had to stay off Mom's radar for a good long while.

As the years passed, these tales became the stuff of family legend, shared at holiday gatherings or over dinner, always with a knowing chuckle or roaring laughter – and no matter how long ago or how ridiculous the story sounded in hindsight, Mom's reaction was always delightfully predictable – "Oh, Irving!"

In Ledyard, Connecticut, playing in the woods at Aunt Irene and Uncle George's house, where George built by hand the rope swing, platform, and ladder seen above. That's five-year-old me on the swing, with Dad getting ready to send me on my way. Next to him are my cousin Jack, Aunt Irene, and Steve. Behind the ladder is my cousin Michael, and at the bottom right corner, holding Pam, is Mom, vigilantly supervising – "Oh, Irving!"

Mom and Dad taking a turn on the rope swing.

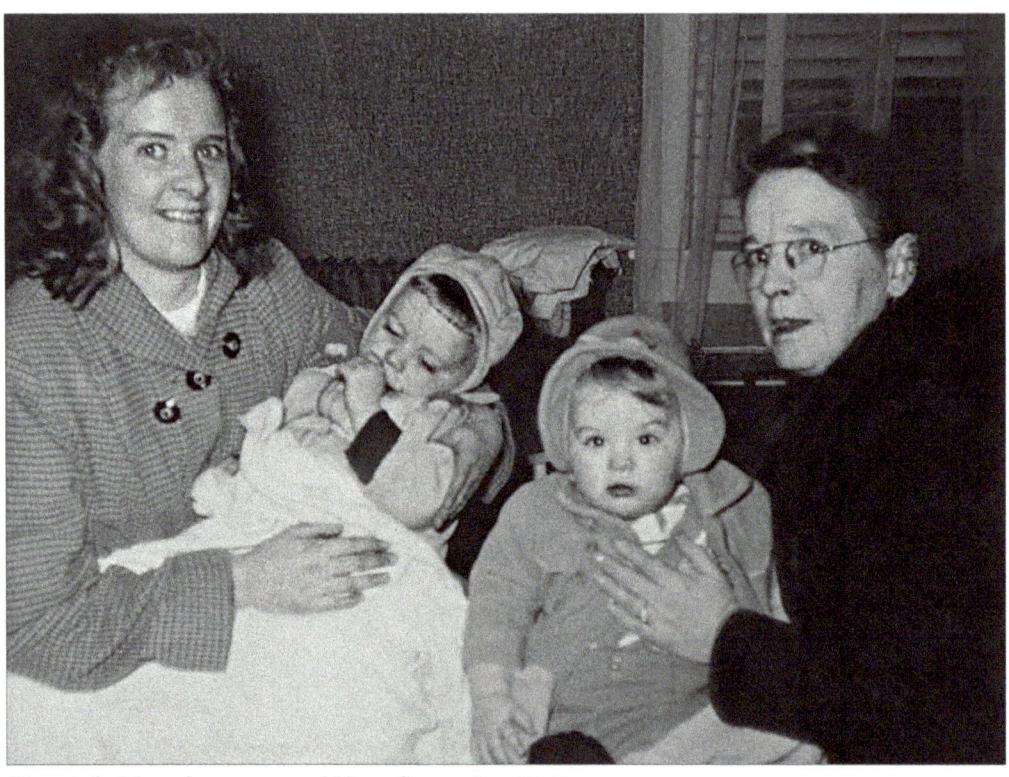

From left, Mom, Steve, me, and Nana Susan circa 1953.

At left, Nana Susan holding me, and Dad with Steve, likely taken the same day as the photo above. At bottom right, a detail of a photo taken Easter Morning 1964 – me, Dave, our cousin Cindy, and Nana Susan.

Nana Susan

Before my siblings and I were old enough to look after each other, if we weren't in the care of our parents, our Nana Susan, Mom's mom, often watched over us. Parts Two and Four of this book will paint a better picture of her early years – before she was our Nana – but my earliest memories of her take me back to New Boston Road in Fall River, when we were living with her while Dad was working out of state.

She was quiet and serious, and it's no wonder we have so few photos of her smiling; but, despite her reserved nature, I always felt the warmth of her deep, abiding love. Even after we moved out, Nana and I stayed close. I often went to visit and stay with her, and we would play 500 Rummy together for hours on end. Sometimes she would give me a dime to buy penny candy at the little store across the street from her house. Along with the candy, this short walk was a special treat for a kid who lived in the Swansea suburbs, where you needed a car (and a parent) to go to the store.

I loved going with her to First Baptist Church. She always sat in the balcony facing the altar, where communion was served in a passed tray with little glasses of grape juice. She knew the words to all the hymns, but I could barely hear her voice. When I stayed overnight I slept in her bed, snuggled up beside her, and as she whispered her prayers, I always listened for my favorite part – "Bless Debbie in her schoolwork."

Nana also made the most delicious doughnuts. I got to help, of course, making the dough with simple ingredients, shaping them by hand and then frying them in a deep pot of lard. The kitchen filled with the most heavenly aroma, and knowing I could barely wait, she would let me eat the centers we poked out to make the donut holes.

Nana's Doughnuts

Makes about 3 dozen medium-sized doughnuts.

Ingredients
- 1 Egg
- 1 Cup Sugar
- 1 Cup Milk
- 4 Tsp. Baking Powder
- ½ Tsp. Salt
- ¼ Tsp. Nutmeg
- 4 ¾ Cups Flour

Instructions
- Beat egg, add sugar & milk
- Sift salt, powder, nutmeg & flour together
- Add dry ingredients to liquid. Mix well.
- Turn out on floured board. Knead lightly.
- Roll to ¼-inch thickness.
- Cut with doughnut cutter.
- Fry in deep fat. Drain on brown paper.

Nana Susan on Christmas at the Kimwell Nursing home – look at that smile!

Steve and I did something very untypical of teenagers when we were in our last years of high school – we visited Nana Susan at the Kimwell Nursing Home in Fall River just before joining our dates at our high school prom.

We were all dressed up in our very best, me in a peachy-pink and white gown that Mom made, and Steve sporting a powder-blue patterned suit jacket.

As the attendant brought Nana out of her room, her face lit up with a radiant smile, beaming at us in our finery, and that moment still shines in my memory.

Steve and I, all dressed up for prom (my junior prom) and an unforgettable visit with Nana Susan.

Nana passed away at the age of seventy-six on March 27, 1973, which also happened to be our brother Brian's thirteenth birthday. I was a senior in college at the time and came right home for the wake and funeral. It was the first time I had lost someone close to me, and the first time I saw a body in a casket. It hit me hard. I loved Nana and she loved me.

In my mind, Nana was a *"fainting robin,"* a reference to one of my favorite Emily Dickinson poems, "If I Can Stop One Heart from Breaking"–

If I can stop one heart from breaking,
I shall not live in vain;
If I can ease one life the aching,
Or cool one pain,
Or help one fainting robin
Unto his nest again,
I shall not live in vain.

I wish I had helped Nana Susan up into her nest again. I wish I had known her better, talked with her more, and spent more time with her at the nursing home. Those thoughts still linger with me, and I hope that, if I'm very lucky, my grandchildren will want to spend time with me, and always think of me with love.

Thankfully, life has a way of surprising us in the best ways, and one of the happiest days in my life wasn't too long ago. My teenage granddaughters, Meriem and Leila, after winning a bronze medal in their volleyball tournament, sent me a video with their entire volleyball team jumping and chanting, "Zizza! Zizza! Zizza!"

Like "Nana" for my grandmother, "Zizza" is their nickname for me – short for *Aziza*, of Arabic origin, meaning "beloved" and "cherished." Their joyful shouts of "Zizza! Zizza! We love you, Zizza!" make my heart soar, just like a perfect batch of Nana's doughnuts, warm and comforting, made with love.

Zizza (me) with my granddaughters, Leila (left) and Meriem (right), in 2024, moments after these two helped lead their volleyball team to the win that sent them to sectionals – a first in team history!

Grandpa & Grandma Cross

The warm and fuzzy memories of my Nana Susan stand in stark contrast to the peculiar and somewhat blurry recollections I have of my paternal grandparents, Cecil and Alice Cross. Though we lived with them in Swansea when I was just a baby, we didn't visit them very often after that.

What sticks with me most is the sharp, unmistakable aroma of Grandpa Cecil's cigars, which he smoked in the parlor, filling the room with the exotically distinct scent. He also had a real fondness for Pickwick Ale, an "old-time" English-style brew from Boston's Haffenreffer & Co., and he drank it by the quart.

Grandpa Cecil had his vices, but the man could really cook. His specialty was making "slop" (a hearty stew of potatoes, pork, and carrots), and when compared with Grandma Alice's skills (and mostly inedible concoctions), Grandpa Cecil was practically a Michelin-starred chef.

While in the army, Dad was the only one who never complained about the food. His brothers-in-arms would wax poetic, misty-eyed over missing their mom's cooking, but to Dad, military mess was a treat, and far better than anything his mother ever produced.

According to Mom, when we did happen to visit with our Cross grandparents at their Harbor Terrace apartment near downtown Fall River, the very suggestion of Grandma Alice preparing a meal would elicit a unanimous response from every single one of us kids – "I'm not hungry, Mom!"

Harbor Terrace was a subsidized housing community that has since been renamed, but back then, I remember going to a nearby playground and walking to the corner store – which sold both candy and alcohol.

Grandpa Cecil passed away in 1969, age seventy. I know I was seventeen, but I didn't attend his funeral, and his death is a blank spot in my memory. And it seems I'm not alone in this forgetfulness – no one I've asked can remember anything about his funeral.

My Aunt Joan, Dad's younger sister, was a new mother when her father died, so she has a good excuse. Mom remembered Dad making the necessary arrangements, and feeling a deep sadness – not so much because Cecil had died, but because he had lived a life with so little kindness, gratitude, or love, a life so few would mourn.

After Grandpa Cecil's passing, Grandma Alice lived alone in her Doyle Street apartment in Providence, Rhode Island, where my cousin Cathy, Joan's daughter, visited her every day after school. For me, my most precious memories of Grandma Alice also come from the time period after Grandpa Cecil passed away, as she was always present at all of our family functions throughout the 1970s – sometimes even the starring act!

One day, Cathy went to visit and found Grandma Alice on the couch, and when she asked her how she was, Grandma replied, "As tired as a cat." It turned out to be an early sign of her first stroke, and marked the beginning of her declining health.

Grandma Alice passed away in 1980 at the age of eighty-one. Her funeral was a mostly solemn affair, until Dad, in a hushed voice (and with hand gestures), informed the mourners that our poor brother Brian was dealing with a "twisted testicle."

Both Grandma Alice and Grandpa Cecil were interred in Oak Grove Cemetery in Fall River, but not together. Before her passing, Grandma Alice arranged to be laid to rest alongside Mom's parents, Nana Susan and Louis. This was Grandma Alice's idea, simply because there was "space available." (And there's still one spot left in that four-person plot, so I might just stake my claim).

Grandma Alice and Grandpa Cecil Cross.

Dad's parents were unusual, but so were Mom's, just in a different way, and the next four parts of this book will hopefully shed more light on the lives and personalities of all four of my grandparents.

But, before I get ahead of myself, let's cruise on back to 1965, the year when Big Mamie came to town – and landed just a short walk down the hill from our Cross Grandparents' Harbor Terrace apartment!

USS Massachusetts (BB-59) – also known as "Big Mamie" – photographed in Boston Harbor in May 1942. Photo source: U.S. Navy archive.

Me giving Clarel a tour of Big Mamie in 2024.

Big Mamie

If there's anything that both my parents inherited from their folks – and passed on to us – it's a relentless work ethic and an unyielding level of stick-to-it-iveness. Steve, for instance, knew he wanted to be a policeman, but he first dabbled in entrepreneurship.

He was brimming with ambition and determined to build his empire by selling magazines, but it wasn't the get-rich-quick scheme he'd hoped for. Even our parents, who would do anything for their kids, could not be convinced to buy a single subscription. When Steve approached Dad and asked how many magazines he wanted to buy, Dad gently rejected him, but Steve was undeterred, and he moved on to Mom, who was also not in the market for magazines. Steve then went door to door to every neighbor on Little Neck Island and still didn't sell a single subscription.

I once hatched my own get-rich-quick scheme with my cousin Cindy Weaver, Uncle Frank and Aunt Betty's younger daughter. We were going to make a fortune picking beans at a farm down on Gardners Neck Road, and our parents, always supportive, let us try it. We got up at dawn and walked to the corner where we waited for the farm truck to pick us up. The other workers looked strong and were much more appropriately dressed in hats, overalls, and sturdy shoes. Cindy and I didn't even last a whole day – sunburned, exhausted, and with a measly half-bushel of beans between us, we realized that farming was not our calling.

For both Steve and me, our first "real jobs" were aboard Big Mamie, the *USS Battleship Massachusetts*. Commissioned in September of 1941, Big Mamie is a behemoth – 681 feet long and 35,000 tons of steel – with a resumé that included action in both the Pacific and Atlantic theaters during World War II. She was decommissioned in 1962 and destined for the scrapyard, but thanks to a heroic fundraising effort by her veteran crew members and Massachusetts school children, Big Mamie was saved and brought to Fall River on June 12, 1965, creating Battleship Cove. All six Cross children were among the 500,000 spectators who lined the shores of the Taunton River to welcome her home, an event immortalized in our home movies.

Not long after her arrival, when Steve was about fifteen, he was hired onto Big Mamie's painting crew. His boss, who Steve thought was mean and demanding, gave him a five-gallon can of battleship gray paint and told him to finish the job by noon. By 11:30, Steve was only a third of the way done. Not willing to lose his job or his precious $1.10 an hour, he decided to dump the rest of his paint overboard to meet the quota and call it a day.

During Big Mamie's first year in Fall River, 250,000 people came to see her, which created a need for more tour guides – and when I was fourteen, I got my first job as an official Big Mamie tour guide. I was a pretty good one, too; armed with a smile and a memorized script, I led groups around the battleship like a pro. Little did I know at the time, this experience was a perfect primer for my future career in teaching. These days, and thanks in large part to my daughter Jessica's work for a maritime nonprofit, my teenage naval knowledge, much like my boating ability, has considerably expanded over time.

Ultimately, Steve was destined for police work, not ship painting, but the beauty of our upbringing was that we were free to do anything – and fail spectacularly – without any pressure to fulfill anyone else's dreams except our own. Whether we were selling magazines, picking beans, or painting battleships, we were encouraged to follow our hearts, respected for our independence, and loved for who were, no matter what.

Dadisms

When it comes to life lessons, my siblings and I struck gold with a treasure trove of what we lovingly call Dadisms. These weren't just any old sayings; they were mini life strategies, each with a unique flavor, and many with a dash of military zest.

Some Dadisms were eloquent and profound, like the one I've leaned on for most of my career: *"A quick and intelligent action is better than a delay in search of the ideal."* Others were more down to earth, but still packed a punch, like the classic: *"You snooze, you lose!"*

Our morning reveille was the old battle cry *"Up and at 'em!"* – and if any of us refused to get up, Dad would repeatedly clang two pans together, an old fashioned but effective method.

Fun Fact: In the industrial towns of nineteenth century England, people could earn extra money by working as "knocker uppers," human alarm clocks that roamed the streets in the wee hours, knocking on windows to wake up the sleeping inhabitants so they wouldn't be late for work.

Most used a long bamboo pole or a soft mallet to tap on windows and doors – some used peashooters – but by the 1970s, with electric alarm clocks so widely available, the knocker upper became obsolete.

A knocker upper in Lancashire, England, circa 1908.

Dad's starting signal for any family game or competitive activity was – *"Let the games begin!"* – and while he was indubitably the king of fun, he still had his boundaries.

When we really misbehaved, he had unique ways of reining us in. *"Stand up. Sit down,"* he'd say, turning it into a drill that reminded us who topped the Cross chain of command – and we would sit and stand, up and down, as many times as Dad thought necessary.

Sometimes our mischief earned us yard work as part of our penance, which we all hated. *"Police the area!"* – Dad would command – *"All I want to see are asses and elbows!"*

That last phrase is a colorful way to order soldiers to get to work, and our army of six would crouch down and crawl around, removing the weeds and tidying the yard to Drill Sergeant Dad's satisfaction.

Excepting Dad's use of the word *"asses,"* we never once heard either of our parents say a swear word, and cursing was a big no-no in our house. I once told my brother Steve to "go to hell," and we were both sent to the cellar to cool off, where we whispered even worse things to each other until we were finally allowed back upstairs. Lesson learned – keep the cursing out of earshot.

Some Dadisms were punctuated with hand gestures. For instance, if you asked to borrow any of Dad's precious tools, he would always remind you there was only one proper place to return it – *"In my hand!"*

Dad also had a quirky way of describing working overtime as earning *"double stamps,"* a reference to the days when Sperry & Hutchinson (S&H) Green Stamps were all the rage.

As a reward for making purchases from supermarkets and other stores, you earned these mint green stamps (double stamps on promotion days), which we saved up to redeem for "distinguished merchandise" from the S&H catalog.

The cover and an interior page from a Sperry & Hutchinson green stamp quick saver book.

My parents were not careful about saving things, but somehow an S&H stamp saver book survived, as well as a catalog – and I can still taste the glue from licking those stamps!

Turning down overtime was practically a crime to Dad, but when he did find time to relax, he described himself as being *"on a loose pulley,"* a mechanical metaphor which refers to the belt system of a machine, in which one of the pulleys simply spins freely – without doing any work.

For Dad, this meant something deeper – that when he was idle or otherwise unengaged, he was free to do whatever he wished. There's a variation of this Dadism I once heard him say while wisecracking on himself – *"Funny how something loose can keep everything together!"*

But Dad rarely indulged in doing nothing, and relaxing for him often meant doing something productive, like his community organizing with the Little Neck Association, and his service as Selectman for the town of Swansea.

My absolute favorite Dadism is his answer to the question, "Are you comfortable?" – with a grin, he'd always reply, *"Oh, I've got a few bucks."* Dad wasn't rich, but he was resourceful. Whether fixing an engine, a toy, or even a scraped knee, he was a master of *"field expedience,"* a skill he honed while in the army. It was all about improvising with what you had on hand, and with our ever growing collection of cars, motorcycles, minibikes, go-karts, bicycles, boats, electric trains, and planes, something was always in need of repair.

Dad taught us that we could fix anything we needed to with a bit of creativity – whether it was repurposing parts from one machine to another or using duct tape to stop a leak. He once saved a family trip by crafting a muffler hanger from a shoelace!

But field expediency wasn't just a handy skill, it was also a kind of coping mechanism for Dad – a way for our perfectionist father to deal with some of the less-than-perfect situations he encountered in his life.

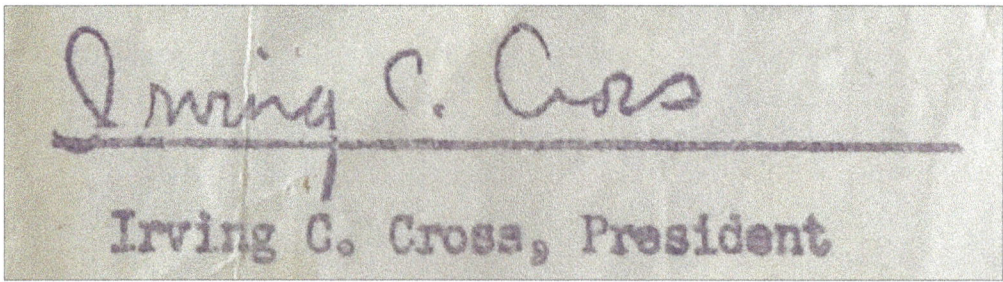

Above, Swansea selectman Dad in the 1960s, and below, Dad's signature on a 1964 letter to the residents of Little Neck Island, while he was serving as president of the Little Neck Island Association.

Going to Butler

I'm now going to peel back some of the more delicate layers of my Dad's complex and spirited personality. He could light up any room with his charm, kindness, and wit, and he was the most entertaining person you could hope to meet. But, as it is with all bright lights, there were some shadows, too – a darker side to his exuberance. There were some times when his boundless energy spilled over into thrilling stunts or wild adventures, and even a few episodes of intense mania.

In one story Mom recalled, I was just a toddler, cradled in one of her arms, Steve in the other, and we were outside of our house, eyes glued to the sky, waiting for Dad to "buzz" the roof by flying over very low and very fast in the small plane he shared with a friend.

"That's your crazy father up there!" Mom exclaimed with a mixture of exasperation and affection, shaking her head – "Oh, Irving!"

This aviation stunt is the more reckless example of his occasional mania, but there was also a more innocuous edge, like his unyielding drive to complete a project. Dad experienced both in different ways at different times throughout his life.

One of these obsessive completion incidents occurred when Dad decided to wallpaper our Swansea kitchen. It was a tedious task, to be sure, but with our brothers, Dave and Brian, as his eager assistants, the work got underway. Dad, however, was quickly consumed by the compulsion to precisely place the feathered heads and tails of the roosters printed on the paper in perfect alignment. Enchanted by a mystifying spell of boundless do-it-yourself mania, the work dragged on into the wee hours of the following morning.

These manic bursts didn't happen often but when they did, they were like fireworks – rare, spectacular, and impossible to ignore. Not often, but several times while we were growing up, Dad's excitement would bubble over into full blown chaos, a trait that runs through the family, especially with our brother Dave.

On at least a couple of occasions, Dad ended up staying a few days at Butler Hospital in Providence, where he received the care and medication he needed to stabilize his mood swings (and for much of his life, Dad took a small dose of Ativan to keep the anxiety at bay).

"Watch out, you're going to Butler," we'd warn Dad – or he'd warn us – whenever things were getting a little too jubilant and rowdy. This phrase became something of an inside family joke, but never said with cruelty or mockery. We were never ashamed of Dad, and his struggles were never a secret to be hidden away. Humor was just our way of sharing compassion and trying to find the light in a situation.

When it became clear that our brother Dave was facing his own mental health challenges, Dad's personal experiences – and our collective experiences as a family – became an unexpected silver lining. We could all better understand what Dave was going through. To that end, Mom served on the board of a local advocacy group, where she continued learning and educating others about mental health, and working to reform the outdated, harmful stereotypes of mental illness that still widely persist.

I'll close this chapter with a particularly funny instance of Dad's more excitable side. Once, as adults, my siblings and I joined our parents at the Foxwoods Casino in Connecticut. We were all at the craps table and Dad was winning – and getting very worked up – when, suddenly, his luck turned, and a controversy arose over the bet. Dad went on and on trying to convince the dealers that he personally knew Jerry Hunt, the casino manager, and demanded to see him immediately.

It became quite a scene when several casino supervisors joined their coworkers at the table to explain that – surprise, surprise – there was no Jerry Hunt! The incident developed into one of those classic family story moments, and now, if anyone's acting a little delusional, one of us might quip – *"Where's Jerry Hunt?!"*

While Dad had his challenges, most of the time he channeled his endless energy into productive and positive outlets, like music – which is also something that has helped our brother Dave. That's when the real magic happened!

Dad and Dave jamming.

Aunt Irene and Dad singing together.

Dad on keyboard and Mom on vocals. The sheet music she's holding is called "His Word Will Stand."

The Cross Family Singers

Mom and Dad were natural-born entertainers who could capture any audience, especially us kids. Dad could even make something as dull as reading the phone book entertaining. We would gather around, and he would use funny voices and facial expressions to read out the phone book entries, making us all erupt with laughter.

Our parents were also good singers! Dad would often serenade Mom around the house with his favorite tunes, and then she would sing back to him in her beautifully sweet voice.

Fun Fact: The eldest child of the real-life Trapp Family Singers, the inspiration for *The Sound of Music*, was not a sixteen-going-on-seventeen girl called Liesl, it was a boy named Rupert. After Nazi Germany's 1938 annexation of Austria, the whole von Trapp family eventually immigrated to the United States, settling in Stowe, Vermont.

After World War II, in which Rupert von Trapp served as an army medic, he got married in Fall River, and in 1948, he bought a house in the historic village of Adamsville, Rhode Island – now part of Little Compton, Rhode Island – where he eventually became a physician and ran a medical practice for three decades. Steve has some early memories from when we lived in an apartment on the same road as Dr. von Trapp, including Mom taking him and toddler me to Dr. von Trapp's home office for a couple of appointments. I wish I could also remember these visits – such small-world coincidences are some of "My Favorite Things."

Unlike the very talented von Trapp children, musicality wasn't distributed evenly among the Crossketeers. Sure, we all loved a good singalong and impromptu dance party, but Dad thought we should all learn how to play an instrument. We had a piano in our house, so I tried that for a while, but our beloved brother Steve chose the clarinet, which proved quite distressing for everyone within earshot.

Steve was tone deaf and rhythmless but determined to learn. During one memorable practice session, Dad tried to help him "feel" the music. Even the neighbors could hear our well-meaning father hopelessly banging on the kitchen table and shouting *"ONE-two-three, ONE-two-three!"*

Steve always came up flat or off-beat, or both, and we did feel sorry for him (and Dad). It was painful to watch and hear, but we all got a good laugh. Years later, Steve showed me his eighth-grade report card: solid F's in both art and music.

The award for natural talent in our family goes to Dave, who is blessed with artistic flair and musical ability – a master of percussion. The rest of us have meager talent, but when we all get together, we can't resist breaking into song. Our go-to anthems include "John Jacob Jingleheimer Schmidt," and our ultimate favorite, the theme from "The Addams Family," always accompanied by enthusiastic stomping, clapping, and snapping!

My granddaughter, Madeline, is one of our Crazy Cross descendants who definitely inherited the music and dance genes, and in another wonderful coincidence, at six years old, she was in a local youth theatre production of, you guessed it, *The Addams Family.*

My granddaughter Madeline in costume for "The Addams Family" in 2024.

They're creepy and they're kooky,
Mysterious and spooky,
They're altogether ooky,
The Addams Family!

Haves & Have Nots

When Steve was out driving around with Dad on stiflingly hot summer days, Dad would joke, "Roll up the windows, son – so people will think we have air conditioning!"

What other people thought of our family really didn't matter to us, but our parents always made sure we were as happy, healthy, and hygienic as a bunch of crazy Cross children could be.

Our family's favorite indulgence was sweet treats – especially candy – but not all luxuries are extravagant and enjoyable, and so it was when we visited our family dentist, Dr. Robinowitz. There were eight of us, each with a sweet tooth and a cavity or two to prove it, but Dr. Robinowitz gave Dad a good deal – just ten dollars per cavity filling. Novocain, however, was five dollars more, so, most of the time, none of us were numbed for our dental work, creating a lifelong fear of going to the dentist for some of us Cross children.

Those of us who were old enough also remember a visit Mom made to the dentist which ended up traumatizing the whole family. I was about ten years old when Mom had to have all of her upper teeth extracted, and while she no doubt splurged on some Novocain for the procedure, she came home crying from the pain, which only intensified when she looked at herself in the mirror. Mom was beautiful, but not vain, and I think anyone would feel how she felt upon seeing her reflection – she was only thirty-five and she looked like an old woman.

We were horrified, and helpless to ease her discomfort, but even while she was in constant excruciating pain, Mom never complained, and she always put the needs and care of her family first.

Still to this day, long after Mom's dentures were in and her smile returned, my siblings and I talk about our shared PTSD of seeing our mother that way – we simply didn't have the emotional tools to process or respond at the time.

All of us Cross kids had crossed front teeth – me more than the others – but I always understood, without ever asking or talking about it, that we didn't have money for braces.

When I look at the photo of my sister Pam and me in our girl scout uniforms, despite our sweet preteen innocence, I recognize that I was already comparing myself to others. I was about twelve, crooked-toothed and completely flat-chested, and it wasn't long after this photo was taken I would begin noticing things while on play dates with girls my age – two bathrooms in Gretchen's home, store-bought clothes, braces, and bras (for breasts I wondered if I would ever have).

And then there was the time in middle school when a friend let me know that I had the imprint of an iron seared into the very cheap fabric of my sweater. She wasn't trying to embarrass me, but I was embarrassed, and the incident, like the iron print, is seared into my memory.

This was the first time I really knew I had "less than" others, and it was also the first time I realized that high quality, stylish – and dare I even think it, expensive – clothing was something I wanted to have. In fact, I wanted it so much, that in high school, I bought a brand-new dress with money I earned from my amusement park waitress job. It cost a whopping twenty-five dollars, but, fearing my mother would disapprove, I lied and said it was only fifteen.

The older I got, the more I understood the disparities – the "haves" and "have nots" – but our family could always laugh about how we compared to those with multiple bathrooms, air-conditioned cars, and closets full of expensive clothes.

We luxuriated in our familial love and joy, and that made us richer than most. And besides – like love, happiness, taste, and manners – some things you just can't buy, and as I was about to discover, not all families are as naturally hospitable as ours was.

Me and Pam wearing our girl scout uniforms in the mid 1960s.

From the Joseph Case High School 1970 yearbook, clockwise from top left – my senior portrait; my class superlative photo – I was voted "Best All Around" with my classmate David Provost; my best friend Karen's senior photo; and my and Karen's varsity cheerleading photos.

Tighty-Whities

Ah, the shock of childhood discoveries. It's right up there with finding out Santa Claus isn't real (thanks to Mom slipping up and asking me to help wrap presents when I was ten). But nothing compares to the first time I realized my family was not the norm. Growing up, I thought every family was like ours – full of laughter, love, and just the right amount of madness – but I was wrong.

The parents of my school friends seemed so stern and strict, with far more rules than I had ever observed or been required to obey, and as I ventured further into the world during my teen years, I sadly discovered there were unhappy and dysfunctional families all around me. Sometimes it was more than sad – it was downright creepy.

The stark disparity really struck me when, at the end of my senior year, I was invited to meet the family of my brand new boyfriend. I had just broken up with my high school sweetheart, Bobby, who was actually my best friend Karen's boyfriend first – Karen and I shared clothes and interests, and our taste in boys, too, I guess!

This new boyfriend wasn't particularly bright, ambitious, or even interesting, and I had forgotten his name until I recently cracked open my yearbook, where I found his signature under a long note he'd written about our "future" together. My parents, especially Mom, had adored Bobby, and they didn't like this new guy at all. But I was on a mission to prove I could make my own choices – and I needed a date for senior prom – so I agreed to meet his parents. They lived in an ordinary-looking ranch house in the Swansea suburbs, and as we entered through the kitchen door, his father greeted me in a way I will never forget.

There he was, standing proudly in his underwear – a sleeveless undershirt taut across his potbelly, and a pair of briefs, the kind my daughters would call "tighty-whities" – *eeew*!

I was mortified. Neither my boyfriend nor his father acted like anything was amiss, and I could barely say hello before I was ready to get out of there. I never did meet his mother, and I still went to the prom with this guy – and what a night that turned out to be!

Among all the girls of my class, I was crowned queen of the senior prom and summoned to the dance floor to the sweet sounds of "This Magic Moment." But dancing with my date was anything but magical, and I knew right then and there that I never wanted to see or hear from him ever again – and I didn't. There are no photos of me on my big night either, because I deliberately destroyed every single shot! In addition to being voted prom queen and "Best All Around" in our class superlatives, I was also the layout editor for our yearbook, and I just couldn't bear photos of the two of us dancing being preserved for eternity.

My teenage granddaughters would call this guy a relationship "pancake" – because when making pancakes, the first one or two are never the most delicious – it's best just to use them to season the pan, and then toss them.

He and his dad were nothing like the "Crazy Crosses" – everyone knows when you invite a stranger to your house, you should put on some pants and perhaps be willing to let them borrow your car for a few days – or at least that's what *my* Dad would do.

Marooned Motorcycle Rescue

While this tale is best told in person by Steve, who was sixteen at the time, what follows is one of our family's all-time favorite stories.

It was a bright and breezy Friday evening in the summer of 1967, Labor Day Weekend, and smack-dab in the middle of the hitchhiking craze of the sixties and seventies. Dad was kind and helpful by nature, and already known locally for giving total strangers a lift, and as he was driving home from his shift at the Brayton Point Power Station on Route Six, he spotted a young man and woman stranded with their motorcycle by the roadside.

These two looked like they had just stepped out of a biker magazine, with leather jackets and windswept hair, real rough-and-tumble types. Or so it seemed, and maybe that's why no one else stopped to help, but not our Dad! He pulled over without a second thought, ready to lend a hand.

After a quick inspection, he concluded that the motorcycle's oil crankcase was cracked and the engine was kaput. Lucky for them, they were just a few minutes away from our house, so Dad asked them to wait while he zipped home to switch vehicles. He roped in Steve and they returned in a bigger car, ready to haul the bike – and the young couple – back to our house. During the drive, they explained that they were newlyweds on their way from New Jersey to Cape Cod for a honeymoon weekend. Dad, ever the fixer, took another look at the bike, but the damage was too much for even a field expedient fix. The crestfallen couple asked for a ride to the bus station, but Dad had a better idea.

Without missing a beat, he jangled a set of keys as he said – "Oh, just take our car!" – and sent them on their way. Disbelieving at first, then overjoyed, the young couple thanked him profusely, tossed their backpacks in the trunk, and drove off. Watching them round the corner and drive out of sight, Steve turned to Dad, a little concerned, and asked, "Do you even know their last name?"

Dad just chuckled. "Don't worry. They'll be back."

When Mom got home later, she noticed that one of our cars was conspicuously missing, and after hearing Dad's explanation, all she could do was smile, and sigh – "Oh, Irving!"

But, sure enough, the very happy newlyweds rolled back into our driveway that Labor Day Monday evening, and with a full tank of gas to boot. Mom invited them in for a hearty family dinner, story sharing, and laughter, and even our dog joined the fun, snatching the meat right off the table. The couple stayed with us that night, sleeping in a tent in our backyard, and the next morning, Dad and Steve chauffeured the very happy campers to the bus station, their motorcycle left behind to be sold for scraps.

After this, for many years, we'd find a Christmas card from them in our mailbox, thanking us for what they called our "radical kindness," but, honestly, it wasn't radical all – it was just another day in the life of our Dad.

Thanksgiving with the Crosses

Radical kindness, generosity, and gratitude – three things Dad and Mom had in abundance, which is probably why Thanksgiving was such a major Cross family holiday every single year.

It was also the only holiday that we Massachusetts Crosses got to spend lots of quality time with our extended Connecticut and Rhode Island Cross families, a tradition which began in the early 1950s with our first Thanksgiving celebration at my Aunt Irene and Uncle George's home in Ledyard, Connecticut.

Everyone played games, told stories, and hiked in the woods until it was time to eat. We were always in suspense when we gathered around the table, as the doneness of the turkey was always a mystery. Sometimes it was undercooked, one time it was burned – that was the time Uncle George looked at the "buzzard," and said, "No, more!" – which started the tradition of having two turkeys every Thanksgiving, just in case.

Aunt Irene hosted Thanksgiving every year, all the way up to 1969, but because Irene and her father, my Grandpa Cecil, stopped speaking to each other when she left home in the mid 1940s, he was never invited to these gatherings. It was like that until Thanksgiving 1969, a few weeks after which, Grandpa Cecil passed away.

The Connecticut, Massachusetts, and Rhode Island Crosses fused feasts in 1970, when my Aunt Joan and Uncle Ed took over hosting Thanksgiving in their home – first on Doyle Avenue in Providence, and then later in picturesque Foster, Rhode Island. We even commemorated our 30th Thanksgiving anniversary in 2000 with a special newsletter that shows some photos from that first Providence Thanksgiving in 1970.

Since the 2000s, there have been a couple of years when our brother Steve and his wife Marcia have hosted the official annual celebration, but there was one Thanksgiving my daughter Allie and I missed when we went to see my other daughter Jessica in Morocco – where we met her future husband, Abdessalam Hamdoun.

Pam and her husband Mark now spend Thanksgiving with their extended Antaya family in Amherst, Massachusetts, and Clarel and I spend the day with our extended Antoine and Laurençon families in Long Island. And, while our tradition of celebrating Thanksgiving together as siblings has faded with time, we always make up for it with the one holiday Cross custom that none of us have ever broken – being together at Christmas!

We give thanks to Uncle George, who started the two-turkey tradition for our annual Thanksgivings.

Thanksgiving 1979. Grandma Alice and Pam on Dad's lap, with my cousin Jenny behind them.

Aunt Irene goofing around for the camera on Thanksgiving.

A holiday family photo from 1960. Standing in the back are my Aunt Irene and Uncle George with my cousin Jack; standing in the middle are Pam, Steve, and Mom; David (standing in front of Pam); Dad holding baby Brian; and then me – always camera shy – in the front.

Thanksgiving at Aunt Joan's in the later 1970s. From left to right are Bob, Uncle George, my cousin Michael, Mom and Dad, and my cousin Jack.

Thanksgiving 2000 flyer, celebrating thirty years of family feasts at Aunt Joan and Uncle Ed's house.

Steve and baby Dave, Christmas morning 1958.

A 1963 Easy-Bake Oven advertisement by Kenner Products (later Hasbro).

Christmas with the Crosses

Like Thanksgiving, Christmas was always extraordinarily merry in the Cross household, and our parents always made sure that it was a magical, exuberant, and unforgettable experience.

For most families, the holiday season is a special time to come together, celebrate their traditions, and bask in the warmth of loved ones. While Mom went to church every Sunday of her life until she was seventeen, our family was not particularly religious, so our church visits were sporadic at best, which is why I so enjoyed going with Nana.

For us, Christmas was all about Santa Claus, a mountain of toys, and a level of excitement that made us feel as if we might just burst. One year, Steve was so electrified by the holiday spirit that Dad had to barricade him in his room, for fear that his contagious enthusiasm would spread like wildfire – and we might all just end up going to Butler.

"We didn't have a lot of money," our brother Brian once recalled, "But we always had a lot of toys, and our Christmases were just amazing. Other kids might get one or two toys, but we'd get, I don't know, at least six. Multiply that by six kids – that's thirty-six toys in one day!"

Ah, the toys! Dad would barely catch a wink every Christmas Eve because, like a one-elf workshop, he stayed up so late assembling our toys.

One of my fondest memories coincides with the Christmas morning my sister Pam and I got an Easy-Bake Oven. Half a million were sold that year, but Pam and I thought we were among a very special few. It was a functional toy version of a grown-up appliance, light blue in color with a little oven door. We would whip up the tiny packets of vanilla cake batter, let them bake under the glow of a 100-watt light bulb, and then top them off with a slather of chocolate frosting. It may have been a humble beginning, but I'm convinced the sheer joy of those early Easy-Bake adventures sparked Pam's culinary passion. Our whole family delights in her delicious cooking, and her legendary pepperoncini cheese dip is an absolute must at every gathering.

Pam's Cheese Dip
(Pepperoncini Dip)

Ingredients
- 1 cup mayo (½ light, ½ regular)
- 8 oz. sharp white cheddar cheese
- ¼ cup chopped black olives
- ¼ tsp. garlic powder
- 1 cup chopped pepperoncini

Instructions
- Mix ingredients together and put in pie plate
- Bake on 350 degrees for 20 – 25 minutes
- Don't overcook!
- Garnish with chopped tomato & scallions
- Serve with tortilla chips

Ranking only slightly above Pam's dip is our most important – and oldest – family Christmas tradition, which is simply being together with our siblings and parents. It's harder than it sounds, and I'm both proud and rather astounded that since 1950, not one of us has missed a single Christmas together. However, there was an instance very early on that nearly broke our streak.

In October of 1970, Steve left our cozy little home for California on his motorcycle with a friend on the back. Though he called and wrote from time to time, we missed him terribly, and as the calendar ticked toward December, it dawned on us that Steve wouldn't be home for Christmas. It was a sad and strange thought. But Steve was about to pull off our very own Cross Christmas miracle, and on the morning of Christmas Eve, he secretly boarded a plane in Los Angeles.

Christmas 1960 – Steve, Mom, Pam, Dad, and me.

At left, Mom and Dad on Christmas 1960, and at right, Dad on Santa's lap in the 1980s.

Steve's plane had to make an unexpected detour to Chicago, so from there, he hopped on another plane, which, after a delay, just barely reached Boston due to extreme winter weather conditions. With snow swirling upon arrival, it seemed like he might not make it home to Swansea after all.

Whether it was good Cross karma or just pure radical kindness, two women Steve met on his second plane offered to drive him – through the raging snowstorm – all the way to our festive Swansea doorstep.

We were already nestled all snug in our beds, visions of new toys dancing in our heads, when Steve sneaked into our parents' room and hopped into bed with them. Mom, half asleep, suddenly realized – "It's Steve!" – and it wasn't long before the whole family was up and at 'em, smothering Steve with love.

It was truly a Cross Christmas miracle, brought to you by our sponsor, radical kindness, the gift that keeps on giving.

Brian, Dad, and Dave on Christmas morning 1966.

The Crazy Crosses on Dad and Mom's 25th wedding anniversary in 1975. From left to right behind Dad and Mom are Dana, Brian, Steve and his wife Marcia, my husband Bob and me, Dave, and Pam.

A candid shot from Dad and Mom's 25th wedding anniversary in 1975. To the right of me (standing next to Mom), from left to right, are my Uncle Frank and Aunt Betty, and at far right, Grandma Alice.

Crazy-Wonderful Crosses

Radically kind and crazy wonderful – an apt description for my parents and the loving family they created. But Mom would say that both she and Dad came from "challenging" families – which is both a tragic and complicated understatement, as I've since learned from all my research.

And while mom and dad's childhoods were trying and troubling in different ways, these formative struggles inspired them to create the warmest most wonderful environment they could for their children, and for each other.

Most of it came naturally, but they worked at it too. Mom and Dad had a policy to never go to bed angry, and even if she knew he was wrong about something, often she would apologize first so they could resolve whatever the disagreement was and get on with being happy.

Somehow, despite the "challenges" of their youths, for Mom and Dad it was as simple as that – a choice to be happy. Crazy!

PART II

Alzada's Weird but Wonderful Childhood

1926 – 1949

Mom's Family Tree

Almost all of Mom's ancestors descend from early English colonists in Massachusetts and Rhode Island, including several *Mayflower* passengers, more of which is featured in Part IV.

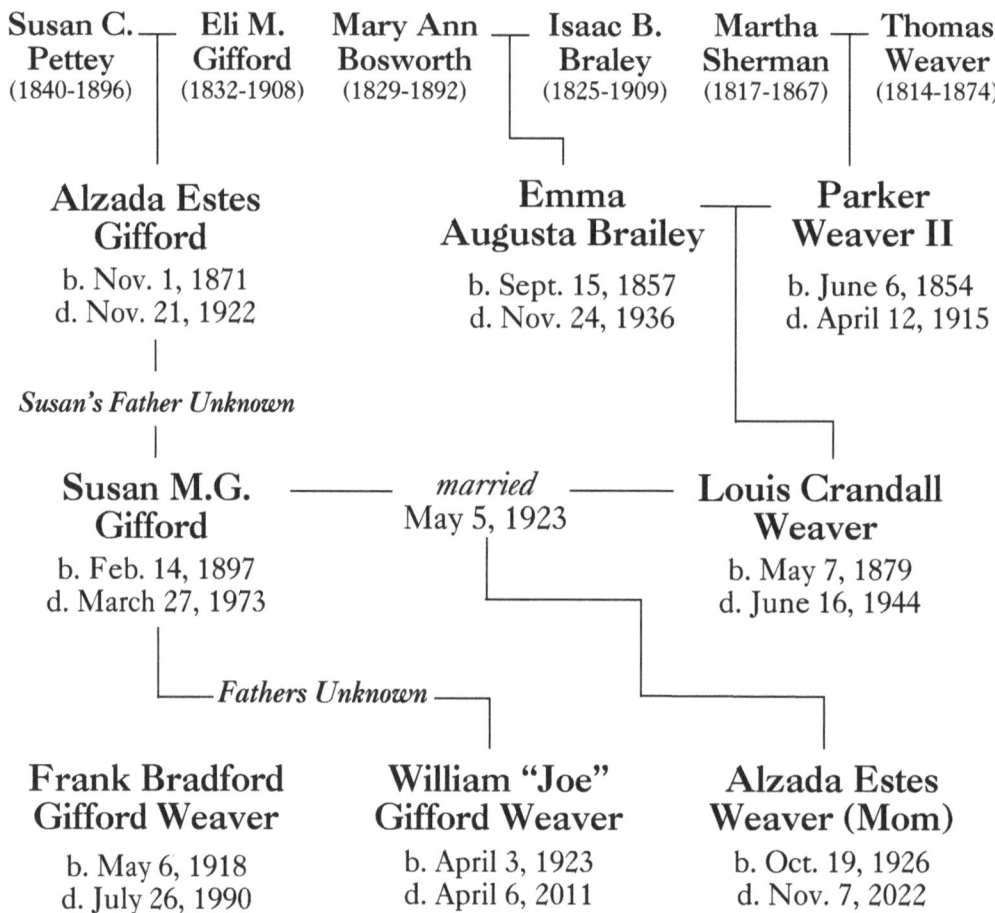

Alzada's Weird but Wonderful Childhood

MY WONDERFUL MOTHER, Alzada Estes Weaver, was born Tuesday, October 19, 1926, in Fall River, to Louis Crandall Weaver and Susan M.G. Gifford Weaver, both lifelong residents of Fall River.

Mom and Dad were natural storytellers, but even if I'd had the foresight to ask all the right questions while they were still with us, there was much they couldn't – or wouldn't – share about their childhoods and families. In the ways that my father experienced a lack of parental warmth and affection, my mother had an abundance of loving family – but her family also had a few secrets.

Mom was named after her maternal grandmother, Alzada Estes Gifford, just as my Nana Susan was named for her maternal grandmother Susan. It's a lovely waltz of names – Susan, Alzada, Susan, Alzada – and in this part I'll be calling Mom by her given name, Alzada.

I'd also like to explain my very intentional use of the word "weird" to describe Alzada's childhood, which, during one of our interviews for this memoir, she herself called "not happy." She didn't say "unhappy," but I do think her childhood was unusual, as well as unfortunate, in a way, as it was for most growing up during the Great Depression. And, when compared to the constant chaotic happiness of my crazy Cross childhood, her definition makes even more sense.

Alzada loved her parents, and they loved her, but she never saw any affection or romance between them – she never even saw them kiss, not even once. There were no lingering embraces or subtle gestures of love, and, for as long as Alzada could remember, she slept between them in the middle of their bed.

Whether it was just their personalities – as in, they weren't the lovey-dovey type – or even if it was a marriage built on convenience, one thing was for sure: seeing her parents' steady but seemingly passionless relationship gave Alzada a clear vision of what she wanted for herself – a secure and stable partnership AND a passionately romantic love story.

Even though her parents weren't affectionate with each other, they lavished their daughter with love and attention. Susan took great care to ensure that Alzada and her brothers were always neat and well-dressed, and whenever Alzada was sick, doting Susan would whip up her favorite custard to comfort her. Her father, Louis, who raised his voice in anger to her only once, was also a masterful storyteller, and he had a talent for spinning epic adventures starring his very own darling daughter.

Alzada had many more memories of magical Christmas mornings and weekly trips to the local amusement park, the highlights of an average happy childhood. Unlike most children, however, Alzada's earliest memory was utterly terrifying.

Frank, William, Alzada, and Santa (yikes), probably in December of 1927.

Conflagration

Alzada's very first memory happened when she was just eighteen months old. It was the freezing cold night of February 2, 1928, and she was huddled in her mother's arms in their Durfee Street home, gagging on thick smoke and crying in terror as the Great Fire of Fall River ravaged the city.

"I could feel my mother trembling," Alzada said when recalling this vivid memory for me. She and her older brothers, Frank (ten) and William (five), clung to their mother as they watched the disaster blaze around them. What a traumatizing moment that must have been for a toddler, to palpably feel and forever remember her mother's terror as their whole world was swallowed up in an inferno.

The fire began in the abandoned Pocasset Mills, a sleeping giant that once thrummed with the lifeblood of the city's textile industry, and on that fateful February night, the giant awoke to spew toxic fumes and roaring flames through the streets of Fall River.

The howling winds whipped the fire into a frenzy, thwarting all efforts to bring it under control, and in just eight terrifying hours, the "conflagration" – as the local papers called it – razed five city blocks to the ground and leveled three dozen structures, reducing most of its businesses to ashes. One popular local columnist reported seeing a stray ember ignite a woman's fur coat as she fled, and a man's hat explode like a box of tinder. Mercifully, no lives were lost, but the stories of that night still smolder in the city's collective history.

Fall River, once the crown jewel of America's textile industry, had been the largest producer of cotton textiles in the United States, with more than 100 mills operating in the late nineteenth century.

Increasingly high demand during World War I gave the city another big boost, but every boom must bust, and by the early 1920s, mill closures were rampant, including the Pocasset Mills, which closed the year Alzada was born. By the time the nation was beginning its descent into the Great Depression, the folks of Fall River were no strangers to hardship and disaster, and families like the Weavers had long relied and survived on their resilience and resourcefulness.

While the 1928 Great Fire of Fall River may have left scars on the city, and Alzada's memory, it also sparked a determination in its citizens to rise from the ashes – especially in Alzada's mother, Susan.

Photos in the Fall River Herald News show the damage caused by the Great Fire of 1928.

Nana Susan's Family Tree

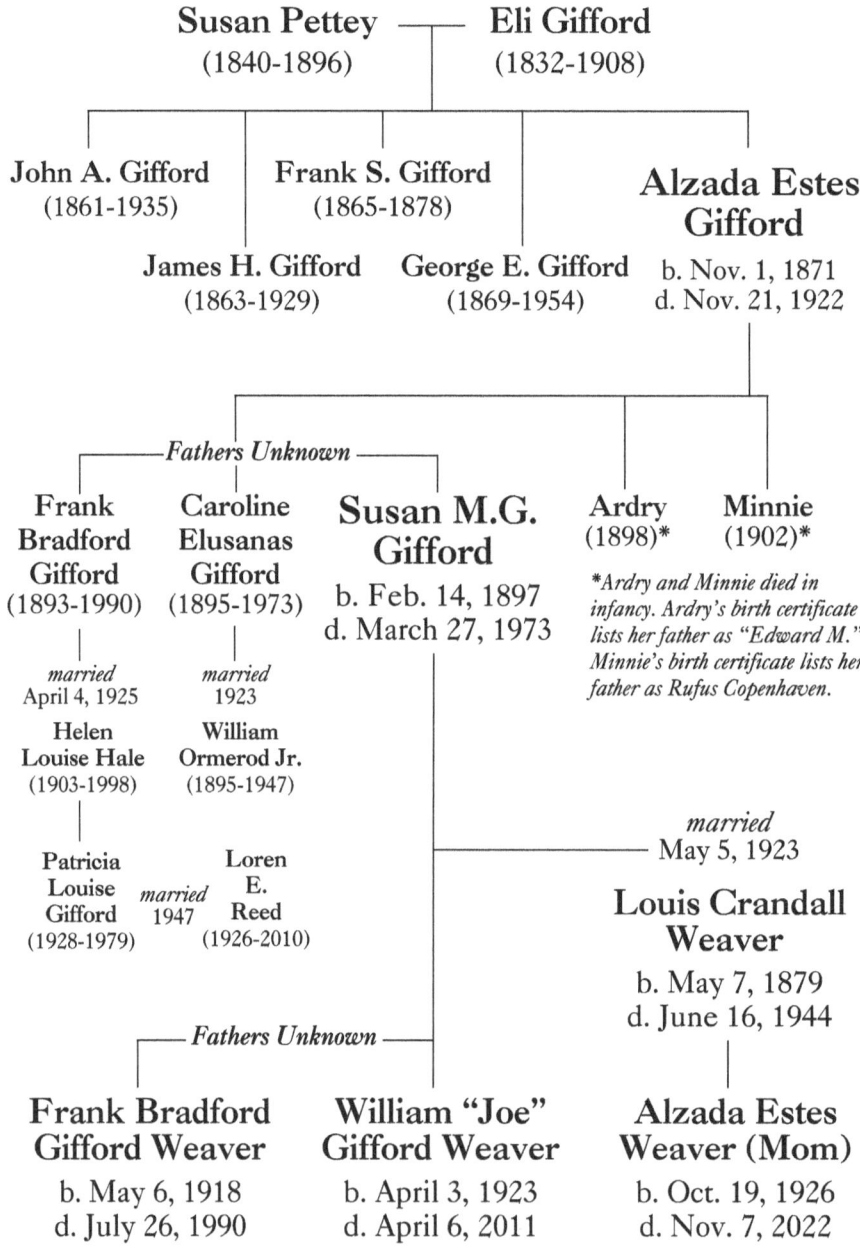

Alzada's Mother Susan

Susan M.G. Gifford was born on Valentine's Day, February 14, 1897, in Fall River, to Alzada Estes Gifford and an unknown father – and if you think that's a pearl-clutcher, brace yourself.

Nana Susan was the youngest of Alzada Gifford's three children who survived to adulthood, all three of whom had unknown or uninvolved fathers, something we'll take a closer look at in Part Four.

Susan's older brother, Frank, arrived in 1893, when their mother was twenty-one, followed two years later by her older sister, Caroline. Family tradition suggests that Frank and Caroline had the same father, but as far as the stories and records go, we haven't yet figured out who it was. That same tradition suggests Susan's father was a different man.

No birth certificate was ever filed for Susan, but her death certificate lists a "George Gifford" as her father. It's possible that this George was a distant relative to Alzada, with Gifford being a common surname in the area, or it could just be an error – two more things we'll explore in Part Four.

All we really know of Susan's childhood are small facts gleaned from inconsistent census records, and assumptions made from reading local newspapers of her day, but the trail picks up once she turns seventeen and is old enough to be listed in the Fall River city directory.

In 1914, Susan made her directory debut as "Susie M G Gifford," and listed her occupation as a "clerk" for an unnamed business at "101 S Main Street." Although she still lived in the Gifford family home with her mother and siblings, at seventeen, "Susie" was considered to be an adult woman, and, as was customary, was listed like her siblings as a "boarder" at their 655 Durfee Street home.

> Rebecca A teacher bds 627 Maple
> Sada Lincoln bds 290 Cambridge
> Sarah widow Daniel h 290 Cambridge
> Susie M G clerk 101 S Main bds 655
>   Durfee   [E Main
> Walter E fish 1010 S Main bds 145
> Walter L clerk house 922 Broadway

Nana Susan's first official listing in the 1914 Fall River city directory.

There's a possibility the "S" for "South" in her work address is a typo, due to the unrelated directory listing below hers (for Walter E. Gifford, a fisherman working at 1010 S Main), but also because located at "101 North Main Street" was Wilmot's, a sporting goods store which specialized in bicycles, as well as typewriter rentals and repairs, and, their biggest sellers, the Edison Diamond Disc Phonographs – plus records.

The two locations, 101 S Main and 101 N Main, were relatively close in distance, so wherever Susan was and whatever she was doing, it must have been exciting to be working in the thick of bustling downtown Fall River. In 1915, Susan is still listed as a clerk in the directory, but no work address is given, and it's the same for 1916 and 1917, until 1918 when her occupation was switched to "stitcher."

The most likely reason for the job change was that, towards the end of 1917, Susan became pregnant with her first child, and with her visibly progressing "condition," she may have been dismissed or asked to resign as a clerk, where she would have been on full display.

Luckily, in March of 1918, C.P. McClellan's started advertising for stitchers to run their power sewing machines, which they used to make automobile tops and seat covers, horse and wagon covers, tents, awnings, canopies, and sails.

Employed but unmarried, Susan gave birth to her first son Frank in Fall River on May 6, 1918, at the age of twenty-one, the same age her mother was when she gave birth to her older brother, also named Frank, for whom Susan named her new son.

According to the city directory, Susan's brother Frank, a printer by trade, moved out of the Durfee Street home before 1916, and had "removed to Springfield" by 1918, where he married a woman named Eliza Millward. Eliza passed away young, and widowed Frank then married Helen Louise Hale, with whom he had daughter Patricia Louise Gifford, my mother's favorite cousin, Patty.

Caroline, Susan, and baby Frank remained with matriarch Alzada at 655 Durfee, where they'd lived since 1900, and by 1919, both sisters were working as stitchers. Susan is listed as a servant in a private home in the 1920 census, but the city directory lists no profession for her in 1920 or 1921.

Tragically, on November 21, 1922, when Susan was twenty-five, still unmarried, and almost five months pregnant with her second child, her mother Alzada, just fifty-one years old, passed away at home. Her death certificate states she was never married, which is probably true, despite the various "widowed" and "Mrs." notations we occasionally find with her name, but it might have just been less of a hassle for her to lie or imply or let people assume.

Alzada Estes Gifford was laid to rest in Beech Grove Cemetery in Westport, Massachusetts, and four months later, Susan gave birth to her second son, William. And then, just a month after that, on May 5, 1923, Susan married forty-four-year-old Louis Crandall Weaver at the First Baptist Church in Fall River, with Rev. Everett C. Herrick officiating.

What a whirlwind it must have been! In the span of just a few months, Susan went from grieving the loss of her mother to giving birth to her second child to getting married and moving out of her long-time family home. By 1926, the new family – Susan, Louis, young Frank, and toddler William – had settled into a small but cozy home at 625 Durfee Street, and it was here that the Weavers would welcome their last child and only daughter, my mother, Alzada Estes Weaver.

The life of Susan Gifford Weaver was anything but ordinary, and she met every challenge with a loving heart and unwavering faith. She embodied a quiet, natural strength, and through it all, stayed connected to her roots, honoring the memory of her mother, and carrying forward the legacy of the Gifford women in her own special way.

Nana Susan in the 1940s.

Betty with Susan and Alzada, who is holding Betty and Frank's first daughter, my cousin Susan.

Grandfather Louis' Family Tree

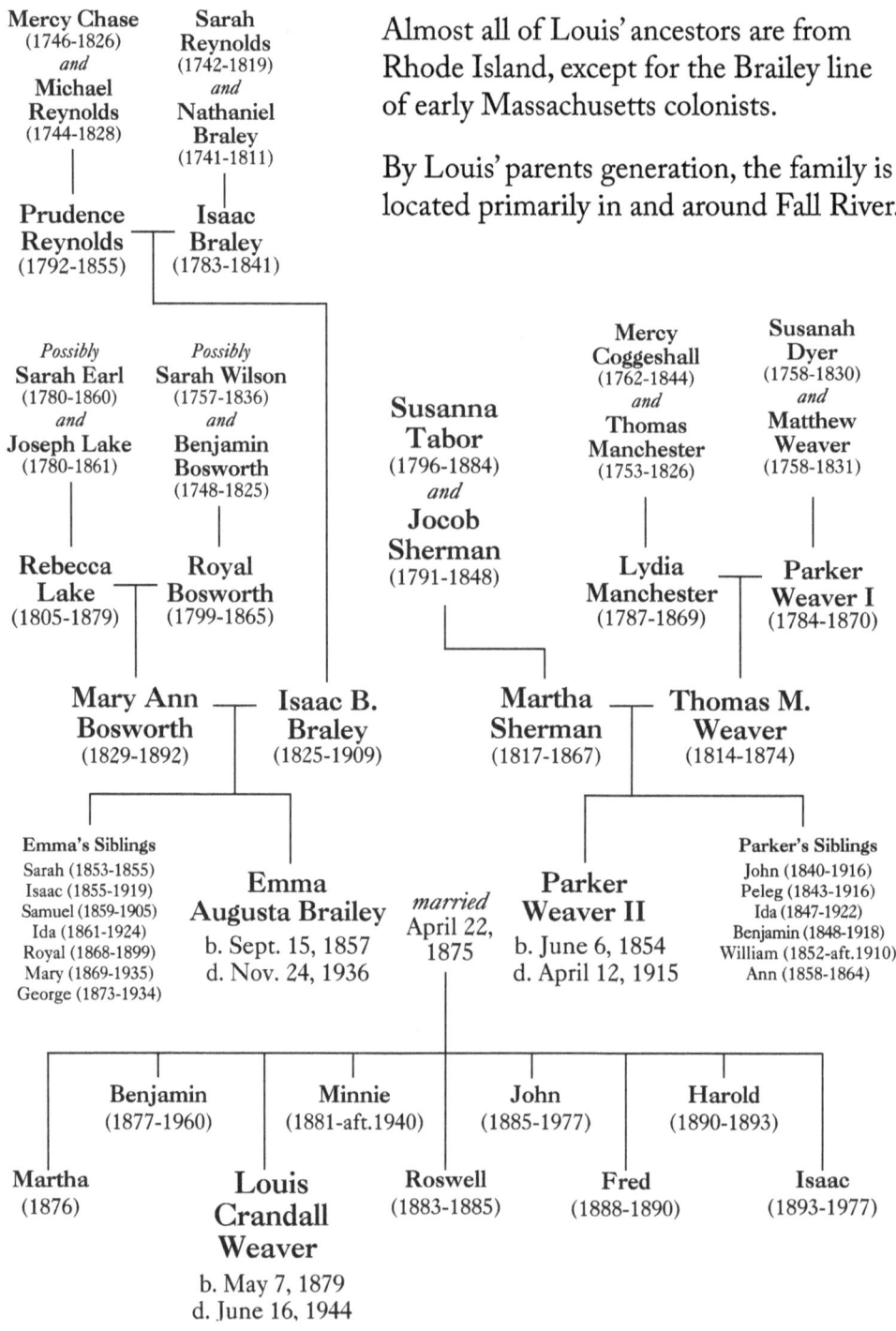

Almost all of Louis' ancestors are from Rhode Island, except for the Brailey line of early Massachusetts colonists.

By Louis' parents generation, the family is located primarily in and around Fall River.

Alzada's Father Louis

Louis Crandall Weaver was born May 7, 1879, in Fall River, to Parker Weaver II and Emma Brailey Weaver, the second of five children who survived to adulthood. Parker was born in 1854 in Swansea, but he descends from a family of eighteenth-century Rhode Island sheep farmers, and Emma was born in 1857 in Bristol, Rhode Island.

Louis' parents were married in 1875 in Swansea and moved to Fall River as a young couple, where Parker worked in the mills, first as a fireman and later an engineer, both in Fall River and New Bedford.

Emma gave birth to nine children, but she and Parker lost four of them very young. We have no record of Emma working for wages, but if she did, she would've already had her hands full running the household and raising five children, two of them with physical disabilities.

Louis' older brother Ben walked with a limp, and beginning in his younger years, Louis developed a similar gait. But unlike Ben, Louis relied on crutches and canes, one of which was always within reach. His World War I draft registration card notes "spinal troubles, lameness," and by World War II, it lists "partial paralysis of the legs."

"It would bother me when kids stared at him," Mom once confided in me, "but he would say that it was OK and it didn't hurt him."

It's possible that Louis had a severe case of scoliosis, and while stares and comments didn't hurt his feelings, every day was probably physically painful for him. In photos, he's almost always with a cane when he's standing – never hiding himself, always smiling – but in photos of him sitting, his condition, whatever it may have been, is pretty much totally undetectable.

His resilience, like Susan's, was remarkable, and he never let his physical pain overwhelm his desire to work and provide for his family. Louis was a talented craftsman and a creative person by nature, but as a young man – and like the vast majority of his family, friends, and neighbors – he had to work full-time in the mills. He then became a brass polisher at a nearby sailmaking loft, and by 1915, he was a polisher for C.P. McClellan, another sailmaker, at 22 Boomer Street in Fall River.

Well before Susan and Louis' brow-raising betrothal, it appears Louis was attached to a different woman in the neighborhood, a newly widowed woman named Sarah "Sadie" Potter, mother of five and several years older than Louis.

In July of 1910, when Susan was thirteen, a society item appears in the *Fall River Globe* detailing a party thrown by a Mrs. Armstrong on Pearce Street, attended by *"Louis Weaver, wife and family, and Miss Grace Potter, all of Fall River."*

The "wife" is likely Sadie, the "family" her sons, and Miss Grace Potter, her daughter, but we have no evidence that Louis and Sadie ever married, let alone proof of a romance. The earliest record I can find that is most likely to be Sadie is the 1900 Newark, New Jersey census, which lists her and her husband George and their two children, Willie and Gracie.

The next reliable record is the 1908 Fall River directory, which lists widowed Sadie at 177 Cherry Street, followed by the Fall River 1910 census, which lists all five Potter children – William (14), Grace (12), George (10), and Ernest (5), all born in New Jersey, and Robert (4), who was born in Massachusetts.

By 1912, Louis and Sadie live in the same building at 205 Durfee Street, and by 1913, Sadie's son William is working at the same place as Louis, C.P. McClellan's. By 1914, Sadie and Louis have moved to 135 Pine Street – although he is officially listed as a boarder at his parents' home.

Louis, Alzada, and Susan in May 1937.

Louis and Alzada with Louis' brother, Ben Weaver, taken May 1937, at their home on New Boston Road.

Intriguingly, another social item appears in print on May 9, 1914, in both the *Fall River Globe* and the *Evening Herald* – *"A tango tea was held in the home of Mrs. Potter on Pine Street, last night, when a Maybasket was hung to Louis C. Weaver of that address. The dining room was tastefully decorated for the occasion, ferns and daffodils ornamenting the center of the table. The presentation of the basket, which was filled with all sorts of good things, took place after tea had been served. Vocal and instrumental selections were next in order and a most enjoyable evening was spent."*

This was no doubt a birthday celebration for Louis, who turned thirty-five just two days earlier. Tango teas were all the rage at the time, and newspaper items from later years depict the Potter children and their friends as quite musical, singing and playing piano at parties they hosted in their home.

After his father passed away in 1915, Louis moved in with his youngest sibling, Isaac, and their newly widowed mother, at 655 Durfee, where Susan lived with her mother and sister on a different floor. My ancestors, and many of their friends and neighbors, moved a lot in those days, but they stuck to the same neighborhoods and streets – Cherry, Danforth, Durfee, and Main – because they already knew people there. So, before they boarded in the same house, Susan and Louis had probably already seen each other around the neighborhood.

By 1918, Louis had moved to Danforth Street, and his job had changed from "polisher" to "sailmaker" – this is also the year that Susan, pregnant with Frank, became a "stitcher" at the same place. Louis and Sadie don't share addresses ever again, and by 1921, Louis is boarding with his mother, Emma, at 683 Durfee, making him practically neighbors with Susan, who is still at 655 Durfee. But, even if it was a fizzled romance, there's no doubt the Potters and Weavers remained friendly, because Sadie's son Ernest was later a pallbearer at the funerals of both Emma and Louis.

By the start of 1923, Susan was in a terrifying predicament: her mother Alzada was gone, her brother Frank was living his own life, her sister Caroline was getting ready to get married and move out, and Susan was more than half-way through her second pregnancy – while trying to raise a five-year-old.

I do wonder if Susan and Louis were advised to wait to get married until after the baby was born, as it could have appeared improper for the pastor to officiate the marriage of a heavily pregnant unwed woman to a lifelong bachelor almost twice her age, a man who may or may not have fathered one or both – or none – of her children.

Whatever the circumstances may have been, Louis embraced his fatherly role with pride, and both Frank and William proudly took on the last name of Weaver. What's most important, simply put, is that Louis was a good father to Frank, William, and Alzada.

Susan, Frank, Louis, and William a few years before Alzada was born.

William, Frank, and Alzada in 1927.

Uncle Frank & Uncle Joe's Family Tree

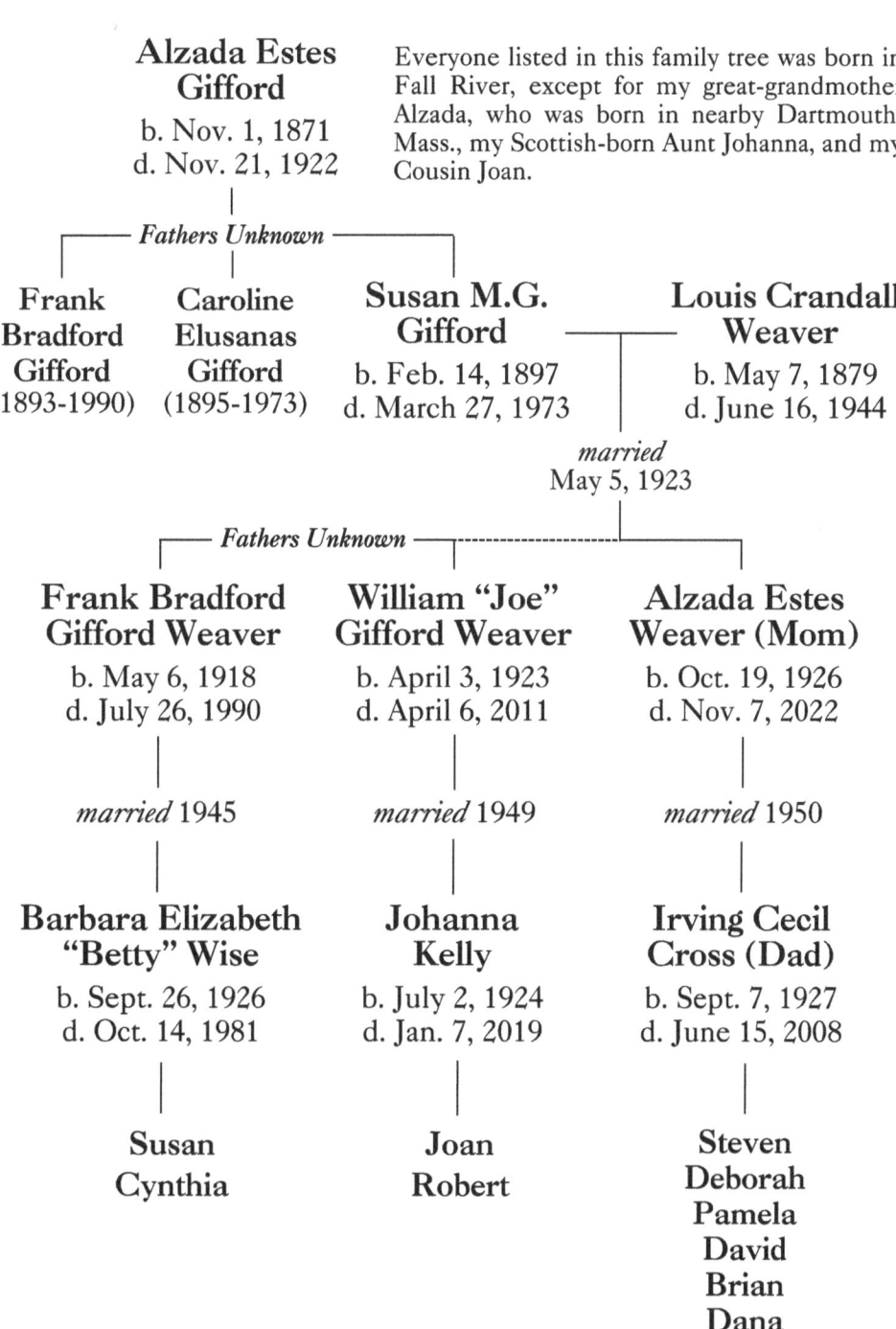

At top left, Frank's senior photo, and at top right, Frank posing with a car. At bottom left, Frank and his wife Betty in the later 1940s, and at bottom right, Frank in 1961.

Alzada's Brother Frank

Frank Bradford Weaver's birth certificate listed no father, but as an adult, Frank officially changed it to name Louis as his father. Though Susan and Louis didn't marry until after middle child Williams's birth, it is possible that Louis is first-born Frank's biological father, due to two major pieces of evidence: geography and genetics.

First, geography: Frank was born in Fall River on May 6, 1918 (coincidentally, one day before Louis' thirty-ninth birthday), putting Frank's date of conception in early August 1917, when Louis and Susan were both living at 655 Durfee Street.

Second, genetics: Frank and Louis both had spinal conditions. We don't know if Frank was born with what was probably scoliosis, or if it developed early in his childhood, but it ultimately affected his height. He had to wear a cast, and then a brace, and while it may have just been a major coincidence, maybe it was congenital, passed down from father to son. Louis' condition seems to have been far more severe, and likely worsened over time, whereas Frank's was milder, but perhaps because he received some medical attention, he was less affected later in life.

My memories of Uncle Frank are of a kind, quiet man with a warm but reserved smile, a twinkle in his eye, and never a harsh word for anyone. He was naturally gifted with anything mechanical or electrical, a true genius with gears and gadgets, and during his high school days he was a proud member of his electrical club.

By the time he graduated from Durfee High in 1936, Frank was well on his way to a long career as a radio repair technician, and within the decade that followed, he'd also found himself a lifelong love.

At left, Frank barbecuing on Ocean Drive in Newport in 1961, and at right, Frank in May of 1964.

After their wedding, Frank and his wife Betty – who was also Mom's best friend – moved in with Susan and Alzada at 733 New Boston Road in Fall River, and it was in this little house that they raised two children, my wonderful cousins Susan and Cynthia.

Alzada remained close with Betty and Frank, and Steve remembers summer days spent at Horseneck beach with our Weaver cousins. Cindy was close to my age, and I remember bonding with both her and Susan during Sunday school at the First Baptist Church of Fall River, where we were all baptized and attended service with Nana Susan – and where my cousin Susan still sings in the choir!

Susan and Cindy both married young, giving Frank and Betty many years with their six grandchildren. Twelve great-grandchildren followed, and, as of this writing, although Frank and Betty have since passed away, they are also the great-great-grandparents of five.

At top left, my cousin Susan at age four, and at bottom left, my cousin Cindy at age nine. At top right are Cindy and Susan around 1960, and at bottom right, Susan and Cindy on Easter Morning 1960.

At top left, William (Joe) in his military uniform, and at top right, Joe's wife, Johanna (Kelly) Weaver, with my cousins, Joan and baby Robert (Bobby). At bottom left is Mom (pregnant with Steve) holding her new nephew, Bobby. At bottom right, a photo of my cousin Bobby in boyhood.

Alzada's Brother William

William's arrival on April 3, 1923, was only weeks before Susan's wedding to Louis, and unlike his fair-haired, light-eyed, pale-skinned siblings, William was born with black hair, deep hazel eyes, and what Alzada called a "year-round tan."

"As a child, I always wondered about this," she once admitted to me. "Joe was very handsome, but he was much darker than I was, and we didn't even look like siblings." Alzada once mentioned this innocent observation to her mother, who got very upset, and told her never to talk about it again. So, she didn't – ever – and when I first revealed my discovery to Mom, that Susan gave birth to two children before her wedding to Louis, her reaction was a mix of tears and relief. She was finally free from a secret she had never even known.

William had a shy and introverted personality for the most part, but he also had a joyful spirit and a playful sense of humor, and he would tease Alzada with brotherly jabs when he and his friends were hanging out at the corner drugstore.

"Get home, fatso!" he would call after her, despite her slender frame – or maybe it was affectionate irony, like nicknaming a very tall person "Tiny." Whatever the case may be, luckily for Alzada, "fatso" never stuck – but "Joe" did for William.

Joe was what the guys on the corner called him, and it might have been because of his so-called "dark" features – and because Fall River has one of the largest Portuguese diasporas in the world, with many coming from places in the Azores and Madeira. It was (and is still) common for names like João and José to be shortened to Joe, but, during Joe's day, there was also a well-known character from John Steinbeck's 1935 novel *Tortilla Flat* – which was made into a film in 1942 – who was called by the derogatory name of "Portagee Joe."

I don't know if the nickname bothered my uncle, but he kept it, and after graduating from high school, Joe enlisted in the military in April of 1943. His departure for basic training sparked a long and near daily exchange of letters with his mother, who carefully preserved many of his replies in a special album, so sweetly demonstrating their close bond – but, oh, how I wish we also had Susan's letters to him!

After the war, Joe married Johanna Kelly, a spirited Scottish woman, and they had two children, my cousins Joan and Robert. I have a couple of adorable photos of Joanie and Bobby in their early years, and in one that is particularly dear to me, Mom is just a few months pregnant with Steve and holding her newborn nephew Bobby in her arms.

Uncle Joe rarely came over to our house, but when he did, he never called in advance. He would just show up, knock, and walk right in – and every time, Mom, upon seeing her brother's mega-watt movie star smile, would light up just as bright. Bobby definitely inherited his father's piercing eyes and good looks – and that smile!

My brother Steve fondly remembers visiting Uncle Joe's house on Wilson Road in Fall River, where they kept animals, from horses and goats to raccoons and rabbits, all in their huge yard, which was also perfect for speeding all over in Bobby's go-kart.

Steve recalls one visit when he and Bobby, who were both about ten years old, decided to amuse themselves – and their fathers – by securing pillows to their backsides with belts, bending forward, and goading the billy goats into charging at them. The goats would run at full speed and headbutt them right in the cushion, which knocked the boys off their feet and sent them flying forward, and the sight of the stunt and the whole

Joe and Johanna on Christmas at the Weaver home on New Boston Road in Fall River.

Joe with one of his raccoons.

crazy scene made Dad and Uncle Joe laugh uncontrollably. I assume the idea for the stunt arose after someone was unexpectedly headbutted *without* a cushion.

Because Bobby and Steve were close in age, they both got their licenses around the same time. Steve remembers Joan, who was only a few years older, getting a brand new Ford Mustang Mach 1, and as he tells it – "One day, Joanie lost her mind and let me and Bobby take her new car out for a drive. She warned us not to speed, but Bobby spun the tires so much that day, when we finally got back, the tires were bald!"

I guess it's no surprise that Bobby ended up with a career in buying and selling restored sports cars, and he is also the proud father of two sons, Spencer and Andrew.

Joe and Johanna were together for more than 60 years, until his passing at age 88 in 2011. Johanna passed away at age 94 in 2019, and both she and Joe were laid to rest in the Assonet Burying Ground in Freetown, Massachusetts.

The Family Business

In 1922, Louis embarked on a new professional adventure when he established his own thriving business at 124 Elm Street. His specialty was crafting awnings, automobile tops, tents, and covers – just about anything made from canvas. By the time he married Susan in 1923, his growing business was quite successful, and the life he provided for his new family was comfortable, with plenty to eat, nice clothes, a reliable car, and a home at 625 Durfee Street.

Sometime between 1932 and 1933, around the same time Alzada was in the first grade at the Westall School on Maple Street, Louis' business was destroyed by a fire. He continued working as a canvas craftsman for other businesses, and the family moved to 40 Charlotte Street around 1933, where Alzada started second grade at Spencer Borden Elementary. By 1935, the Weavers had moved to 733 New Boston Road, where Alzada's father – and later, her brother Frank and best friend Betty – would live for the rest of their lives.

Around 1936, in a cozy room at the back of the house on New Boston Road, Louis and Susan – who both had extensive experience with high-powered sewing machines – set up shop, and the two of them resumed crafting beautiful custom awnings for the homes of wealthy customers. This family business became a busy enterprise, and they did it for many years, until 1942 when Louis was back at C.P. McClellan's as a sailmaker.

There are very few keepsakes left behind from my grandparents' lives, and I especially cherish two such heirlooms that Mom entrusted to me – her mother's handwritten cookbook (where Nana's doughnut recipe comes from), and her father's "sailmaker's palm," which is engraved with his initials, LW. A sailmaker's palm is a leather strap with a metal plate embedded in the palm area, that when worn, helps to distribute pressure across the hand, and, like a giant thimble, makes it easier to push needles through heavy canvas.

The sailmaker's palm that belonged to my grandfather Louis Weaver (LW).

Alzada loved some of the adventures that came along with the family business, especially the time her father was commissioned to make a circus tent. When it was ready, Alzada proudly rode along with her mother, who did all the driving, to deliver it to the grounds.

The circus was a major event during this era, and huge crowds would gather to witness the excitement of parades, exotic animals, and thrilling performances. On that particular day, Alzada met another little girl, and the two of them spent hours exploring the circus together – she even got to be in the grand parade with her new friend!

She also remembered her father once making a kite out of canvas sailcloth, but it was way too heavy to fly – until one blustery afternoon in September of 1938. Alzada, a seventh-grader, was hurrying home from school in the middle of a raging storm, and as she struggled to open the door in the walloping wind, she caught sight of her father in the backyard. There he was, finally able to fly that magnificent kite – during what turned out to be the deadly and massively destructive Great New England Hurricane of 1938.

Island Park

The Great New England Hurricane of 1938 caused catastrophic storm surge throughout the area, destroying the Weaver family's favorite destination, the one place they could all go together and have fun – Island Park, an amusement park located just fifteen minutes away in Portsmouth, Rhode Island.

Island Park opened in 1898 as a "trolley park," a concept electric streetcar companies devised to boost ridership – by luring people out of their everyday routines and onto a trolley for a day of delight. When a new trolley line opened between Newport, Rhode Island, and Fall River, Island Park sprang up at the perfect midway point. And while there were grumblings about all those new power poles popping out of the ground, the modern magic of electricity had the whole of Portsmouth buzzing by 1911.

Island Park added new attractions over the years – carousels, a shooting gallery, and in 1926, "The Bullet" roller coaster, the second largest wooden frame coaster in New England at the time.

But it wasn't just rides and games – there was a dinner hall for hearty meals, a beer hall for the adults to enjoy, and a dance hall that extended out over the water. Big name bands played live music, and the dance marathons of the 1930s – which sometimes lasted for more than 100 hours straight – required special approval from the town council!

Susan and Louis would take Alzada and her brothers to Island Park several nights a week, and during the day on the weekends, especially when the weather was nice and breezy. They went so often that the park staff knew all the Weavers by name, and with her golden curls and bright smile, little Alzada was adored by everyone.

She was allowed to run free throughout the park, zipping from ride to ride, always protected by the workers watching over her. One day, however, Alzada dozed off at one of the carnival game stands.

A drunken but jovial sailor saw her rosy cheeks and ringlets, and thinking she was a porcelain doll, he tried his luck at winning her as a prize! The sailor had to settle for a consolation prize, but the memory of that mix-up became one of Alzada's countless cherished moments from her family trips to Island Park.

By Alzada's girlhood, multiple storms and fires had already taken a tremendous toll on this magical place, and the 1938 hurricane closed Island Park for good. But for thousands of people, maybe millions, with Alzada and her family among them, the continued sharing of fond memories and photos will preserve the joy of long-gone Island Park for generations to come!

Alzada with her brother William (Joe), their father Louis, and a family friend – and a dog!

Alzada with two Island Park workers.

At left, Alzada is pictured in the Sunday school nursery of the Fall River First Baptist Church, ca. 1928.

Alzada's seventh grade class photo; she is in the third row, right of center.

Banana Curls

As soon as Alzada had enough hair to style, she was subjected to a time-consuming daily ritual – one that she obediently endured well into junior high school. Every single morning, her mother would sit her down and meticulously sculpt banana curl after banana curl – thick, bouncy coils of hair – all around her head, which Susan sometimes topped off with a giant frilly bow.

One of the earliest snapshots of this ritual dates to around 1928, and was taken in the Sunday school nursery of the First Baptist Church. There's little Alzada, the only child with defined ringlets, perched like a doll on a tiny wooden chair. Like my Weaver cousins and I, Alzada went to church with Susan every single week, and Mom's dedication eventually earned her a certificate for an impressive ten years of perfect attendance.

Another charming photo from around 1929 captures little Alzada with her signature curls and a more serious expression, and she sports a little gold ring on one finger while clutching a tiny trophy – her very own "beauty cup." I wonder if she won it an Island Park contest, which would certainly add a dash of glamour to her childhood.

Fun fact: American beauty pageants have roots in amusement park history, and over the last century, both pageants and theme parks have transformed into multi-billion-dollar extravaganzas.

For more than a decade, Alzada's curls grew longer and longer, though they never reached more than five inches past her shoulders. In her seventh grade class photo from Morton Junior High School, she's one of very few girls still sporting perfectly coiffed banana curls in a sea of blunt bobs, pageboys, and bowl cuts.

At top left, Alzada with her beauty cup, and at top right, Alzada with a doll. At bottom left, Alzada with Santa Claus, and at bottom right, Alzada in sixth grade.

Perhaps it was just one way for Susan to make sure Alzada always looked polished and presentable. Or maybe it was an attempt to keep her beloved and only daughter frozen in time – forever young and innocent, a protective shield of sorts. Perhaps it was something Susan had experienced herself, or perhaps longed for, from her own mother.

Eventually, Alzada decided it was time for a change, and in a burst of teenage rebellion, she convinced her Aunt Carrie, Susan's older sister Caroline, to cut her hair and give her a perm. It was a less than flattering look, but Alzada didn't mind one bit – she was thrilled to finally leave those babyish banana curls in the past.

Teenage Alzada and Susan.

Alzada's Uncle Frank Gifford and Aunt Helen (Hale) Gifford, pictured at top left in the 1950s, were the parents of Alzada's dearest cousin, Patricia "Patty" Louise Gifford. At top right, nine-year-old Patty got her picture in the newspaper when she won a limerick writing contest (and a new bicycle). At bottom left is Patty in her preteens, and at bottom right, her senior photo.

The Prim & Proper Giffords

Alzada absolutely loved visiting her extended family of aunts, uncles, and cousins, but there was a distinct difference between her mother's Gifford side and her father's Weaver side.

On Susan's side, they most frequently visited Alzada's Uncle Frank and Aunt Helen Gifford's house in Springfield, Massachusetts. Susan was a good driver with a keen sense of direction, so traveling over 100 miles from Fall River to western Massachusetts was no sweat.

Their journeys would have been quite the adventures, with some taking four or five hours, depending on road conditions, not to mention navigating all those winding New England roads.

Uncle Frank and Aunt Helen were very proper people, and there were rules and regimens for absolutely everyone that came to their house. But it was a happy place, and best of all, they had a daughter, Patty, who was just two years younger than Alzada.

Unlike Susan and Louis, Frank and Helen were very lovey-dovey, so much so that Alzada remembers her mother and Aunt Carrie teasing Frank and Helen about their mushiness. It never bothered Alzada, of course, and if anything, it inspired her daydreams of the ideal marriage she would one day create.

Aunt Helen was very sweet and affectionate, but she was also very neat and structured, with a strict code of conduct that left no room for deviation. Whenever Alzada stayed at Patty's house, naps were mandatory, bedtimes were early, and mealtimes were an extra stressful test of proper table manners. But the worst challenge was the dreaded morning ritual – a compulsory spoonful of castor oil. *Yuck!*

This old remedy, which tasted awful, was supposed to keep a person healthy, but it always felt punitive to Alzada. Fun Fact: used medicinally as a stimulant laxative since antiquity, castor oil got a glamorous rebranding in the late nineteenth century by medicine peddlers traversing America – *step right up, get your miracle cure here!*

But because of its terrible flavor, especially to kids, a spoonful of castor oil soon became a common punishment for misbehaving children. The practice became so widespread that in 1919, the American Medical Association began warning parents against using castor oil as a disciplinary measure, emphasizing its use as a curative for ill health, not ill behavior.

A less fun fact: Castor oil was also used to lubricate plane engines during the World Wars and, horribly, Mussolini's regime was known to force-feed mass quantities of castor oil to captive political dissidents, an interrogation tactic and humiliation technique perfected (but not invented) by Il Duce.

Despite the ripples and ravages of the Great Depression – and all of Aunt Helen's rules – Alzada and Patty always had great fun when they were together. Patty was just nineteen when she married Loren Reed in 1947, and her wedding was a big event in the family, with both Susan and Alzada in attendance. In a fascinating coincidence, after Alzada and Irving got married three years later, they went to visit Patty and Loren for the first time, and upon meeting, Irving thought Loren looked very familiar. And then it came to him – they were in the army together, stationed in Gorizia, Italy, and Loren had been his radio school instructor!

Loren and Patty went on to have seven children – Holly, Carol, Anne, Bradford, Jonathan, Janice, and Matthew – filling their home with the kind of love that Alzada cherished, and eventually the Reed family was blessed with more than a dozen grandchildren, and, so far, three great-grandchildren.

The top photos are of Patty in 1947 — at left, driving a tractor, and at right, on a visit to a farm in Stillwater, New York. At bottom left is Loren Reed in Grado, Italy, and at bottom right, Patty and Loren on their wedding day in 1947.

The Reed family in the late 1960s. In the back row from left to right are Bradford, Carol, Holly, and Anne. In front are Janice, Jonathan, Patty, and Loren, who is holding Matthew.

Carrie at the table with her great-niece Holly Reed in the early 1950s.

Sadly, Patty passed away at the age of fifty-one in 1979, the same age as her grandmother, Alzada Gifford, but her cousin Alzada forever carried the warm memories of their time together in her heart.

I'm very grateful to my fourth cousins, Loren and Patty's children, especially Carol and Matthew, for sharing their photos and memories with me. It was among Matthew's collection of inherited Gifford family artifacts that he found what might be a picture of Carrie, Frank and Susan's middle sister. The photo, which is probably from the late 1890s, is mounted in a gold locket ornately inscribed with the initials CG.

Caroline Elusanas (Gifford) Ormerod moved in with Frank and Helen in 1947 after her husband William Ormerod passed away. Aunt Carrie had no children, and Alzada remembers her spending her free time sewing and reading by a single dim lamp. She was also very particular about tidiness and table manners, and while Alzada found her a bit odd and boring, this was the very same Aunt Carrie who cut and permed her hair in junior high!

Chief among Alzada's oddest memories was her recollection of being at Carrie's house the night her husband died. The next morning, Carrie said, "I never let Bill go to bed without washing up after coming back from the cellar. I didn't do it last night." And then she ordered one of her nephews to wash the feet of their deceased Uncle Bill.

Carrie was still living with Frank and Helen when she passed away at the age of seventy-eight in May of 1973, two months and a day after her sister Susan, and she was laid to rest with her husband in Oak Grove Cemetery in Fall River.

Matthew told me that, several years ago, his sister Carol made the trek to Fall River to find family graves, and when she discovered there was no marker for her beloved great-aunt, she had a headstone made for Carrie and her husband William.

Carol said nothing at the time, she just did it! And I could relate, as I had done the same thing for two of my great-grandmothers and my own great-aunt, Lillian – relatives I'd never met yet felt so close to.

But Carrie was very involved in her great-niece Carol's life, and the Reed kids grew up in an even bigger family than ours! They lived in a house built for two families, and at one point, Patty and Loren, all seven of their children, their Grandpa Frank and Nana Helen, their Great-Grandmother Hale, and of course, their Great-Aunt Carrie, were all living together under one roof.

While Susan and Carrie only lived into their seventies, Frank and his wife Helen lived well into their nineties, and were laid to rest together in Springfield Cemetery.

Frank and Helen (Hale) Gifford on their 50th wedding anniversary in 1975.

Above are images of a locket that was kept and passed down by Frank, Carrie's brother, to his grandson, my fourth-cousin, Matthew Reed. The engraved initials, CG, and the similar appearance of the woman in the photos to my Nana Susan suggest that it indeed belonged to my Great-Aunt Carrie Gifford.

Joe (far left), Alzada (center), and Louis (far right), with Weaver cousins in Sturbridge, MA.

Alzada's father Louis Weaver.

The Fun & Fearless Weavers

It was Alzada's father's side – the energetic, down-to-earth, free-spirited Weavers – that she enjoyed visiting the most. Both sides were kind and caring, but compared to the prim and proper Giffords, the fun and fearless Weavers were boisterous and wild, full of personality and laughter – and probably a few cuss words.

The Weavers were a spontaneous bunch and always ready for fun, so, naturally, Alzada relished visits to her Uncle Raymond Weaver's farm in rural Sturbridge, Massachusetts. Louis could really let loose with his family, and there were always lots of jokes and stories being told, usually embellished with a bit of colorful swearing.

"It was part of his language," Alzada once recalled with a laugh, as even her friends from more refined families found it oddly endearing.

Uncle Raymond and his wife Catherine produced six rambunctious children – John, Parker, Emma, Beatrice, Harold, and Ida – giving Alzada plenty of playmates, and the Weaver farm was truly a kid's paradise! Alzada and her cousins could run wild, ride ponies, and invent fun new games. Best of all, they were allowed to jump on the beds and furniture to their hearts' content.

"Let them have fun," said Uncle Raymond and Aunt Catherine. "When they grow up, we'll get new furniture."

One cherished photo captures Alzada, about seven years old, holding a kitten and squinting in the sunlight. Next to her is her brother Joe, grinning, with a few of their cousins, along with her father Louis, who stands behind her next to a large, dark cow. The names of the kitten and the cow are lost to time.

Another set of photos shows Alzada, nearly eleven, with Louis and his brother Benjamin, proudly posing with their family Buick, which Susan drove anywhere and everywhere. The car allowed them to generate more business and visit with friends and family without having to rely on trains and buses. Susan, who was both a caring soul and an intrepid driver, would often travel hundreds of miles to take food and lend a hand to friends in need – sometimes as far as New York City!

Uncle Ben and his wife Edith didn't have children of their own, but they sure had plenty of nephews and nieces to dote on. Uncle Isaac, the youngest Weaver sibling, and his wife, Alzada's Aunt Annie, lived in Lexington, Massachusetts, with their three children, across the street from a huge hill that Alzada and her cousins loved to slide down.

It was while visiting these Lexington Weavers that Alzada created one of her fondest childhood memories – sitting very properly on the bench in front of their player piano, moving her wiggling fingers up and down the self-playing keys, pretending to be a concert virtuoso.

Happily, Alzada ended up a beautiful blend of both sides – the warm and well-mannered Giffords and the loving, lively Weavers.

Louis (right) with one of his brothers.

Louis, Alzada, and her Uncle Ben Weaver in 1937.

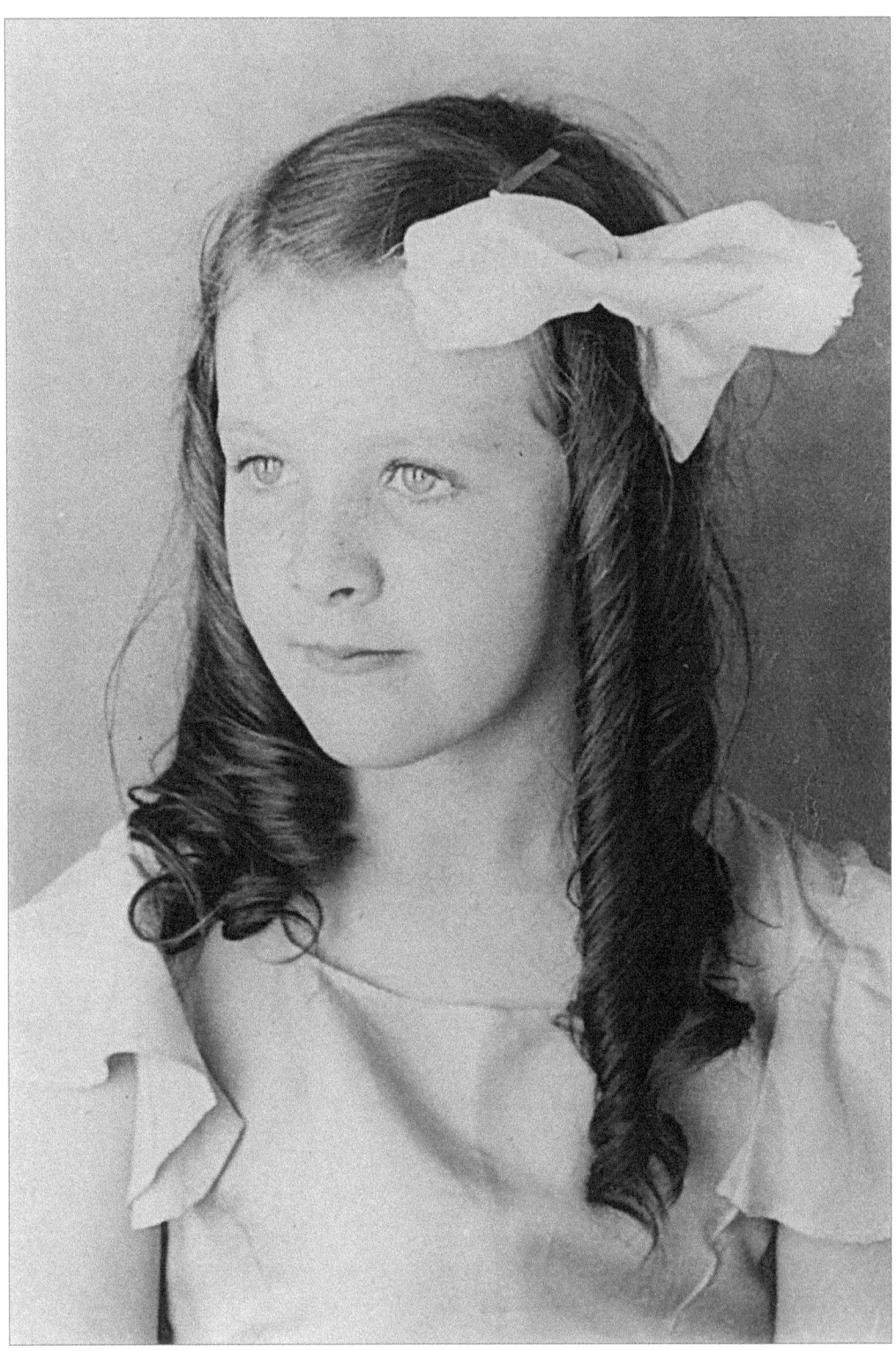

Alzada, age ten.

Alzada's Solo Debut

Alzada had a beautiful singing voice, and she was just ten years old when she made her grand musical debut in front of her classmates with the performance of a song called "When I Grow Too Old to Dream."

Because of its mature emotional theme, the song was an odd choice for a child, but it was very popular at the time, published by Romberg and Hammerstein in 1934 and featured in the 1935 romance musical *The Night is Young*. The movie is about an Austrian archduke, played by Ramon Navarro, who falls in love with a common ballerina, played by Evelyn Laye, and their love story unfolds to the sounds of the enchanting melody.

It's a curious but very catchy mix – part lullaby, part Viennese waltz, part drinking song – and it weaves throughout the entire film, from the tinkling tune of a child's jewelry box to the sweeping bittersweet strains at the end. Alzada must have been captivated by the dreamily romantic film, which her mother probably took her to see. And while the movie isn't very well-known today, the song was an instant hit, and it remains a classic, especially in the jazz world.

While reminiscing with my brother Brian and me, Mom once gave us a kitchen table performance of the entire song. She was in her nineties – eight decades on from her junior high debut – but to me, it felt like time had folded in upon itself. Neither Brian nor I had ever heard the song before, but her sweet voice carried the same tender notes she sang as a child, and she still remembered every word.

When I heard the lyrics, I was struck by the somber realization that preteen Alzada had been prophetically singing about her very own future – a future in which she would outlive the love of her life.

Here are the lyrics –

We have been gay, going our way
Life has been beautiful, we have been young
After you've gone, life will go on
Like an old song we have sung

(Chorus)
When I grow too old to dream
I'll have you to remember
When I grow too old to dream
Your love will live in my heart
So, kiss me my sweet,
And so let us part
And when I grow too old to dream
That kiss will live in my heart

After you've gone life will go on
Time will be tenderly melting our tears
Yet will I find you in my mind
Beckoning over the years.

"When I Grow Too Old to Dream" has since become a timeless standard and has been crooned by countless artists. It even had an Irish folk music revival in the 1980s, and continues to be sung by new generations.

It's a rather simple song, but it so perfectly expresses the joys and sadness of love and loss, and of a life lived fully and deeply – and those few precious minutes of Mom singing it will forever echo in my heart.

A British cover of the sheet music for "When I Grow Too Old to Dream" from the movie, The Night is Young. The song was – and is still – popular in both the U.S. and the U.K.

Promotional poster created by Joseph Binder for the 1939 New York World's Fair.

The World's Fair

While trips to the amusement park and the movies were fun, one of Alzada's biggest and best memories was going with her mother to the 1939-40 New York World's Fair.

The fair's themes of "World of Tomorrow" and "Dawn of a New Day" promised new beginnings, excitement, and, as its organizers were hoping, the stimulation of a sputtering economy. Raised from the ashes of an actual dump for coal furnace ashes, the fairgrounds spanned 1,200 acres, totally transforming a rat-infested wasteland into a playground of dreams, at the center of which stood the towering Trylon and the massive Perisphere.

For Alzada and her mother, the "Food Zone" was nothing short of heaven. Hot dogs, hamburgers, doughnuts, and Coca-Cola – what more could a young girl ask for? They savored every bite and soaked in all the sights, exploring the various rides, exhibits, and attractions.

The "Amusement Area" was designed to lift spirits and ignite imaginations, and some of it was rather risqué, thanks to Salvador Dalí's surrealist display of living statues – along with those mysterious "peep shows" that kept getting raided by the New York City vice squad.

Beyond the entertainment, the cotton candy, and the carousels, the New York World's Fair offered a peek into the future, a place where people could marvel at new technologies and dream of what was to come. Imagine the thrill of Alzada seeing herself on a television screen for the very first time at the RCA Pavilion, where, during the opening ceremony on April 30, 1939, President Franklin Roosevelt made the first national telecast.

Despite the dark clouds of impending war, even after Hitler invaded Poland in September of 1939, the fair pressed on with optimism, and began its second season in 1940 with a new theme – "For Peace and Freedom." But as the war escalated, public interest shifted, financial difficulties led to bankruptcy, and the last day of the fair was October 27, 1940.

Twenty-five years after twelve-year-old Alzada went to the World's Fair in 1939, I got to go to the 1964 World's Fair, also at the age of twelve! Mom was unaware of this serendipitous coincidence when I told her about it decades later, but with five other kids in the house at the time, I suppose it's no surprise she didn't even remember giving me permission to go to New York City!

Accompanied by my older cousins, Susan and Cindy, I traveled on a rickety church bus for the 200-mile ride. We had hours to chat and whisper about "the birds and the bees" – which was all news to me – and I remember feeling distinctly "grown up" for the first time in my life.

The 1964 theme, "Peace Through Understanding," continued the futuristic optimism of the 1939 fair, but just like the 1939 fair, real-world challenges were already casting a pall of gloom. The shadow of President Kennedy's assassination loomed, and civil rights demonstrations were in full swing, including a protest against President Johnson during his speech for the fair's opening ceremonies.

The 1964 fair was ultimately another messy financial failure, but even among the turmoil, there was joy to be found. The fairs gave us young girls – both Alzada and me – a glimpse into a whole new world of wonders, and for me, it fostered my belief in the power of knowledge, discovery, and possibilities. It also gave me the hope that a girl from a big family in a small New England town could one day be a proud New Yorker.

The Boarder

Alzada's early teenage years were blighted by a dark presence in the Weaver's home on New Boston Road – the boarder.

Their home was small and modest, with only two bedrooms and two beds – and, if you'll recall, Alzada's brothers shared one, and the other she shared with her parents.

Alzada was thirteen by the summer of 1940, and it was around this time that the boarder moved into the Giffords' spare bedroom. He was a sixty-three-year-old World War I veteran, the widowed husband of Susan's best friend Mabel, who had passed away in 1935, and with nowhere else to live, Susan offered to help.

"He was an evil person. And a drunk," Mom once told me, still disgusted even after all those years.

The boarder was unemployed and unable to work, yet always able to find his way to the bar, where he would always get too drunk to get home. Susan had to go retrieve him and bring him back to their home, a once sacred place that had always been safe and secure.

Worst of all, he would try to chase Alzada when she came home from school, attempting to molest her when no one was home. Ashamed and scared, she kept the burden of those dark moments to herself, and never told her parents – or her brothers – or anyone until she told me. But she did want this story to be included in the memoir, as a reminder that painful truths are often buried deep and kept hidden, even from those closest to us.

We don't know how long this awful man stayed with the Weavers, but records show that he passed away in 1947, the same year Frank and Betty moved back into the family home on New Boston Road.

An Elizabeth Arden ad for "Montezuma Red" from Vogue (issue 103, no. 8, April 15, 1944, page 115).

Lipstick

Susan's protective nature and strict parenting style likely stemmed from a belief that by keeping Alzada in the safe cocoon of childhood, she could somehow shield her from the world's challenges and prevent her from making adult mistakes. Because of this, Alzada was forbidden to go on dates or wear makeup until long after her friends had begun to do so – and even the most well-behaved young ladies in the mid-1940s couldn't resist the allure of lipstick.

From the factory workers of the home front to the servicewomen at the front lines, during World War II, red lipstick was much more than just a fashion statement – it was a symbol of bravery and patriotism. In fact, it was considered so important that it was officially incorporated into the U.S. Armed Forces standard issue uniform, coordinating with the color of the *"hat cord, scarf and chevrons of the Women in the Marines."*

Created by trailblazing cosmetics magnate Elizabeth Arden, the name of the signature shade – Montezuma Red – was an homage to lyrics in the "Marines' Hymn," and available as lipstick, blush, and nail polish.

But with Susan's strict no-makeup rule still in effect even after she graduated from high school, Alzada had to be creative. She'd slyly apply her lipstick after leaving the house, and dutifully wipe it off before returning home. Her plan worked flawlessly, until the day her mother surprised her by showing up at the end of her shift, hoping to escort her lovely daughter home for the evening. To Susan's shock, there was her precious little Alzada, sporting bright red lipstick – in public!

"You wipe that right off," her mother demanded, but Alzada courageously stood her ground.

Once home, Susan complained loudly to her oldest son, Frank, whose opinions she held in high regard.

"Just look at her – your sister! She has makeup on her face!"

Frank reverently acknowledged his mother's request, and then he locked eyes with Alzada – and grinned. Turning back to their fuming mother, he finally responded – "Well, fine! It's about time!"

And that was the end of that. The ban was lifted, and Susan never again scolded Alzada for wearing lipstick.

Alzada with her oldest brother Frank, with whom she always remained close.

Alzada at age sixteen.

Alzada's high school senior portrait from 1944.

You Can Call Me Albatross

Alzada's sense of independence and hopeful determination carried her through her teen years, but there was something that always bothered her – her name. Because she was born four years after her namesake died, the two Alzadas never met, but her mother Susan frequently took her to visit her Grandmother Alzada's gravesite in Westport, Massachusetts.

Despite Susan's efforts to cultivate a connection between her daughter and her departed mother, there was no denying that Alzada Estes Weaver absolutely HATED her first name.

The Social Security Administration recorded only 337 babies named Alzada between 1880 and 2015, and because it's so rare, it's difficult to pin down a definitive meaning and origin. Even pronunciation can vary – our family says *al-ZAYD-uh*, but others say *all-ZAH-dah*, both with the emphasis on the second syllable.

The name's earliest roots seem to be Arabic, meaning "exalted" or "elevated," and in Portuguese, the word *alzada* translates to "dawn," the rising of the sun. Similarly, in Spanish, *alzada* is the feminine form of the adjective *alzado*, meaning "height" and "elevated," and relates to the Spanish verb *alzar* which, at its simplest, means "to raise."

If we dig a bit deeper into all of the various translations and interpretations, it could also mean to raise oneself up, to amplify one's voice, or to rise against something – to revolt or rebel.

Naturally, teenage Alzada "rose" to the challenge. Anyone who's ever disliked their given name can empathize with how Alzada felt about hers, especially during her teenage years. At school, she would always cringe with embarrassment whenever her unusual name rang out for morning roll call. To escape the discomfort, she nicknamed herself "Al" and went by that name exclusively among her friends; even her 1944 senior yearbook photo is captioned "Al."

Her mother disapproved of that boyish nickname, but Susan was also disappointed by Alzada's rejection of her beautiful name. One might assume Alzada finally accepted her name as she got older, preferring a more mature moniker as she transitioned into adulthood, but it wasn't until my second child, Rebekah Alzada, was born that she finally came to love her unconventional name.

Over the years, Mom collected a few other nicknames, including "Albatross," which was also the operator "handle" she used for her and Dad's shared hobby of amateur ham radio.

She never thought it was particularly flattering to be likened to this enormous bird, but it suits her quite well. The albatross, you see, has an extraordinarily long lifespan, and the largest (11-foot) wingspan of any living bird. With these formidable wings, they effortlessly glide on ocean winds for hours at a time without ever flapping. And, just like Alzada, the albatross mates for life and breeds every two years – in Mom's case, 1950, 1952, 1954, 1958, 1960, and 1962, with just one skip in 1956.

The English poet Samuel Taylor Coleridge cited the albatross as a good omen in his epic poem, "The Rime of the Ancient Mariner." In it, the sight of an albatross through blinding fog was a sign of good luck, protecting and accompanying ships for days at sea, in glorious as well as tempestuous weather.

Under Mom's expansive, unflappable, inexhaustible wingspan, all six of her children – and many of our friends and neighbor kids – were always nurtured with warmth, love, and wisdom, and we're all so fortunate to have blossomed under her generous wings. Perhaps Alzada can also mean "to soar."

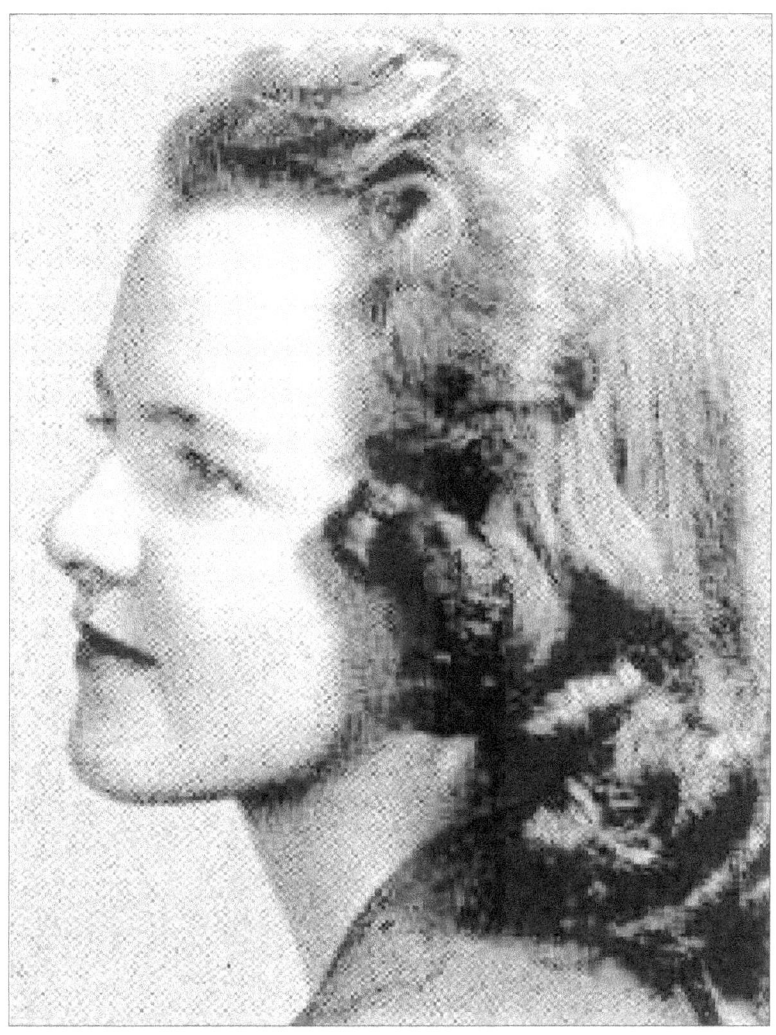

Alzada's 1944 Durfee High School senior yearbook photo.

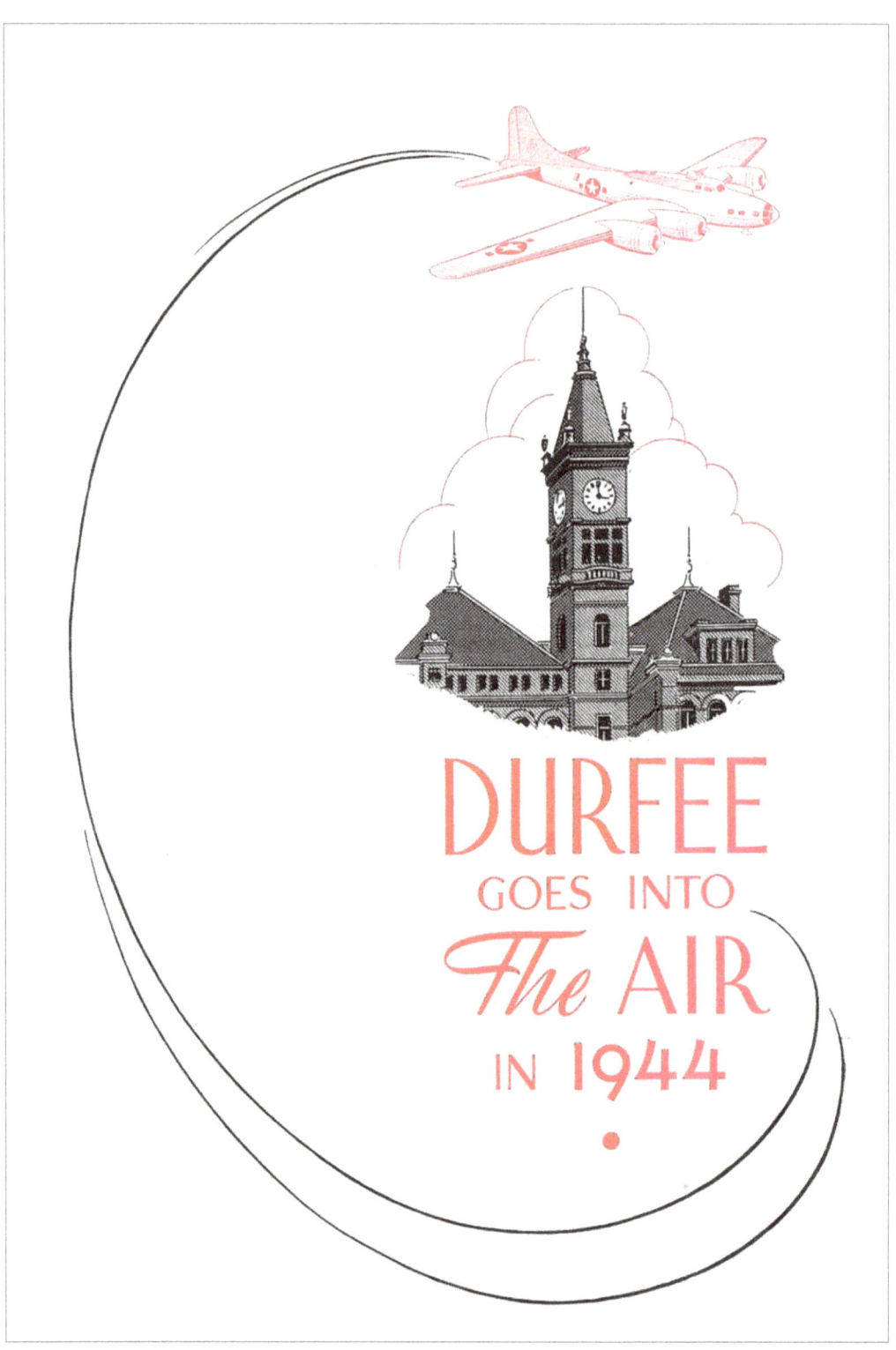

Cover of the 1944 Durfee High School yearbook.

Class of 1944

Speaking of soaring, the yearbook theme for Durfee High School's graduating class of 1944 was "Durfee Goes into the Air."

The senior class photos of these young men and women are striking not just for their style, which reflected the trends of the day, but also for the maturity etched into their faces, including that of "Al Weaver." This was a generation coming of age in a time of war, and it shows.

Durfee High principal, Charles V. Carroll, beautifully captured the spirit of the moment in his heartfelt message to the Class of 1944. His words, full of admiration and hope, remind us of the strength and resilience of these young people as they faced a world in turmoil:

"To you, members of the Class of 1944, I give hearty congratulations from the faculty on the completion of your high school years, unusual years in which you have been forced to meet unusual situations, and you have met them well.

Forty-five boys from your class have already gone from Durfee's portals to enter military service, and they are but the vanguard of many more of you, both boys and girls, who will soon be enrolled in the armed forces of our country. In addition to your regular school program, many of you have helped on the home front by working in the various war industries of our city.

The patriotism that all of you have displayed, when called upon to aid in any way the war effort, has been a splendid example for classes to come. This height to which you have risen in your patriotism and loyalty to your school is the symbol of the skyward flight of the pilot who will guide your bomber in one of the theaters of war. As that pilot for the safe accomplishing of his mission will take his bomber high above the clouds, so may you keep high your ideals of courage, patriotism, and right living to guide you safely through the years ahead – hard years of war and still harder years of peace with problems which will require love of country, integrity of character, clearness of vision, and the courage to follow that vision.

Upon you, the men and women of the immediate future, depends the solution of these problems. Upon your loftiness of purpose depends the retention of the democratic principles of our founding fathers."

Leaving high school is always a mix of excitement and nerves, a thrilling leap into the unknown, but for Alzada and her classmates, the stakes were unimaginably high. The world was in the throes of World War II, and the allied invasion of Normandy was fully underway.

This was also a hard time for those unable to serve, including Alzada's brother Frank, likely due to "curvature of the spine," which is noted on his 1940 draft registration card. He was twenty-two at the time, and listed Susan as his emergency contact – a poignant reminder of the realities of wartime, as all registrants were required to list *"The person who will always know your address"* (the one to notify if you were injured – or worse).

Alzada's brother Joe registered in June of 1942, age nineteen, and served from 1943 until the end of the war. He listed their father, Louis, as his emergency contact, but thankfully, no notifications were necessary.

Alzada, meanwhile, stayed safe on the home front, living with her parents, contributing to the war effort by making gas tanks, and enjoying time with her friends. The world of tomorrow was waiting for her with open arms. But on Friday, June 16, 1944 – ten days after D-Day and eight days before her high school graduation – Alzada's father Louis passed away.

She had gone with a friend to the cinema, where a variety of westerns and war dramas were showing, films like *Sonora Stagecoach* and *Days of Glory*, as well as new musical comedies, like *Two Girls and a Sailor*.

Alzada had told her family she was going to see one specific film, but ended up watching a different one, and this last-minute change in plans made it much harder to find her in the movie theater. By the time she got home, she was among the last to learn that her father had passed away earlier that day from heart failure, and she always felt a deep sense of regret for not being with her father in his final moments.

Louis was sixty-five, and just a few days after his funeral and burial in Oak Grove Cemetery, Alzada graduated from high school. She was only seventeen.

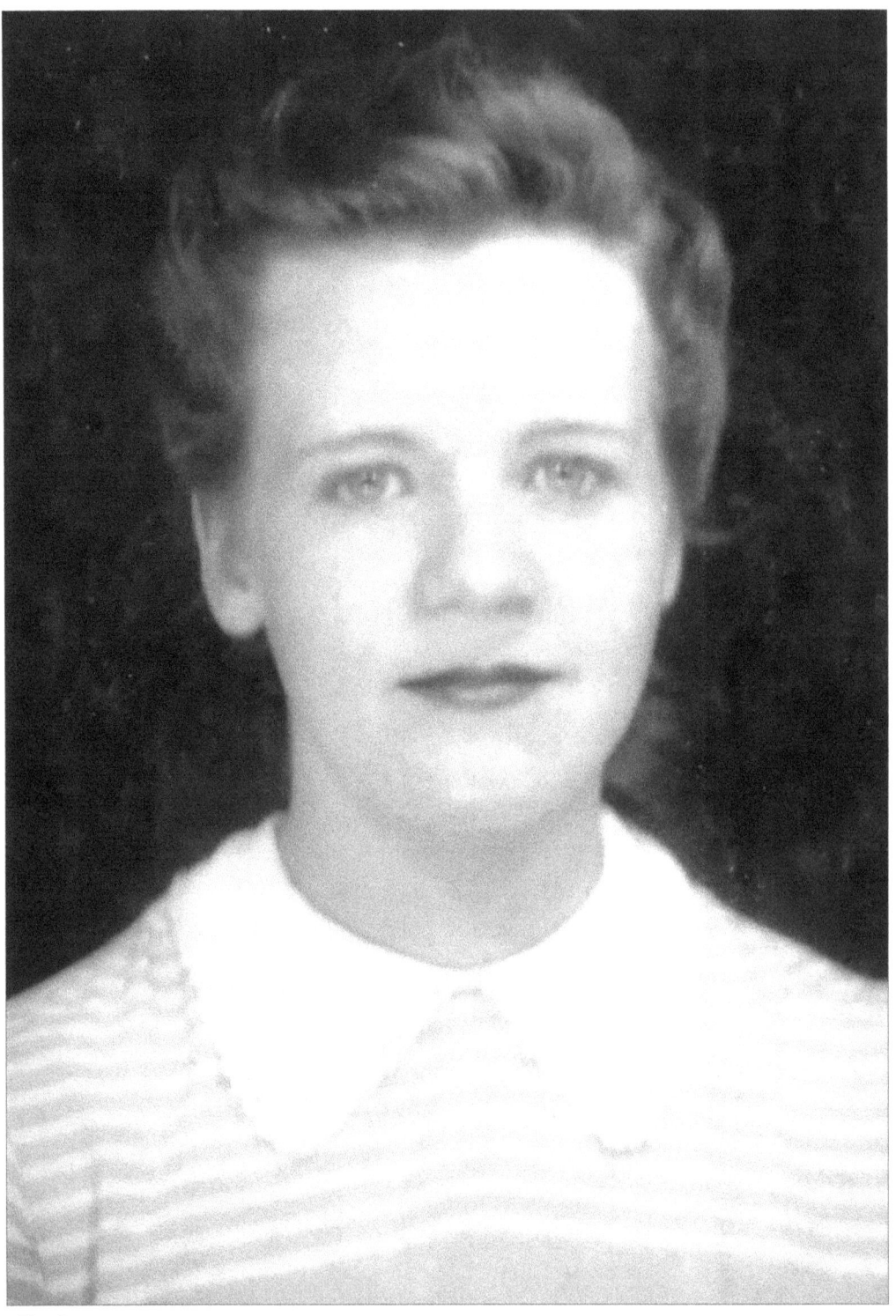

Alzada as a young woman.

Secret Smokers

The loss of her father was devastating, but life goes on, and Alzada kept moving forward, buoyed by daydreams of brighter days ahead – and, as it would turn out, her mother's adventurous streak.

Alzada turned eighteen in October of 1944, and to celebrate, Susan planned a trip for just the two of them to go see Frank Sinatra perform at the Paramount Theatre in Times Square – what a gift!

I'm not sure exactly which performance they attended, but the day Sinatra arrived in New York City for his first show of the season – October 12, 1944 – was when "Sinatramania" really exploded, propelling him into pop star status, and becoming an iconic moment in his early career, as well as American history.

This was Frankie "The Voice" Sinatra! Before Elvis ever swiveled his hips, before the Beatles took the world by storm, there was Frank Sinatra, the original heartthrob. In 1944, at twenty-nine years old, he had "bobbysoxers" – and their mothers – completely captivated.

It wasn't his first time performing at the Paramount, so no one could have predicted the hysteria that unfolded that day, which is now known as the Columbus Day Riots. Lines to get into the theater started forming the night before, and by show time, 30,000 swooning women and screaming adolescent girls had swarmed Times Square.

The commotion caused traffic jams and made headlines across the country, and while I don't think Alzada was there for the so-called riot, the Paramount remained packed to capacity for every Sinatra show that season. The excitement was electric, and for Alzada and Susan, it was going to be a magical moment shared in a city that never slept.

Alzada was practically floating as she and her mother boarded the bus for the four-hour ride to New York City, but almost immediately there was a bit of a snag – Alzada liked to smoke cigarettes, and her mother was dead set against it. Now, even though Alzada was on the cusp of adulthood and officially old enough to be listed in the city directory, when it came to her mother's rules, she didn't want to push too hard. So, she tried asking permission.

"Ma, can I smoke?"

"No," Susan emphatically replied. "No, no, no!"

Alzada dutifully obeyed her mother, but as the bus crossed from Massachusetts into Connecticut, she tried again with a different angle.

"Ma, you know I smoke – why make me sneak it?" she asked, hoping for a more favorable response.

Susan quietly considered her daughter's plea and, with a reluctant sigh, she caved – "Well, all right…" she said, her eyes flicking toward Alzada's pack of Chesterfield cigarettes, "But give me one of those."

The shock and satisfaction of sharing a forbidden activity with her own mother was a delightful surprise – and unchartered territory. Susan might as well have asked to borrow a tube of Montezuma Red!

For Alzada, this celebration of her eighteenth birthday – mother and daughter, sharing secrets, smoking and swooning – was both a rite of passage and a revelation.

Alzada's BFF Betty

Susan was loving and caring, but she was a parent first – not a confidante, not a sister, not a friend. Luckily, Alzada found someone else to fill all those roles and so much more – her best friend in the whole wide world, Betty.

Barbara Elizabeth Wise, was born September 26, 1926, in Fall River, making her only one month older than Alzada.

Betty grew up on President Avenue with her parents, Henry and Irene, and her younger brother Charles, whom everyone called Bud. According to family lore, Betty loved jumping rope, an activity which often sent her glasses flying, and so her father was constantly replacing her cracked spectacles.

Tragically, when Betty was eight, her mother Irene passed away at the age of forty-two, and her father hired a housekeeper to help with Betty and Bud.

Betty and Alzada's friendship first blossomed when they met in high school, but it really flourished when Betty became Alzada's sister-in-law in 1945.

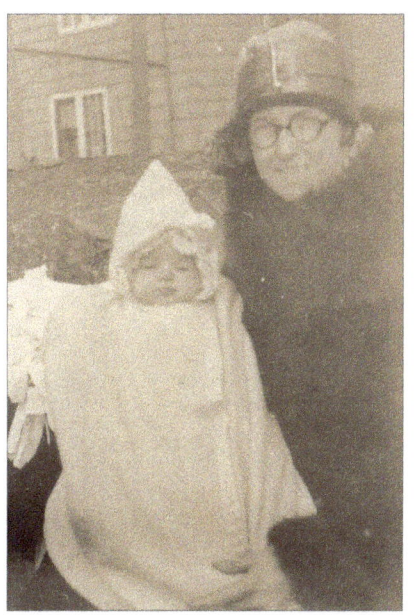

Above, baby Betty with her mother Irene, and below, Betty around age sixteen.

Betty and Frank's wedding in 1945. Standing at left is Susan, third from left is Alzada, and to her right, Betty's father, Henry, then Betty and Frank, and standing next to Frank, Betty's brother Bud.

World War II had a funny way of shuffling love stories around. Before the war, Betty was dating Joe, but after he joined up and left Fall River, Frank and Betty got to know each other – and they fell in love!

After their wedding, Betty and Frank honeymooned in New York City, and they just so happened to be among the many thousands of people in Times Square on August 14, 1945, when the news broke that Japan had surrendered. That same day, Alfred Eisenstaedt took his iconic photograph, "V-J Day in Times Square," capturing the moment a young sailor spontaneously grabbed and kissed a stranger wearing an all-white nursing uniform (the stranger was actually a dental assistant). The photo was published in *Life* magazine, and quickly came to symbolize the ecstatic joy Americans felt upon hearing that the war was over.

At left, best friends and soon-to-be sisters-in law, Betty and Alzada. At right, Betty in 1981 (and that's Dad standing behind her).

Betty was a classy, educated professional, and when I knew her, she was a bank teller at Fall River Trust Bank. She was beautiful, and she had the most delightful smile and a lovely gentle laugh. I also vividly remember how friendly she was to absolutely everybody.

Betty and Alzada remained the best of friends – sharing recipes and laughs, talking on the phone and going to the beach together – until Betty passed away at the age of fifty-five in 1981. I was fortunate to be able to visit my Aunt Betty shortly before she passed, and I remember sitting at her bedside and telling to her how much I loved her.

She was laid to rest in Oak Grove Cemetery, which is located in the very same neighborhood where she grew up, and in 1990, her beloved husband Frank was laid to rest beside her.

In 2023, I was deeply saddened to learn that my cousin Cindy had passed away at the age of seventy-two. Of all my cousins, I was closest in age to Cindy, and along with the many memories I have of spending time with her and our Nana Susan at church, I also fondly recall all the Christmases we exchanged gifts, and that one time we put curlers in our hair before going to the movies together.

Cindy was there with me picking beans on Gardners Neck, and she was there with me at the New York World's Fair. We saw each other become mothers and grandmothers, and then suddenly she was gone, and I'm so grateful for all the wonderful memories.

At left, my cousin Cindy, age nine, with Goldie, the family dog. At right, Cindy in 1963, one year before we went to the New York World's Fair together.

Letters Home

During World War II, from April 1943 through September 1944, Pvt. Wm. G. Weaver – Alzada's brother Joe – wrote more than 230 letters home, creating a treasure trove of stories that their mother Susan lovingly preserved in a cherished commemorative scrapbook.

The letters begin with a postcard on April 23, 1943, just a week after Joe's twentieth birthday. He had just arrived at Camp Devens, Massachusetts, and soon after, he was writing from Atlantic City. The boys in his unit, all part of the Air Corps ground crew, were living it up at the Ritz Carlton Hotel.

Joe's letters are brimming with humor, questions about folks back home, and heartfelt thanks for the treats that his mother and Aunt Carrie sent his way. He also writes about his ailments, mainly his teeth, which required extensive dental work, all described in vivid detail.

Throughout his first several dozen letters, he addresses Susan variously as *Mother*, *Mom*, and *Ma*, and while he always asks about *"Pa,"* it's not until November of 1943 that Joe starts opening every letter with *"Dear Mom & Dad."*

Joe also wrote to Alzada, their cousins, and his friends – and Betty, of course. Sometimes he would include a sketch of the person the letter was addressed to – and we happen to have one of Joe's sketches of Betty!

In February of 1944, Joe proudly announced his graduation and promotion to "Corporal" in Fort Myers, Florida. From there he went to Columbia, South Carolina, to study chemical warfare. In March, he wrote *"Why hasn't Betty written?"* – clearly curious about her silence – but as we now know, Betty's heart had moved on.

By August, Joe was in Florence, South Carolina, his letters still full of charm and affection. He had met a girl named Sue, and told his mother, *"I call her Sweet Sue. She's a really nice girl and I wish you could see her."* He jokingly refers to himself as *"Just a wolf,"* but adds, *"Don't you worry about me. She is a nice girl, but I have to teach her how to talk like I do (ha ha)."*

The last letter in Susan's scrapbook is dated September 7, 1944. There may have been more, but that's all we have. Joe would write whether there was anything to write about or not, and his letters also reveal his serious side, filled with words of love and support, especially when his father passed away.

Joe got leave for the funeral, and as soon as he got back, he wrote to let his mother know he arrived safely. He brought the letter to a close with an assurance – *"Don't you worry, Ma, everything will be alright. Alzada, Frank and I will take good care of you."*

A day later, June 29, 1944, Joe wrote again to tell Susan about a monthly allotment of fifty dollars that would be deducted from his pay and sent to her, and from that day forward, for each and every letter in the remainder of the collection, he uses only one way to end – *"Lots of Love, Wm."* – and only one way to begin – *"Dearest Mom."*

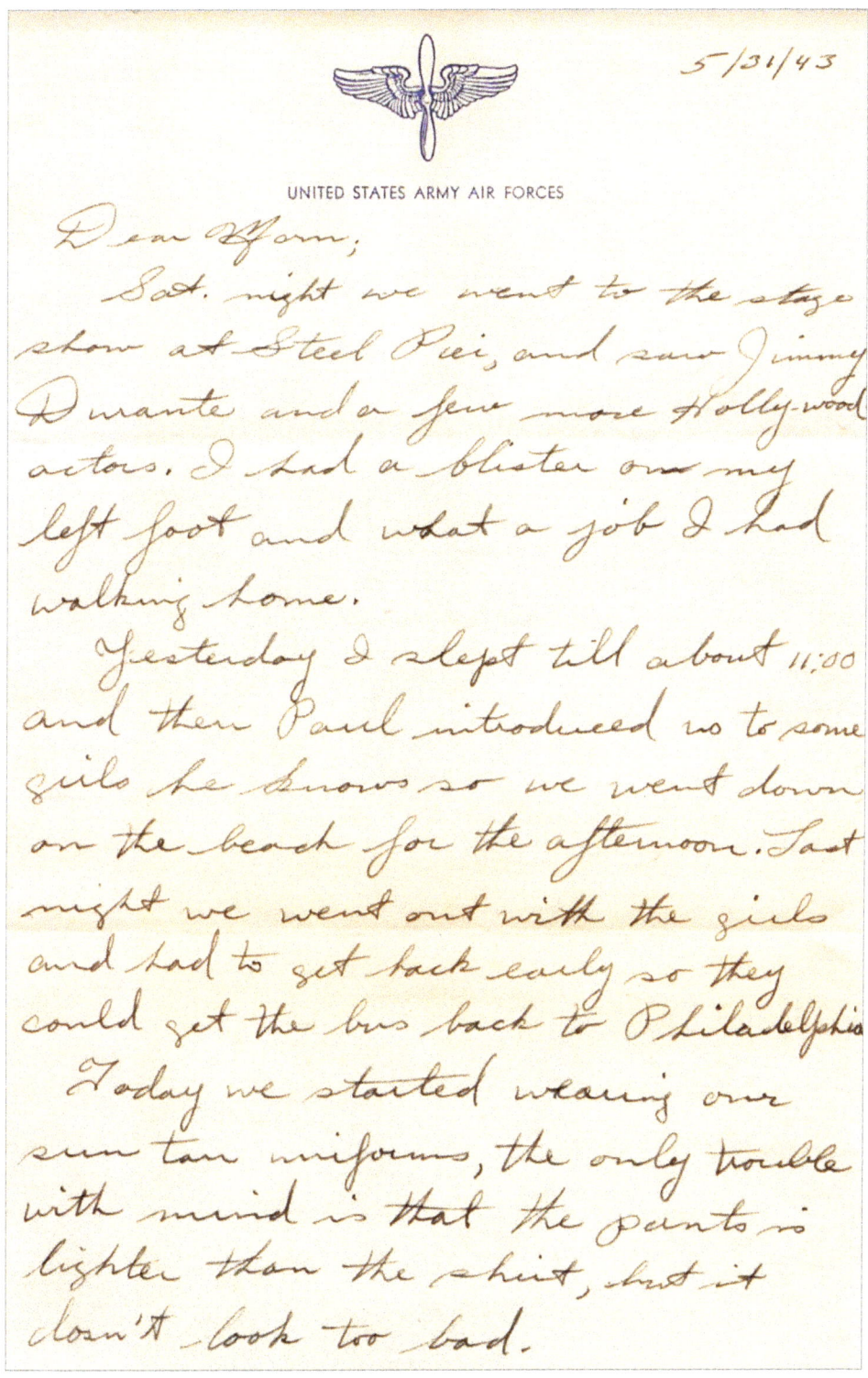

The front of one of Joe's letter home, dated May 31, 1943.

Alzada, possibly Cal Thomas, an unknown friend, an unknown sailor, and Betty.

Irving with an unknown friend – perhaps a girlfriend – sometime in the late 1940s.

A Broken Engagement

So, what *if* Betty had married Joe instead? Or what if Alzada and Irving had never crossed paths? It almost played out that way.

One evening, when Alzada was out roller skating with a church group, she met a handsome young Navy man named Calvin Alfred Thomas, who just so happened to be on shore leave in Fall River.

Born in 1925 in Chamblee, Georgia, Cal was only sixteen – but eager to serve his country – when he joined the U.S. Navy. He was too young to serve legally, but he wasn't the only one who fudged dates and forged signatures to enlist early, and he ended up a torpedo man on a PT boat during the taking of the Solomon Islands in the South Pacific.

Alzada and Cal's romance was swift and intense. They were both so young, and they both wanted to be in love, even if they were separated by thousands of miles. Like many starry-eyed young people during wartime, Alzada said "yes" when Cal proposed to her with a diamond ring just before he shipped back to the Pacific.

They wrote to each other, and when Cal returned – almost two years since they'd gotten engaged – he invited her to travel down to Georgia to meet his parents and family. Alzada went, but things had changed between them, and once she got home to Fall River, she returned the ring and called off the engagement.

Cal eventually married and had his own big family, but it's still a fascinating "what if" – what if Alzada had married the fair-haired, gray-eyed sailor instead? While she didn't know it at the time, Cal was just a pancake, preparing her for the fair-haired, blue-eyed Mr. Wonderful who would one day come her way and love her for a lifetime.

PART III

Irving's Not so Wonderful Childhood

1927 – 1949

Dad's Family Tree

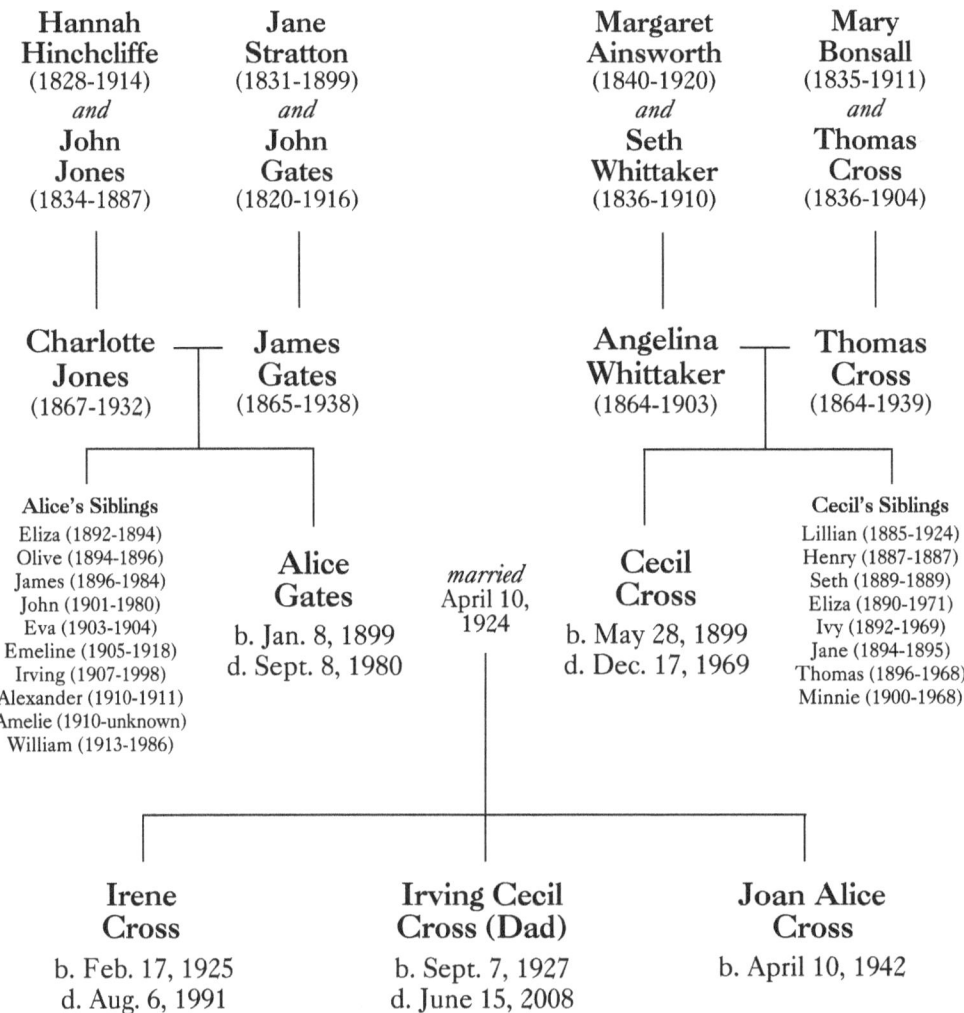

Irving's Not so Wonderful Childhood

WE KNOW SO little about Dad's upbringing compared to Mom's, and I think that's partly because he didn't like to talk about his childhood, as it wasn't exactly a happy one.

His mother, my Grandma Alice, was very different from other moms, with a quirky personality that could be both charming and a bit bewildering, but never cruel. Grandpa Cecil, on the other hand – well, at his worst, he could be just plain mean.

Dad and Cecil were both brilliant inventors and electricians, clever and crafty, with minds innately inclined to the mathematical, mechanical, and musical – but that's where the similarities ended.

After Dad got out of the army, he moved back in with his parents and worked for his father, which, as one might guess, proved to be an all-around unpleasant experience.

Their worlds just didn't align. Dad joined the union, Cecil absolutely did not; Dad was warm, chatty and friendly with customers, Cecil not so much. But that was Cecil; he preferred the predictable, the reliable, the fixable – numbers, formulas, machines.

But people are not machines – they can't be rewired like a lamp or tuned like a piano – and while Cecil was a stable presence in the home, he offered little emotion, affection, or encouragement to his children.

It saddens me that I have so few nice stories about Cecil, and it's a stark contrast to the volumes of praise I could write about Dad. However, I'm compelled to offer Grandpa Cecil a little grace, as his childhood wasn't very happy either – it was tragic, in fact, beginning with the loss of his mother, Angelina, when he was just a toddler.

But here's the beautiful twist – despite his upbringing, Dad was the kindest person I have ever known, and I'm amazed that he came out of such a gloomy environment with a heart so big and full of love.

Dad grew into someone completely different from his own father, becoming a loving husband and an adoring father who always wanted to be close to his children – children who stayed, children who brought over their friends, children who filled his life with warmth and laughter.

Irving with his sister Irene, sometime in the mid-to-late 1930s.

Irving's final 9th grade report card from Henry Lord Junior High in Fall River.

Irving's Boyhood

Irving Cecil Cross was born in Fall River on September 7, 1927, to Cecil and Alice (Gates) Cross. Sadly, we know nothing more than that about his early childhood. There are no baby pictures, no stories handed down about him as a toddler or young boy, and the one extremely precious memento we have of Irving as a baby is his Certificate of Dedication, from when he was baptized by his grandfather, the Rev. Thomas Cross.

We only have one childhood photo of Irving, which was taken when he was about eleven or twelve years old. He's smartly dressed and smiling, standing next to his older sister, Irene, in front of their Plymouth Avenue home in Fall River.

Along with the certificate and photo, however, we also have Irving's ninth grade report card – a bittersweet relic of the time just before his father forced him to drop out of school and start working.

From 1941 to 1942, Irving attended Henry Lord Junior High School on Tucker Street in Fall River. He did well there, keeping up solid A and B averages in all his courses – Civics, English, Math, Mechanical Drawing, Music, and Gym. He got straight A's in science, of course, and his lowest grade was a C average in Printing class, but what stands out the most is his report on citizenship and conduct – straight A's in Courtesy and Personal Appearance, A's and B's for Cooperation, and a C average for Self-Control.

This little piece of paper is just more proof that Irving always wanted to look nice, be nice, and have fun. But after he finished his freshman year, his father made a huge decision, and at just fifteen, Irving was pulled out of school and sent to live with a family friend in Newport, Rhode Island, where he worked at the Naval Torpedo Station on Goat Island.

While this forced him to grow up fast, Irving's kind and joyful nature as child would carry through into the adult he was becoming – a person very different than his father.

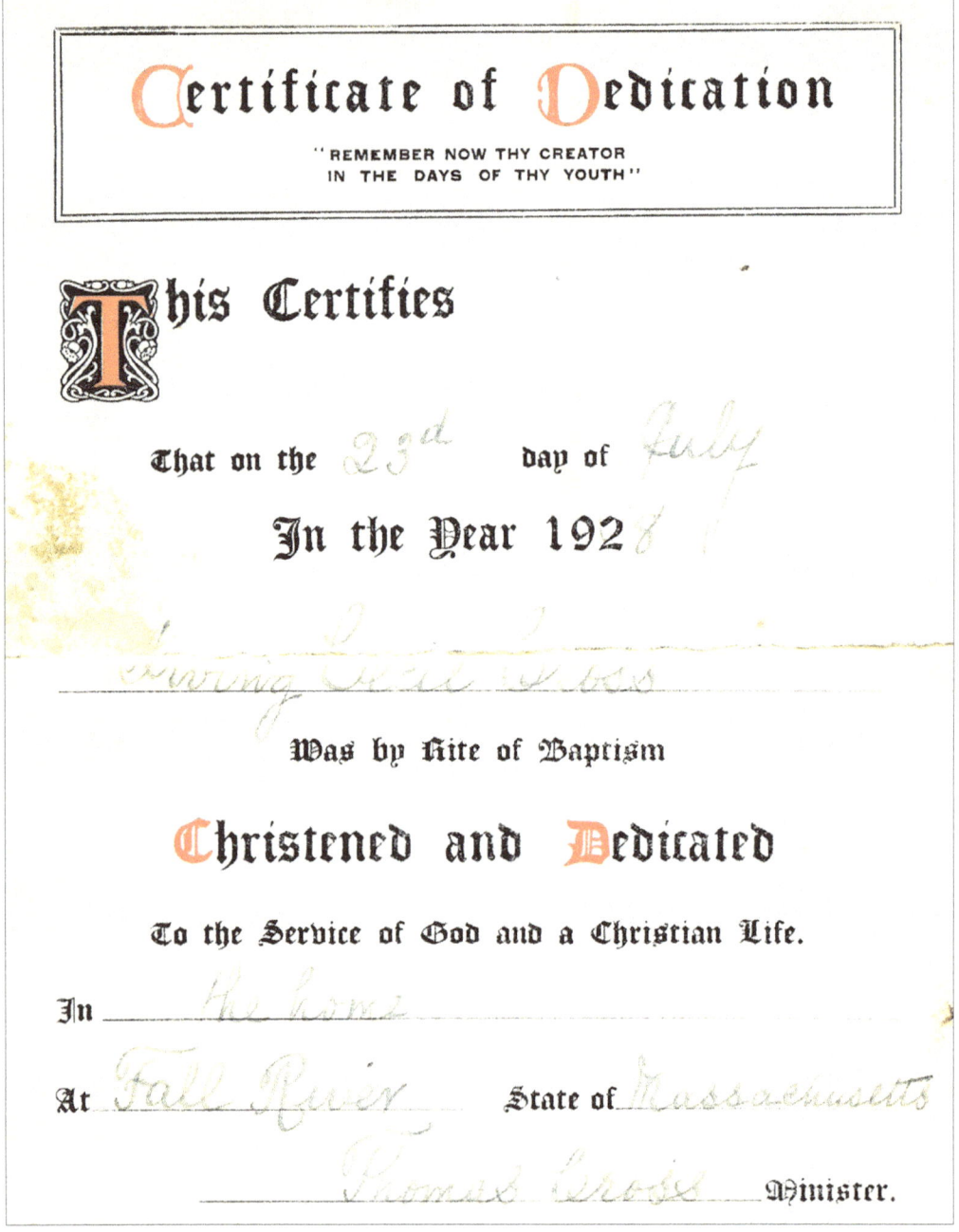

Dad's certificate of dedication from 1928 when his grandfather, Rev. Thomas Cross, baptized him.

Irving's Father Cecil

John Cecil Cross was born May 18, 1899, in Rishton, England, to Thomas and Angelina (Whittaker) Cross, one of six children who survived to adulthood.

Cecil was just a toddler when his mother and four siblings set sail for America in 1902, destined for Fall River, where his father and older sister had already laid the groundwork for a new life. But tragedy struck not long after their arrival when Cecil's mother, Angelina, fell ill and passed away.

This early loss set a somber tone for much of Cecil's life, and as time passed, each of his sisters took on parental roles in the absence of their mother, caring for the house and the children until they were old enough to work in the mills. The first to take charge was Lillian, the oldest, who balanced working and running the household with the help of her younger siblings, until she married John Haworth in 1907. Next was Eliza, who married Albert Ashworth in 1911, and then Ivy, who remained unmarried and stayed with her father until his death.

By September of 1912, things changed for the Crosses when their father, Thomas, a hard-working mill worker and part-time inspirational speaker, became an ordained minister in Albion, Maine, where he moved from congregation to congregation as a traveling preacher.

By the time Cecil is sixteen, the 1915 directory for Augusta, Maine, lists his sister Ivy as a clerk and Cecil as an axe painter. Fun Fact: Maine was once known as the axe manufacturing capital of the world. Both Cecil and Ivy were boarding with Rev. Thomas Cross at 35 School Street. Their sister Minnie was probably with them, but too young for the directory, and Thomas Jr. was serving in World War I. It was while Rev. Thomas was preaching in Maine that he met Nettie Holmes, a devoted churchgoer and twice-widowed Canadian-born woman with no children. In 1916, Thomas married Nettie in Eastport, Maine, and they lived together for a while – but not forever – in Oakland, Maine, where Thomas had a pastorage.

By 1920, Ivy, Thomas Jr., Cecil, and Minnie had settled back in Fall River, and Cecil's life took a pivotal turn in 1924 when he married Alice Jane Gates in Orleans, Massachusetts. His father, the reverend, officiated, and Cecil's sister Eliza signed as witness.

Cecil and Alice's marriage certificate. The Rev. Thomas Cross officiated, and Cecil's sister, Eliza, witnessed.

Cecil and Alice in the 1930s.

Alice was soon pregnant, but in December of 1924, their happiness turned to heartache when Cecil's oldest sister Lillian passed away at the age of thirty-nine – the same age at which their mother Angelina passed away.

After Cecil and Alice's first child, Irene, was born in 1925 in Rhode Island, the little family moved back to Fall River, where Irving was born in 1927 – and baptized by his very own grandfather the following year. But it wasn't until 1942, as Irving was finishing ninth grade, that his baby sister Joan was born.

According to those who knew him best, Cecil was a glum and very difficult man to live with, and his temper and drinking often darkened the mood at home. But Cecil had positive traits, too. He was a talented musician, having taught himself how to play the organ, and every once in a while he would shed the gruff exterior and show how funny he could be. We have one hilarious skit on Super 8 film of Grandpa Cecil entertaining us Cross kids, dancing with a mop on his head and sporting a magnificent mustache made from black electrical tape.

Cecil also had an undeniable flair for meticulous record-keeping, and he tracked it all: household expenses, addresses, obituary clippings, family haircuts, freezer defrosting dates – even Grandma Alice's dress size, a detail that feels both excessive and endearing, especially if we consider that Alice might have had trouble keeping track of it herself.

Cecil, always with his cigar.

Alice Gates Cross as a young woman.

Irving's Mother Alice

Alice Jane Gates was born January 8, 1899, in Fall River, to James and Charlotte "Lottie" (Jones) Gates, the second of their six children – out of eleven births – who survived to adulthood.

Alice's father James was born in 1865 in Liverpool, England, to Irish parents, John and Jane, the youngest of five, with two older brothers, Thomas and William, and twin sisters Effie and Eliza. James was just two years old when his family arrived in New York and settled in Fall River.

While the Gates family was preparing to cross the Atlantic, Alice's mother Lottie was being born in Rhode Island to English immigrants, John and Hannah (Hinchcliffe) Jones, the youngest of their five children. The Jones family had also settled in Fall River, where Lottie's father John worked in the mills until his passing in 1887 when Lottie was twenty.

Lottie's mother Hannah, however, lived well into her eighties, and became a respected figure in her Fall River neighborhood. Sadly, in a terrible accident, Hannah set herself ablaze while lighting a fire at home and quickly succumbed to her extensive burns in the hospital. The *Fall River Globe* reported the tragic news, and called Hannah *"one of the foremost residents of the Flint during her life in this city whose death will cause much regret."*

Both the Gates and Jones families lived in the Flint neighborhood of east Fall River, which is likely where Alice's parents first met, though they may also have crossed paths while working in the mills. Alice's father James had a long career as a loom fixer, and her mother, Lottie, worked as a weaver – when she wasn't busy caring for the children. Like many families of that time, neither of Alice's parents were educated beyond middle school, and neither were Alice and her siblings, but they all could read and write.

As soon as Alice was old enough, she found steady work in the mills, and lived with her family on Quarry Street until she married Cecil in 1924 and moved out. According to the 1920 census, when Alice was twenty-one, her youngest sibling William was only six, meaning that Lottie had given birth to him at the age of forty-six – a bit of family history worth noting, especially since Alice gave birth to her third child, Joan, at the age of forty-three.

Grandma Alice is remembered fondly in family memory as a quirky, unpredictable, and "simple" person, a description that applied to both her intellect and her emotions.

She wasn't overly affectionate, and she didn't exhibit the common social graces or sensibilities of other women her age. She's often described as completely innocent – someone who didn't harbor a single bad thought in her head. But, while she may have been uninformed and a bit inept in some areas, her heart was absolutely pure.

Joan's daughter, my cousin Cathy Pereira, was much closer to Alice than we Cross kids were, and she has many stories and memories of her time with Grandma Cross, most of them from after Cecil's passing.

For example, while Grandma Alice was living in an apartment on Doyle Avenue in Providence, she pulled out her vacuum cleaner one day and started pushing it across the floor, fully believing that she was cleaning the place – despite the fact that the machine wasn't even plugged in. When this was pointed out to her, Grandma Alice replied – "Well, I'm not going to vacuum it all over again!"

Now, if you'll recall, my highly intelligent and very sociable mother Alzada never had much luck with the vacuuming either, but as Cathy recalls, Grandma Alice had many other endearing idiosyncrasies, some of which could be quite heart-wrenchingly humorous – like how she would clip the grass outside her apartment with a pair of scissors.

Alice and Cecil in 1939, possibly taken while attending the funeral of Cecil's father, Rev. Thomas Cross.

Grandma Alice Cross with two dogs. This photo was taken in front of our Swansea home when Alice and Cecil were living there with their youngest daughter, my Aunt Joan.

Alice on a bicycle behind our Swansea home.

Grandma Alice also smoked cigarettes, but she never inhaled, and when it came to food, she simply lacked the need, desire, and ability to cook. Instead, she would just pop over to the convenience store to get her essentials – Lipton tea, white bread, ham, and American cheese.

She never drove, preferring to walk everywhere she needed to go, but sometimes she would take the bus. One day, she missed her ride into downtown Providence, so she decided to walk the entire way through the East Side Transit Tunnel – a passage for buses only!

When Grandma Alice was living in Harbor Terrace in Fall River, Cathy remembers taking the bus with her to visit her brother John, a Navy veteran who was both blind and hard of hearing. John lived alone, and when they arrived, Grandma Alice had to bang on the door and yell that she was there. The door was unlocked, so in they went, and there sat John; to his side was a large metal bucket full of water and cigarette butts – to ensure he wouldn't burn the house down – and in front of him, a blaring television set.

And speaking of televisions, here's another story courtesy of Cathy, whose parents once bought Grandma Alice a TV set of her own. Several months after they set it up for her, Cathy's older brother Eddie went to visit Grandma Alice, and when he changed the channel on the TV set, Grandma Alice, astonished, exclaimed, "Would you look at that!" – she had been watching the same channel for months, completely unaware there were other options.

But not all of the stories are lighthearted. My Aunt Joan recalls something about her mother Alice's so-called "simple" nature resulting from being "kicked in the head by a horse" when she was a child. Whether that was a serious claim or a cruel joke, no one ever knew, but in 2023 we unearthed a Fall River newspaper article that revealed a much more likely cause – a sailboat accident when Alice was just three years old.

The article from the May 26, 1902, edition of the *Fall River Daily Herald* described how a fun family boat trip ended with a terrifying tragedy involving Mr. and Mrs. James Gates, residents of Fall River's Flint neighborhood, and one of their young unnamed children.

The headline reads, *"Father Saved Child – Gibing Boom Knocked Little One Out of Mother's Arms,"* and the personal details match James and Lottie, my great-grandparents, which means the *"two-year-old child"* in the article could have only been three-year-old Alice.

According to the article, a small single-mast sailboat *"filled with a merry sailing party, had been down to the south end of the pond on an outing,"* the location given as *"near the boat landing of the Davis pork packing establishment"* on Jefferson Street, where the Gates family lived.

The man on the bow was picking up the mooring when a sudden gust of wind caused the boom to suddenly swing wildly across the hull. He shouted for everyone to watch out, and while most of the passengers jumped out of the way, *"Mrs. James Gates, however, who was sitting in the stern with her two-year-old child,"* did not hear the warnings.

Lottie may have been distracted, probably engaged in one of the most timeless and surefire entertainments from the parenting playbook – lifting the little one into the air to make them giggle and squirm and babble for more – and it could be the reason why she didn't hear the desperate shouts of "Look out!"

The boom swung hard and fast, striking little Alice *"squarely"* and sending her *"whirling over into the water."* As Alice was knocked from her mother's arms, Lottie screamed and dashed forward to jump into the water to rescue her, but she was held back by others on board.

Fortunately, Alice's father was on a skiff tied to the boat, and, having witnessed the whole accident, he immediately dove into the water to save Alice.

FLINT VILLAGE.

FATHER SAVED CHILD

Gibing Boom Knocked Little One Out of Mother's Arms.

Boatmen and others who happened to be near the boat landing at the Davis pork packing establishment late yesterday afternoon witnessed a father's prompt action that saved his child from drowning. A small catboat filled with a merry sailing party had been down to the south end of the pond on an outing. The catboat was about to pick up her mooring when a sudden gust of wind caused her to gibe. The man stationed on the bow to pick up the mooring shouted loudly for everybody to look out. Most of them saw the danger and got out of the way of the flying stick. Mrs. James Gates, however, was sitting in the stern with her two-year-old child raised in her arms. The boom struck the child squarely and sent it whirling over into the water. With a scream the mother started to follow her child, but with great presence of mind those in the boat held her back. Fastened to the stern of the catboat was a skiff in which sat Mrs. Gates' husband. He was preparing to take the party off when the boat was made fast to the mooring.

The gibing of the boat caused his painter to part and left him free. No sooner did he see the accident to his child than he dove into the water, which is particularly filthy at this point. He was but a moment in reaching the child and getting a firm hold on it. He then swam to his small boat, raised the child in and climbed in himself over the bow. He had but one oar and the boat was drifting away rapidly. Those in the larger boat steered their craft close enough to pass him in another oar and he went ashore, neither he nor the child being the worse for their adventure.

Fall River Daily Herald, May 26, 1902

While the article claimed neither Alice nor her father suffered any lasting harm, *"neither he nor the child being the worse for their adventure,"* we now suspect that Alice may have sustained brain damage from either the severe blow to the head or the oxygen deprivation from near drowning.

Oh, Grandma Alice. We might giggle at her quirks, but we always remember her with compassion, with gratitude, and for the profound yet "simple" joy she brought to all those around her.

Grandma Alice Cross in the late 1970s.

Aunt Irene & Aunt Joan's Family Tree

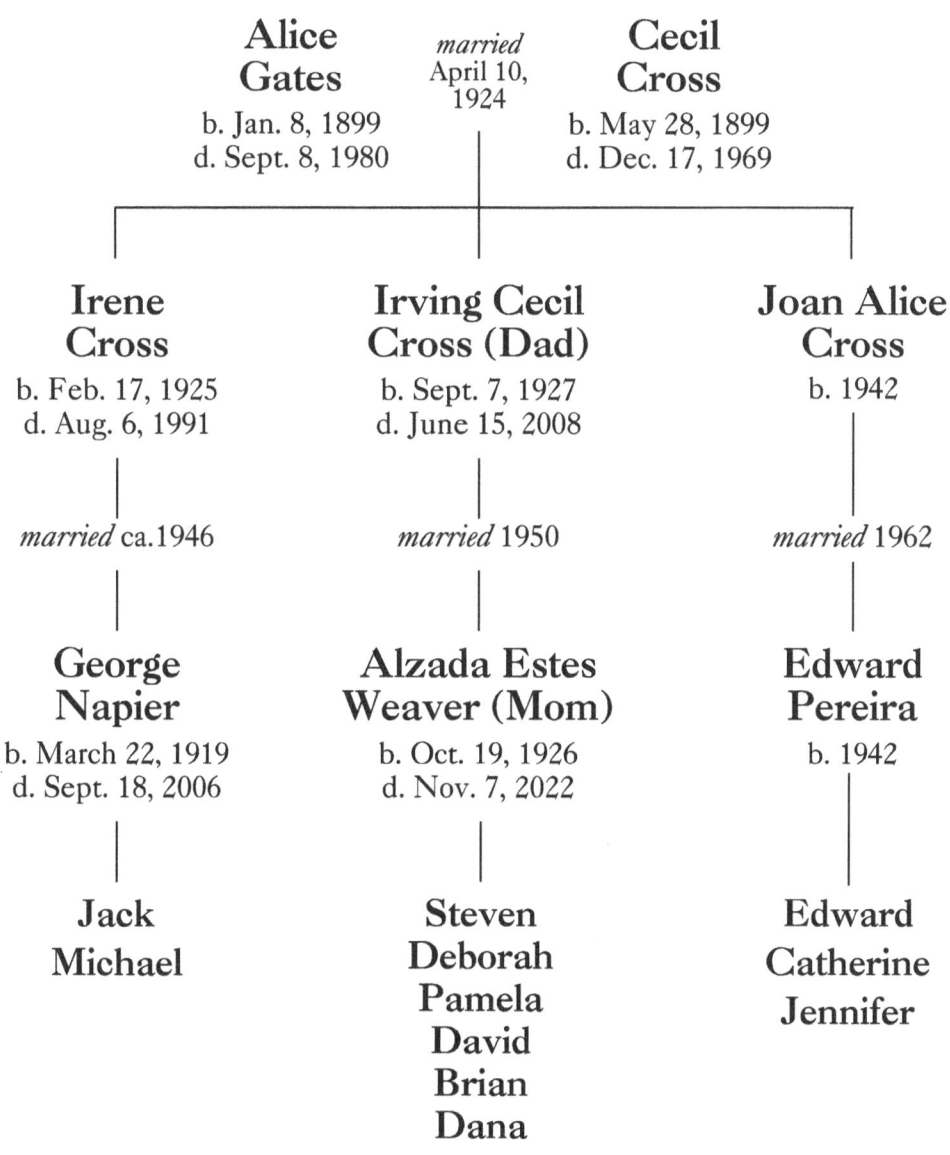

At top left, Irene's senior yearbook photo, and at right, Irene as a young woman. At bottom left, Irene and George on their wedding day in 1946, and at bottom right, Irene dancing on Christmas morning.

Irving's Sister Irene

Irene was born on February 17, 1925, in Providence. A lively, lanky brunette with a sparkle in her eyes and a sweet but mischievous smile, Irene's 1942 Durfee High senior yearbook listed her nickname as "Squealy," an apt description of her exuberant personality.

But Irene's vivacious spirit often clashed with the stern ways of her father – like confiscating all of her earrings and insisting that she do all of the housework. Though teenage Irving didn't have a choice, Irene escaped the family home as soon as she could, first by moving in with her best friend Peggy Driscoll, and then by moving to Newport in 1944 to work as a typist at the same torpedo station where Irving worked.

It was in Newport that Irene met the love of her life, George Napier, at a dance for servicemen. George had a thing for tall women, and when he spotted the lithe and willowy Irene, it was love at first sight.

They got married in 1946, and their first son, Jack, arrived in 1947, followed by Michael in 1948, who was born in the Panama Canal Zone. By 1950, the Napiers had settled in Ledyard, Connecticut, where George himself built their home – and that epic playground set in the woods – all on his own, and continued his work for the Navy.

Always delightfully dramatic and exceedingly hilarious, Irene's quick wit and sense of humor made her the Phyllis Diller of the family. Whenever we went to visit the Napier family, we were always guaranteed to have a wonderful time.

Irene and George eventually retired to sunny Florida, and in 1991, Irene passed away at the age of sixty-six. She left us way too early, but the memory of her fiery spirit still warms the hearts of all those who loved her.

At top left, George with Jack and Michael, and at right, Irene with Jack. At bottom left, Irene with Jack and Michael at the beach, and at bottom right, Irene and her long legs at Christmas time.

At left, George and Irene, and at right, Steve on his motorcycle with George and Irene.

Irene and Joan in 1980.

At top left, Alice, Cecil, and Joan visiting a duck pond, and at top right, Joan with a neighborhood kitten in Swansea. At bottom left, Joan at the beach, and at bottom right, Joan's senior yearbook photo.

Irving's Sister Joan

Joan was born in Fall River in April of 1942, when her parents were both in their early forties. Irene was seventeen and Irving was fourteen, and because of the large age gap, little Joanie practically grew up like an only child. By the time she was old enough to walk and talk, her siblings were already out of the house, living and working in Newport.

When Joan looks back on her solitary childhood, she can't recall much of a family life, not at home, and not socially; they seldom visited with even their closest family members, let alone friends. Cecil was not the jolliest of men, nor was he big on celebrations, and there was rarely a party or special occasion in his gloomy home, which no doubt influenced Irving to make every Christmas super spectacular for his own family.

One especially heartbreaking memory for young Joanie was when she was about nine years old. Her father had promised her a kitten, and she was bursting with excitement – her own little purring friend to love and cuddle. But without explanation, Cecil changed his mind, and just like that the dream of a furry new friend vanished.

Joan, much like her sister, Irene, fought with her father about anything and everything, and she could go for months at a time without speaking to him – and Cecil was the same. Even if Joan was standing in the same room, he would only speak to her through her mother – "Alice, tell Joan to wash the dishes" – which only made it worse.

Despite these difficulties, Joan emerged as a bright and active teenager by pouring her energy into school clubs and activities, and she graduated from Durfee High School in 1960 with the proud distinction of being a member of the National Honor Society.

Two years later, Joan was at a Catholic Youth Organization dance in Fall River when she met the love of her life, Edward Pereira, a marine on leave from boot camp at Camp Lejeune. The young couple eloped to Rochester, New Hampshire, and then, after a celebration hosted by Ed's sister, the newlyweds ventured off to North Carolina in Joan's Studebaker, loaded with wedding gifts.

Joan and Ed's first child, my cousin Edward, was born on the base, followed by my cousin Catherine (Cathy), and eventually they returned to New England – specifically Rhode Island, first to Providence, and then to Foster, where they had a large home with fireplaces and lots of land. It was while living here that their third child, my cousin Jennifer, was born.

Irving always thought of Joanie as his beloved little sister, and they grew even closer as adults, with a bond that steadily strengthened over the years. Joan and Ed shared a long marriage before parting ways, and together they were blessed by three wonderful children, who in turn, blessed them with six grandchildren.

To me, Aunt Joan is the epitome of elegance and kindness, with a beauty that radiates from the inside out. In remembering these stories, it reminds me that both Irene and Joan represent the incredible strength and spirit that runs through our family – women who embraced life with humor, resilience, and love.

Cecil, Alice, Irving, and Joan on Christmas 1952.

In the photo on the left (ca. 1963) are George and Irene, who is holding Joan's baby, my cousin Eddie; Joan is on the right, and behind them is my cousin Jack. The photo on the right (ca. 1969) shows Alice with Joan, who is holding her new baby daughter, my cousin Jenny, and in front is Eddie.

For a period of time in the 1980s, the Pereira family lived in Thailand for Ed's work. The two pictures above were taken once they arrived back home to New England. On the left, Ed, Jenny, and Eddie. On the right, Joan with her arms around our cousin Mike, and her daughter Cathy.

Ed and Irving.

In front, Alzada, Joan, and Ed; in back, Irving, Irene, and George.

Irving and Joan in later years – on the left, embracing; on the right, embracing and singing!

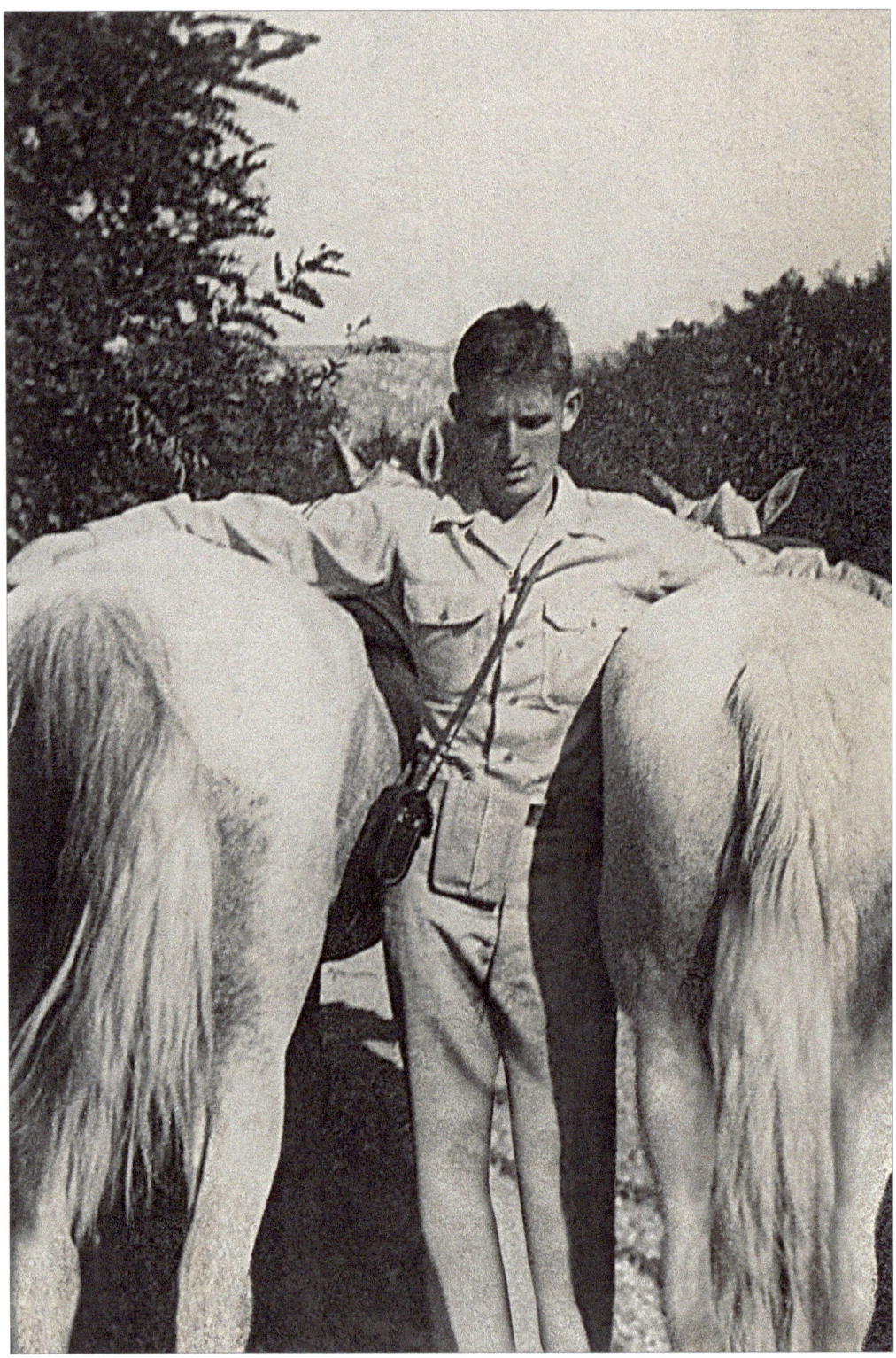

"Three of a kind"– taken at Fort Banks in Massachusetts, 1945–46.

Private Cross

Out of the nearly fifty million who registered for the U.S. draft between 1940 and 1946, more than ten million were inducted into service, and Irving was proudly one of them.

Feeling a sense of duty and eager to join the U.S. Armed Forces, Irving promptly registered on his eighteenth birthday. It was his own choice, not his father's demand, even if it meant swapping the strict command structure at home for another equally strict command structure in the military at a time of war.

For Irving, the army was a way out of town, a chance to travel, and a ticket to a fresh start, just as it had been for his sisters, who both married military men and left the only home they had ever known. And for many like Irving, those who were lucky to make it back home again, the Servicemen's Readjustment Act of 1944, known as the G.I. Bill, opened doors for education, home ownership, and a future that may have otherwise been out of reach.

Irving's only other option was staying in Fall River, getting his electrician license, and working for his father's successful business – all of which he eventually did – but he first chose the army. And so, on December 13, 1945, he was inducted into the 88th Division's 351st Infantry Regiment at Fort Banks in Winthrop, Massachusetts.

While training and preparing for deployment at Fort Banks, Irving also worked in the 88th's horse stables. On the battlefields of WWII, horses had already been replaced by tanks, but they were still used on all sides for transporting supplies, artillery, and personnel. There's a very funny photo of Irving standing between the rear ends of two horses, and on the back of it, his sister Irene wrote "three of a kind." Irving was probably tasked with feeding and grooming, and, judging by his expression in the photo, mucking duty.

By the time Irving joined up, the Third Reich had already surrendered, but the war wasn't over, especially not along the hotly contested and highly confusing borders of northeastern Italy and Yugoslavia. The rapid expulsion of German troops left a mix of various armies from various countries, all uncertain how to proceed, and as their respective governments scrambled to sort it out, weary U.S. troops were sent home and small waves of fresh new recruits were sent back in their place, with Private Irving Cross among them.

Irving was stationed in Gorizia, Italy, eighty-five miles northeast of Venice and about twenty-eight miles north of Trieste, at the foot of the Julian Alps near the border with what was then Yugoslavia, under the control of rising dictator Josip Broz, also known as Tito.

In Gorizia, small attacks and skirmishes among all the various factions in the area were common enough to keep U.S. troops on high alert, but as 1946 progressed, it seemed as though the major fighting had truly and finally ceased. It was no longer about storming battlefields – it was about being vigilant, keeping the peace, and navigating the complex post-war landscape.

Fun fact: It was in Gorizia where Irving trained in a radio service school under instructor Loren Reed, who later married Patty Gifford, the favorite cousin of Irving's future wife.

Another fun fact: General Eisenhower toured this area in 1946, during which he visited the newly established Morgan Line, a tentative territorial border which ran right by Gorizia, unofficially demarcating Western and Eastern Europe. The future President cracked jokes with the soldiers, teasing them about their good fortune – *"I have heard much concerning the hardships of life in the Alps, but I see you have the greatest*

Private Cross in uniform, 1945-46.

scenery in the world, you are warm, the food is good, and the girls are good looking. Things look so good here that I am going to Washington and learn what the prospects are for me to enlist in the 88th Division."

In the spring of 1947, the Paris Peace Treaties were going into effect, and the Selective Service Training and Service Act was expiring, so the 351st Regiment was relieved of assignment, and Irving reached Bostonian shores on April 3, 1947.

Irving's service to his country taught him some valuable lessons about loyalty, chain of command, and discipline, and these military lessons later influenced his many Dadisms. Among the most important of these lessons was personal grooming, especially taking care of his feet! For the rest of his life, Irving was obsessed with keeping his feet in pristine condition – which is why it was so incredibly shocking when he lost both feet later in life due to circulation issues and diabetes.

Enlisting may have been Irving's way of declaring his independence from his father Cecil, but it was also an expression of his deep sense of duty to serve his country, the experience of which helped him learn and grow. He was one of the lucky ones; he made it home and thrived – and he never forgot that not everyone was so fortunate.

Irving in 1948, standing next to his brother-in-law George's new convertible.

Irving's Uncle Red

With his military service complete, Irving returned to Fall River, where he moved back in with his family, became a licensed electrician, and joined his father's business. As a duo, they did business under the name of "Installation by Cross," specializing in residential wiring.

Despite working and living together, Irving and his father were never close, and Cecil wasn't close with his other family members either. But Cecil's siblings, especially his sisters, Eliza, Ivy, and Minnie, quite literally remained close to each other throughout their lives, all three living in separate homes which shared the same yard.

Of his dozens of relatives on both sides, Dad was fondest of his Uncle Red, or, more formally, Irving Jones Gates (1907-1998), Grandma Alice's younger brother – Irving's Uncle Irving. Uncle Red was a real fixture in his namesake's life; once, he even gave Irving a car!

Cecil and Irving's business card from the late 1940s.

Above, Uncle Red with Irving and Alzada in the later 1970s. At bottom left, Uncle Red and Aunt Aggie at Grandma Alice's funeral in 1980 (with Dana in the background), and at right, Mom dancing with Uncle Red at Pam's wedding in 1987.

In 1947, when Irving came home from the army, Uncle Red and his wife Agnes were living with Irving's parents, his sister, and his Great-Aunt Eliza, all in the ancestral Gates home on Bullock Street. The house had seen four generations of Gates since 1897, and passed down from patriarch and matriarch, John and Jane Gates, to their youngest daughter, Eliza, who had lived in the house since the family first moved in.

Irving's Great-Aunt Eliza passed away in the fall of 1947, and in 1949, while Irving was still living there, Cecil and Red had a disagreement, which led to Cecil throwing Red – with his wife and young child – out of the house. Alice and Red's Aunt Eliza was gone, possibly without leaving a will, and in a bit of a karmic twist, the house was ultimately left to Red, so Cecil had to move out – with his wife and young child – and Red moved back in with his family.

This awkward eviction from Fall River, however, happily resulted in Irving acquiring for his parents and sister what would later become our ancestral Cross home in Swansea. And, despite this early drama, Irving's bond with Uncle Red only strengthened over time. He was more than just Irving's uncle – he was a beloved mentor, friend, and enduring presence.

Red passed away in October of 1998, and his wife Aggie followed in September of 1999. Like Grandma Alice and my Great-Uncle Red, Great-Aunt Aggie was also an American-born first generation child of immigrants (from the Azores). Grandpa Cecil was born in England, but he was only three when he arrived, and likely remembered very little of his life before Fall River.

While Irving descends from the "Great Wave" of industrial era transatlantic immigration that spanned from the mid-nineteenth to early twentieth century, Mom's immigrant ancestors date back to the "Great Migration" of the early seventeenth century – Protestants and Puritans and Pilgrims, oh my!

PART IV

The Ancestors of Alzada the Wonderful

1620s – 1920s

Alzada the Wonderful's Family Tree

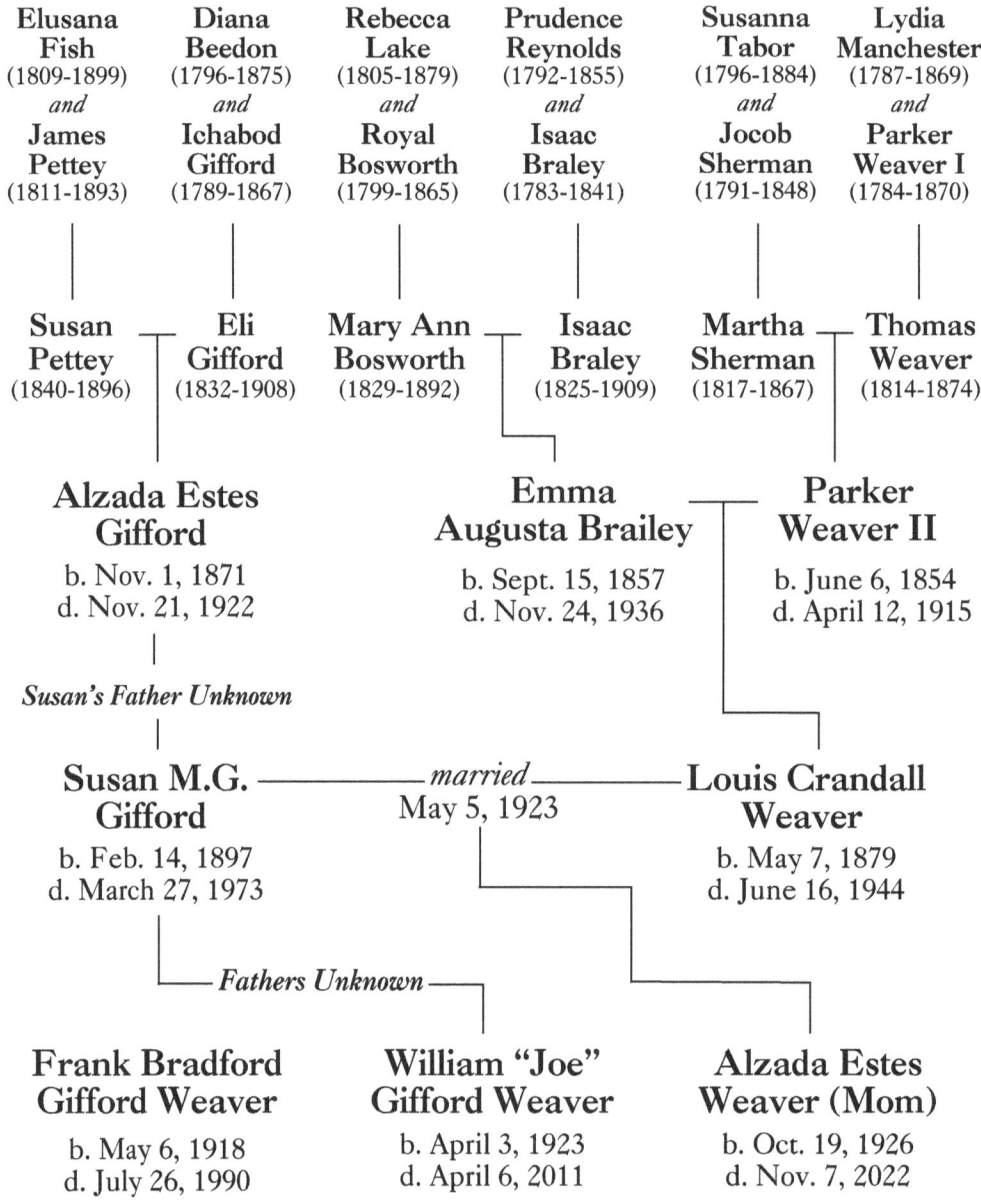

The Ancestors of Alzada the Wonderful

MY FAMILY TREE flourishes with triumphs and tragedies, tales of love and loss, uncanny similarities and coincidences, and lots of surprises! Biologically, a person has four grandparents, eight great-grandparents, sixteen great-great-grandparents, thirty-two great-great-great-grandparents, and so on.

With every generation, our roots spread wider, and while I would love to write about every single one of them, as each is deserving of their own detailed chapters, we've only got so many pages and only so many records to work with.

This part of the book begins with Mom's colonial ancestors, but do remember, dear reader – I am neither a historian nor a professional genealogist, and there are already entire volumes about the Giffords, Braileys, Weavers, and many other early New England families, from whom millions of Americans descend. There are hundreds of books on this period, and I encourage anyone interested in colonial New England – or any topic – to keep reading and learning. And for those of you who are history buffs, while you might find my retellings more storybook than textbook, I hope you'll enjoy them, nonetheless.

Mom's ancestors were among the first waves of seventeenth-century English colonists to arrive in what came to be known as New England, beginning with passengers aboard the *Mayflower*.

These early families expanded and intermarried, so many of our early branches intertwine over time; and to make things even more confusing, some surnames mutated over the generations – like Brayley, Braley, Brailey, for example.

The name of my great-grandmother – "Alzada the Great" – lived on through my mother – "Alzada the Wonderful" – and though they never met, in some mystical way, the two Alzadas were always connected.

As I've mentioned, when Mom was a child, Nana Susan often took her to Beech Grove Cemetery in Westport, where they visited the grave of Alzada the Great. Nana Susan never shared memories or stories about her mother with her daughter, but young Alzada the Wonderful could always sense the heartfelt love and deep reverence Nana had for her mother, especially in those moments at Alzada the Great's graveside, even without hearing any stories.

What a contrast compared to our current Cross generation, as we have more stories than we know what to do with – so many, in fact, that we've had to start numbering them just to keep track!

However, like any family history, some stories were meant to be forgotten, some records are incomplete or intentionally incorrect, and some secrets remain buried for good reason. Alzada the Great, for instance, didn't leave much in the way of official documents – she filed no marriage certificates, and, of all her children, only Frank, her firstborn, had a birth certificate on record. This gap in the record has left me with a major unanswered question about Nana Susan's biological father, which means one-eighth of my great-grandparentage remains a mystery.

But before we delve into the life of Alzada the Great, let's travel back to the earliest colonial roots of the Alzada legacy.

Nonconformists

Almost all of Alzada the Wonderful's English ancestors were known as "Nonconformists," a seventeenth-century term which came to describe the "dissenters" and "separatists" who refused to follow the Church of England, a product of King Henry VIII severing all ties with the Catholic Church in 1534. But for centuries before this historic break with Rome, and for decades after – and depending on the reigning monarch – these religious dissenters were sometimes labeled "heretics."

In England, Nonconformists were primarily Christians who would not conform to the Church of England, devotees of "other" Protestant denominations, many of which share principles but are distinct, including the Anabaptists, Baptists, Calvinists, Methodists, Presbyterians, Puritans, and the Society of Friends, also known as Quakers.

For these individuals, their so-called nonconformity was a way of life, and living by their faith sometimes meant defying the law of the land – for them, the ultimate authority was God.

This kind of nonconformity was a dangerous way to live, but there was no other option – besides, how could any man, even one wearing a crown, control both the life and soul of another? Henry VIII felt this very same way about the Pope, and by the time King Henry's daughter, Queen Elizabeth I, ascended to the throne, tensions with Catholic Spain had developed into a full-blown – but unofficial – naval war.

Spain had been brutally colonizing Central and South America for almost a century when, in 1584, Queen Elizabeth issued Sir Walter Raleigh a royal charter to establish a colony in this "New World." Raleigh never actually set foot in modern-day North America, but he was the one who sent teams of explorers to first survey and then colonize the land they were calling "Virginia." This area is now referred to as the Outer Banks of North Carolina, and history remembers this early effort as the ill-fated Roanoke Colony, also known as the "lost colony," which failed due to numerous challenges, including food shortages, isolation, and tension with native people. When colony governor John White returned in 1590 after a three year absence, he found the settlement deserted.

Queen Elizabeth died in 1603, and in 1604, her successor, King James I signed a peace treaty with Spain. Two years later, King James signed the royal charters that would lead to the first permanent English settlement in the New World – Jamestown, established in 1607 in what became known as the Virginia Colony.

Among the founders of Jamestown was the famous English explorer Captain John Smith, who also surveyed the coastlines of what would become the Plymouth Colony to the north. Smith's 1616 publication, *A Description of New England*, became a powerful marketing tool for the fledgling colonies, and the pitch had two distinct appeals – one worldly, and one spiritual.

A 1624 portrait of Captain John Smith.

The worldly appeal was economic prosperity, and Smith painted a picture of pure paradise on earth, with fertile soil, vast forests, and abundant fish and game, the fruits of which – acquiring land and wealth – would only come to those willing to work hard. This angle enticed many to settle in the southern Virginia Colony.

The spiritual appeal, on the other hand, attracted settlers to the northern Plymouth Colony, framing colonization as a divine mission, and encouraging people to see themselves as instruments of God's will in pursuing religious freedom.

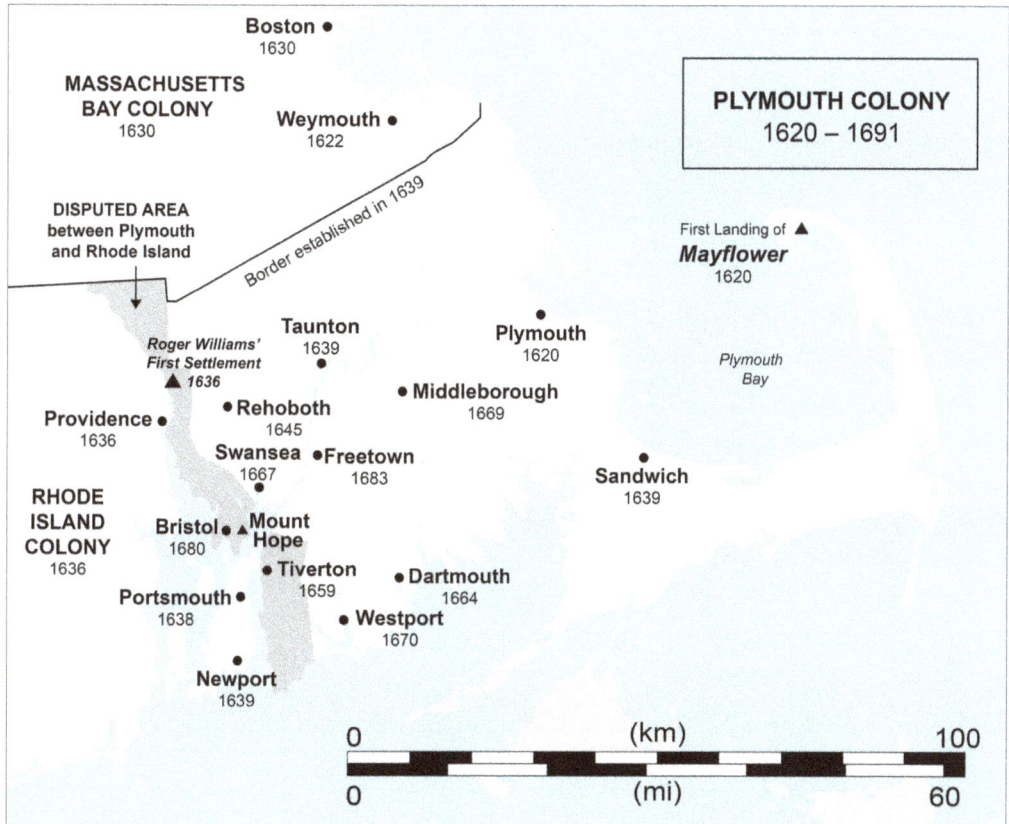

Map of the Plymouth Colony, Massachusetts Bay Colony, and the Rhode Island Colony in the 17th century. This map is for illustrative purposes only, highlighting only the places where Alzada the Wonderful's ancestors lived, and does not include all of the many early settlements in the colonies. Many New England settlements were named after existing cities back in England, including Boston, Weymouth, Plymouth, Sandwich, Dartmouth, Tiverton, Taunton, Bristol, and Portsmouth. Swansea and Newport share names with cities in Wales.

Mom's Maternal Mayflower Ancestors

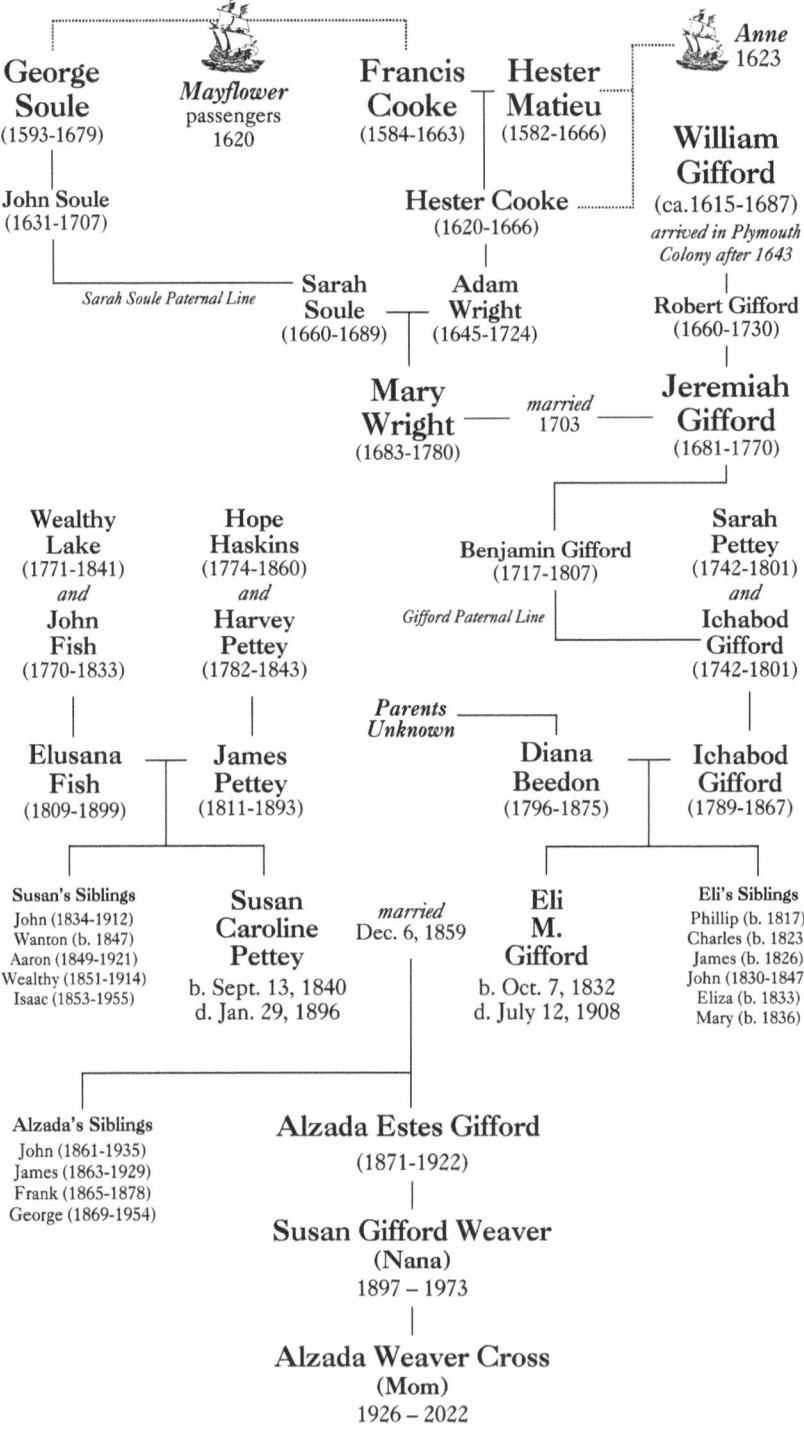

The Mayflower

One of my delightful discoveries through genealogical research is my distant cousin, Lynne Gifford, whom I met online through Ancestry.com. Lynne has a wealth of knowledge about the Gifford family and has traced our lineage all the way back to two of our common ancestors: Francis Cooke and George Soule, who were both passengers aboard the *Mayflower*.

In 1620, Francis Cooke and George Soule set sail with 100 other passengers for the New World, leaving behind everything they knew. The *Mayflower* itself was a merchant ship, built to hold products, not people, who all had to live below deck where conditions were cramped, damp, and dark. Families huddled together with no privacy or fresh air, storms battered the ship, and many passengers fell ill during their sixty-six long days at sea. Remarkably, despite these harsh conditions, only one passenger died during the voyage.

On November 21, 1620, they finally arrived at Cape Cod, but before they went ashore, they drafted the Mayflower Compact – an *Agreement Between the Settlers of New Plymouth* – which would help them govern their new colony under a unified, civil structure. Both of my ancestors, Francis Cooke and George Soule, were among the forty-one signers of this historic document.

While his ancestry is unknown, Francis Cooke was part of the Separatist movement, a group of Puritans who sought to separate from the Church of England to freely practice their faith. He traveled on the *Mayflower* with his eldest son, and was later joined by his wife, Hester, and their younger children in the Plymouth Colony. Cooke became respected in the community for his hard work and humility, contributing to the colony's success and living to be about eighty years old. And just to drop a few names, among his many descendants are President Franklin Roosevelt, Orson Wells, and Marilyn Monroe.

Unlike Francis Cooke, who was a "freeman," George Soule was the indentured servant of another Separatist freeman named Edward Winslow. In exchange for working a certain number of years for the Winslow family, Soule received passage, food, and shelter; but despite his status as a servant, he also signed the Mayflower Compact, giving him a voice in how the colony would be governed.

George Soule was eventually made a freeman, and he settled into a prosperous life as a farmer with plenty of land, becoming an influential figure in colonial society and living until the age of eighty-five. He and his wife, Mary Beckett, had nine children and forty-four grandchildren, creating countless descendants, among them, General George Custer, Laura Ingalls Wilder, Richard Gere, and me!

"The Mayflower on Her Arrival in Plymouth Harbor" – an 1882 painting by William Halsall.

Mayflower II, a replica of the Mayflower, in Plymouth, Massachusetts. Photo by Paul Keleher.

Clarel and I visiting the Mayflower II in 2024.

Giving Thanks

Though they survived the perilous journey, the Pilgrims' first winter proved far more brutal than their time at sea, and they soon realized they were entirely unprepared for the harsh New England winter. It was bitterly cold, the soil was frozen, and their hastily built shelters were inadequate.

They lacked fresh fruits and vegetables, allowing scurvy to take hold, and within the first four months, nearly half of all the *Mayflower* passengers perished from exposure, malnutrition, pneumonia, or other diseases. Of the fifty colonists who survived the winter, twenty-two were men, twenty-five were children or teenagers, and only four were women. Among the fourteen women that perished was the wife of Edward Winslow, to whom George Soule was indentured.

But with the spring came new opportunities, and local members of the Wampanoag nation taught the colonists how to hunt, farm, and fish. They worked hard throughout the summer, and that autumn, in November of 1621, the colonists – including George Soule and Francis Cooke – gathered together with members of the Wampanoag tribe to celebrate their first successful harvest.

Celebratory feasting was one of the few customs the colonists had in common with native people, and nearly everything we know about this gathering comes from a letter written by, once again, Edward Winslow.

The letter, dated December 11, 1621 – a year after the *Mayflower* arrived – is a lengthy and very optimistic epistle, addressed to his *"loving and old friend,"* in which he describes bringing in the harvest and hunting fowl *"…so that we might, after a special manner rejoice together, after we had gathered the fruits of our labors."*

Some ninety Wampanoag accompanied the Pokanoket chieftain, *"their greatest king Massasoit,"* to what became three days of feasting and entertainment. *"And although it be not always so plentiful, as it was at this time with us, yet by the goodness of God, we are so far from want, that we often wish you partakers of our plenty"* – the Puritan way of saying "Wish you were here!"

This occasion became known as the "first" Thanksgiving, especially throughout New England, but our modern concept of Thanksgiving as a fixed federal holiday on the last Thursday of November took centuries to develop, and continues evolving year after year.

In 1846, New Englander Sarah Hale began a long letter-writing campaign, in which she lobbied five consecutive Presidents to establish an official "Thanksgiving Day." Hale, a poet and author, among many other distinctions, is perhaps best known for authoring the nursery rhyme, *Mary Had a Little Lamb*, and in 1863, President Abraham Lincoln received one of her letters – and just a few days later, he proclaimed Thanksgiving Day an official national holiday.

Thanksgiving has always been a happy holiday for the crazy Crosses, because for us, it's a time to be together and celebrate our blessings. But not all Americans commemorate the last Thursday in November the same way. For them, it's a "National Day of Mourning," and in 1998, a monument was placed in Plymouth.

In 2009, President Obama signed the Native American Apology Resolution, and in 2024, President Biden issued a "National Apology." These long overdue federal gestures acknowledged the violence and trauma inflicted upon generations of Native American people, but it's the many descendants of these people who are actively working for change.

My daughter Alexandra is married to JP Prettybull, an enrolled member of the Ponca Tribe of Nebraska, and a dedicated activist working to preserve the cultural heritage of their ancestors. In the late 1870s,

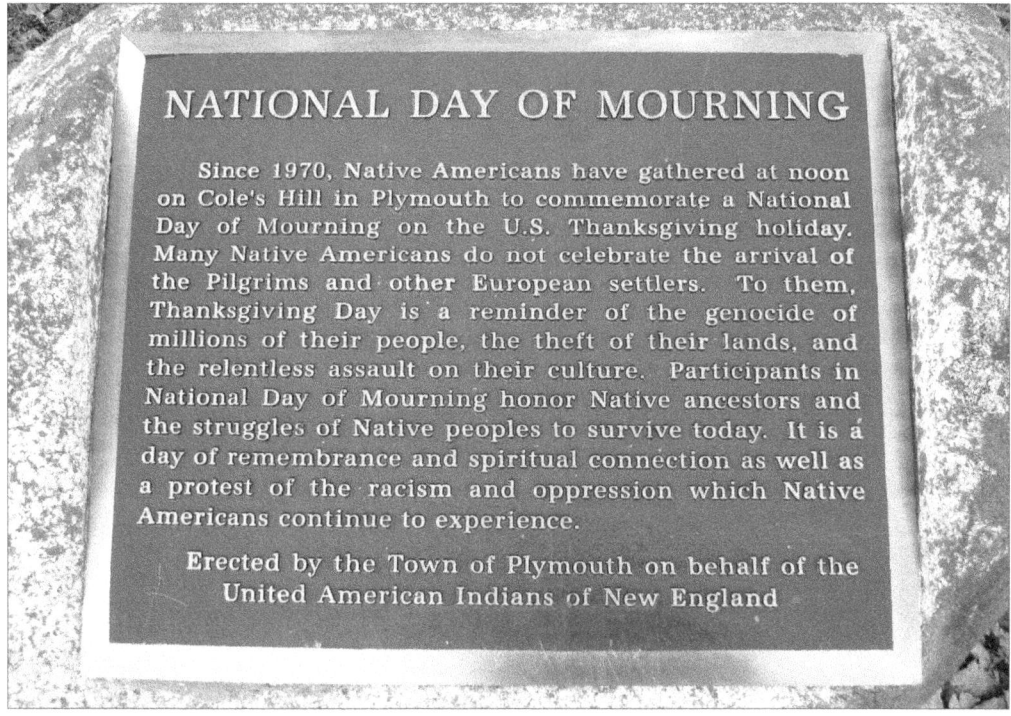

The "National Day of Mourning" plaque in Plymouth, Massachusetts.

the Ponca were forcibly relocated south, driven from their homelands in modern day Nebraska to a reservation in what is now Oklahoma, a harrowing journey known as the Ponca Trail of Tears, which caused the catastrophic loss of nearly a third of the tribe.

In 1879, Ponca Chief Standing Bear, after losing both his son and daughter, returned to Nebraska with a small group of Ponca, including JP's family, and the Northern Ponca and Southern Ponca have remained separated since. It was Standing Bear who led and won a landmark case in 1879, in which the U.S. district court recognized the Northern Ponca as human beings under U.S. law.

This ruling only applied to Standing Bear's people – neither the Southern Ponca nor any other indigenous groups were included – but it was a catalyst for the eventual passing of the Indian Citizenship Act in 1924, more than six decades after the celebration of the first federal Thanksgiving.

Mom's Maternal Gifford Family Tree Branch

William Gifford
(ca.1615-1687)
|
Robert Gifford
(1660-1730)
|
Jeremiah Gifford
(1681-1770)
|
Benjamin Gifford
(1717-1807)
|
Ichabod Gifford
(1742-1801)
|
Ichabod Gifford
(1789-1867)
|
Eli M. Gifford
(1832-1908)
|
Alzada Estes Gifford
(1871-1922)
|
Susan Gifford Weaver
(Nana)
1897 – 1973
|
Alzada Weaver Cross
(Mom)
1926 – 2022

The Gifford Line

While the *Mayflower* is the most famous ship associated with the early colonists, it was far from the only one, and from 1620 to 1640, many more ships carried many hundreds of families across the Atlantic, including dozens from whom Alzada the Wonderful descends.

After 1640, the flow of immigrants from England slowed as the mother country was plunged into the turmoil of a bloody civil war. New England was left to fend for itself for a while, but the early colonists thrived and multiplied, and among these hardy souls was a man whose legacy still resonates in our family history – the famously formidable William Gifford of Sandwich, Massachusetts – my great-times-eight grandfather.

Born around 1615 in England, William arrived in the Plymouth Colony in the 1640s with his wife and several children. While records suggest he might have been a tailor's apprentice, much about his early life remains a mystery. One thing is certain, however – William Gifford was a man of unyielding principles, a Nonconformist who defied the rigid Puritan orthodoxy that dominated New England at the time.

To be anything other than a Puritan in seventeenth-century New England was to openly invite scrutiny and persecution. As Quakers, a religious group considered heretical by the Puritans, it would have been a very frightening time for William and his family.

His refusal to take the oath of fidelity to the colony, and to England, led to repeated harassment and lawsuits, and his defiance came at great personal cost. One incident saw him fined for *"committing fornication before marriage"* with his own wife, as the colony refused to recognize Quaker marriage traditions.

Many dissenters fled – or were exiled – from Puritan communities, but William Gifford chose to stay. He never renounced his faith, despite decades of conflict, endless mistreatment, threats of violence, hefty fines, and public scorn, and eventually he became a wealthy landowner.

By the time of his death in 1687, however, his hard-earned fortune had been eaten away by legal fees – and yet, he had just enough money left to make a final bequest to the Society of Friends.

It's through my great-great-grandfather Eli Gifford – Alzada the Great's father – that I descend from William Gifford's sixth child, Robert. And, while the specific details of William's origins remain elusive, even after centuries of research by historians and descendants alike, the principles he lived by have survived.

William Gifford's legacy is one of moral courage, independent thought, and spiritual resilience, values that have flowed down through the generations – but he's not the only brave soul we'll see in my family tree.

An illustration entitled, "Whipping Quakers at the Cart's Tail in Boston," one of many punishments for belonging to the Society of Friends. From the 1881 book, "Young Folks' History of Boston."

The Weaver Line

The story of my Weaver line begins in 1645 with the marriage of Clement Weaver Jr. and Mary Freeborn in the settlement of Portsmouth, Rhode Island, just as the colony was beginning to take shape.

Mary was the daughter of William Freeborn, another Englishman in search of religious freedom, and she was only seven when her family arrived in 1634 aboard the *Francis*. The Freeborns originally settled in the Massachusetts Bay Colony – first Roxbury, then Boston, and when Mary was about twelve, her father moved the family to Pocasset, a new settlement on Aquidneck Island, the big "Rhode Island" in Narragansett Bay.

The Pocasset settlement, which was later renamed Portsmouth, was established in 1638, with my ancestor William Freeborn among the founders who signed the Portsmouth Compact. This document made Portsmouth the second official settlement in what was unofficially called the Rhode Island Colony.

The first settlement was Providence, founded in 1636 by Roger Williams, another Nonconformist constantly at odds with the Puritan establishment. After being banished from the Massachusetts Bay Colony for his *"new and dangerous opinions,"* Williams fled Salem on foot during a blizzard, escaping just days before the sheriff arrived to arrest him.

Williams trekked more than fifty miles south, and was given refuge in a Wampanoag settlement for the rest of the winter. When spring came, Williams went west, toward the northeastern shore of Narragansett Bay, where he and a small group of fellow exiles from Salem purchased land from the Narragansett – just one of his many "dangerous" beliefs (that colonists should compensate native people for land instead of just taking it).

Mom's Paternal Weaver Family Tree Branch

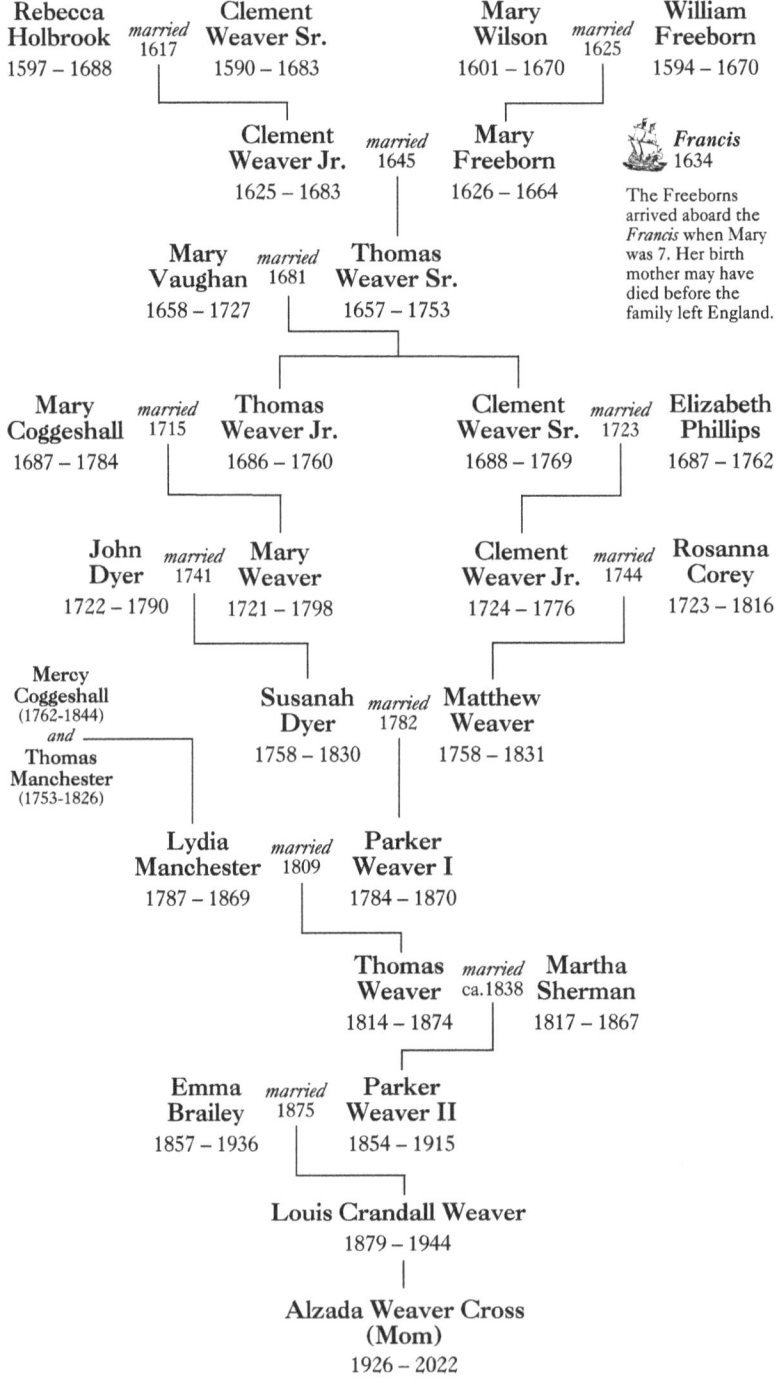

Rebecca Holbrook (1597 – 1688) *married* 1617 Clement Weaver Sr. (1590 – 1683)

Mary Wilson (1601 – 1670) *married* 1625 William Freeborn (1594 – 1670)

Clement Weaver Jr. (1625 – 1683) *married* 1645 Mary Freeborn (1626 – 1664)

Francis 1634 — The Freeborns arrived aboard the *Francis* when Mary was 7. Her birth mother may have died before the family left England.

Mary Vaughan (1658 – 1727) *married* 1681 Thomas Weaver Sr. (1657 – 1753)

Mary Coggeshall (1687 – 1784) *married* 1715 Thomas Weaver Jr. (1686 – 1760)

Clement Weaver Sr. (1688 – 1769) *married* 1723 Elizabeth Phillips (1687 – 1762)

John Dyer (1722 – 1790) *married* 1741 Mary Weaver (1721 – 1798)

Clement Weaver Jr. (1724 – 1776) *married* 1744 Rosanna Corey (1723 – 1816)

Mercy Coggeshall (1762-1844) and Thomas Manchester (1753-1826)

Susanah Dyer (1758 – 1830) *married* 1782 Matthew Weaver (1758 – 1831)

Lydia Manchester (1787 – 1869) *married* 1809 Parker Weaver I (1784 – 1870)

Thomas Weaver (1814 – 1874) *married* ca.1838 Martha Sherman (1817 – 1867)

Emma Brailey (1857 – 1936) *married* 1875 Parker Weaver II (1854 – 1915)

Louis Crandall Weaver (1879 – 1944)

Alzada Weaver Cross (Mom) (1926 – 2022)

Providence soon became a place of peace and a sanctuary for other religious dissenters, including Baptists, Quakers, and Jews, setting the tone for the many Rhode Island settlements that would follow.

Around the same time the Providence settlement was established, the Massachusetts Bay Colony was embroiled in what historians refer to as the "Antinomian Controversy" – *antinomian* is Greek for "against the laws."

At the center of the controversy was Anne Hutchinson, a respected midwife who often hosted unsanctioned spiritual and Biblical discussion groups in her home – sometimes for women only. The bigger controversy, however, revolved around her specific beliefs on faith and salvation, and it resulted in her banishment by the Puritans in 1638.

Hutchinson fled to Rhode Island, accompanied by her family and followers, among them the Freeborns. Guided by Roger Williams, they settled on Aquidneck Island, forming Pocasset (Portsmouth).

An 1856 illustration of Roger Williams seeking refuge among the Wampanoag, by J.C. Armytage.

Clement Jr. was a preteen boy when he arrived in the Massachusetts Bay Colony sometime before 1639, accompanied by his parents, Clement Weaver Sr. and Rebecca Holbrook. Rebecca's brother, Thomas, had arrived in 1635 and settled south of Boston in Weymouth, and the Weavers established themselves nearby.

While records of the Weavers' early religious affiliations are scarce, there is evidence that Clement Sr. was once fined for drunkenness by the colony court around 1640.

In 1643, the Weavers moved from Weymouth to Portsmouth, where Clement Jr. married Mary Freeborn, and it's from this union I trace my lineage back to one of their sons, Thomas Weaver Sr.

Fun Fact: In 1743, Thomas Sr. was among the petitioners who established Middletown, a community nestled between Portsmouth and Newport. Along with Thomas Sr., the names of his sons and grandsons are recorded in the list of freemen at Middletown's first official town meeting.

Unfortunately, many early records from Newport and Middletown were seized by the British during the Revolutionary War and eventually destroyed, making it challenging to trace some of the Weaver history.

Fortunately for me, however, in addition to my well-documented Freeborn forebears, I also have a couple of Coggeshall connections!

The Coggeshall Connection

When Anne Hutchinson fled to Providence in 1638, among her faithful followers was her neighbor from Boston – John Coggeshall, a successful English silk merchant who had arrived in 1632 aboard the *Lyon*, the very same ship that brought Roger Williams the year before.

John Coggeshall was also one of the few people with the courage to testify in Anne Hutchinson's defense during her trial in 1637. He was among the founders of both Portsmouth and Newport, and in May of 1647, he was elected the very first President of the newly united Colony of Rhode Island and Providence Plantations.

John died just six months after taking office, and little is known of his wife, Mary, but their surviving children and many of their grandchildren became actively involved in their communities, including their son Joshua Coggeshall, who was among the founders of Rhode Island's first Quaker meeting house.

Joshua served as an assistant deputy in Portsmouth, but he still had to occasionally deal with the increasing anti-Quaker sentiment sweeping the Puritan colonies – like the time in 1660 when, while riding to the Plymouth Colony, his horse was seized because he had broken a law prohibiting *"any strange Quaker to ride within that jurisdiction."*

The Coggeshalls (and Freeborns) intertwined with several big Rhode Island families, from Newport to Middletown to Portsmouth, and it's through two of Joshua's sons, Joshua and John, that I trace my double Coggeshall connection down to two of my great-great-great-grandparents – Lydia Manchester, who descends from brother Joshua, and her husband, Parker Weaver I, who descends from brother John.

Mom's Paternal Coggeshall Family Tree Branch

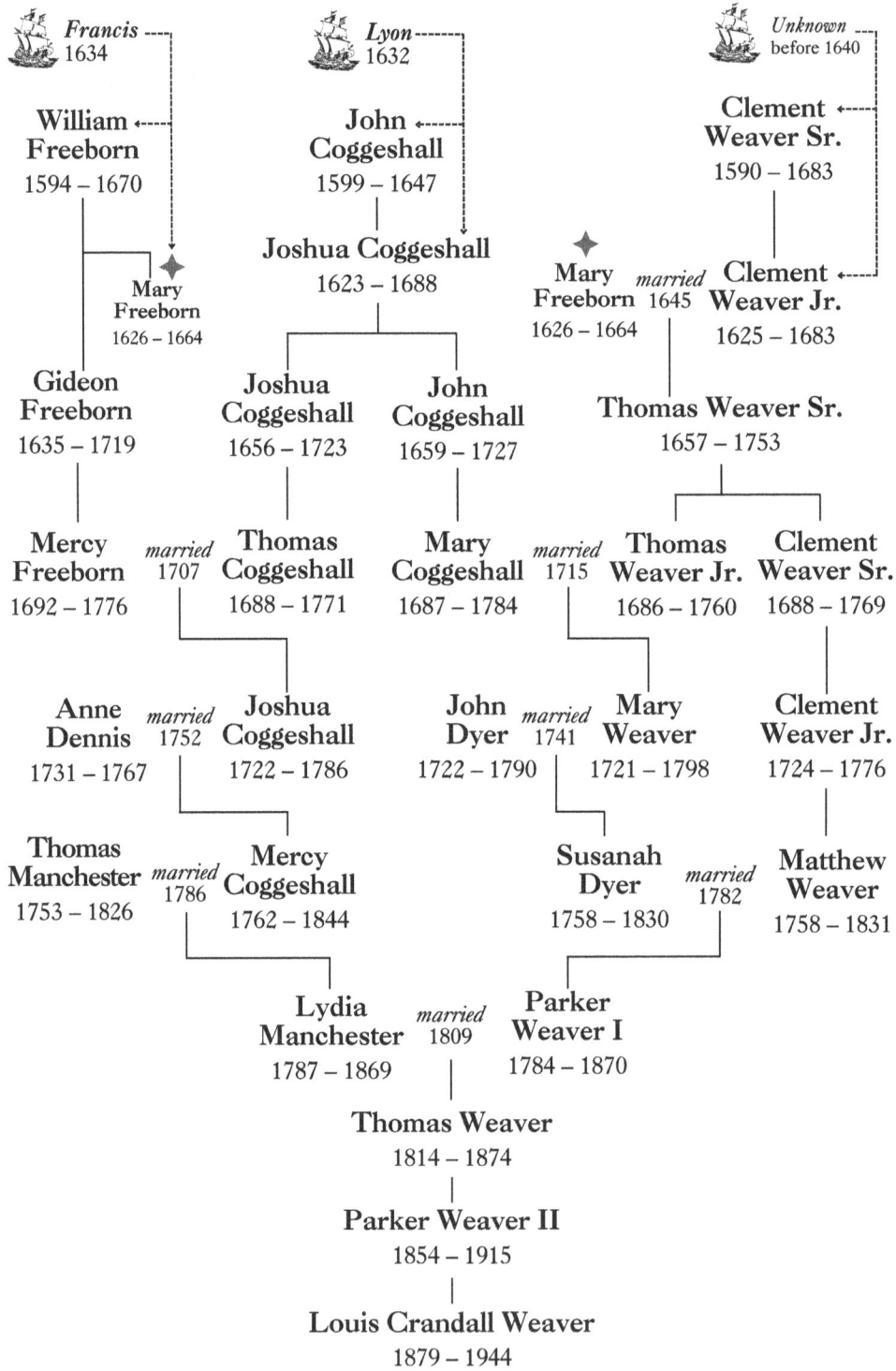

Parker and Lydia's son, Thomas Weaver, moved from Newport to Bristol County in Massachusetts around 1838, settling in Swansea, where in 1875, Thomas' son – my Great-Grandfather, Parker Weaver II – married my Great-Grandmother, Emma Augusta Brailey.

A detail of the Portsmouth Compact, signed by my ancestors, John Coggeshall (fourth signature from top) and William Freeborn (second from bottom). Two other notable signatures belong to William Hutchinson (third from top), husband of Anne Hutchinson, and William Dyre (third from bottom), husband of Mary Dyre (Dyer), who was one of the "Boston Martyrs," a Quaker executed by the Puritans in 1660.

Mom's Paternal Brailey Family Tree Branch

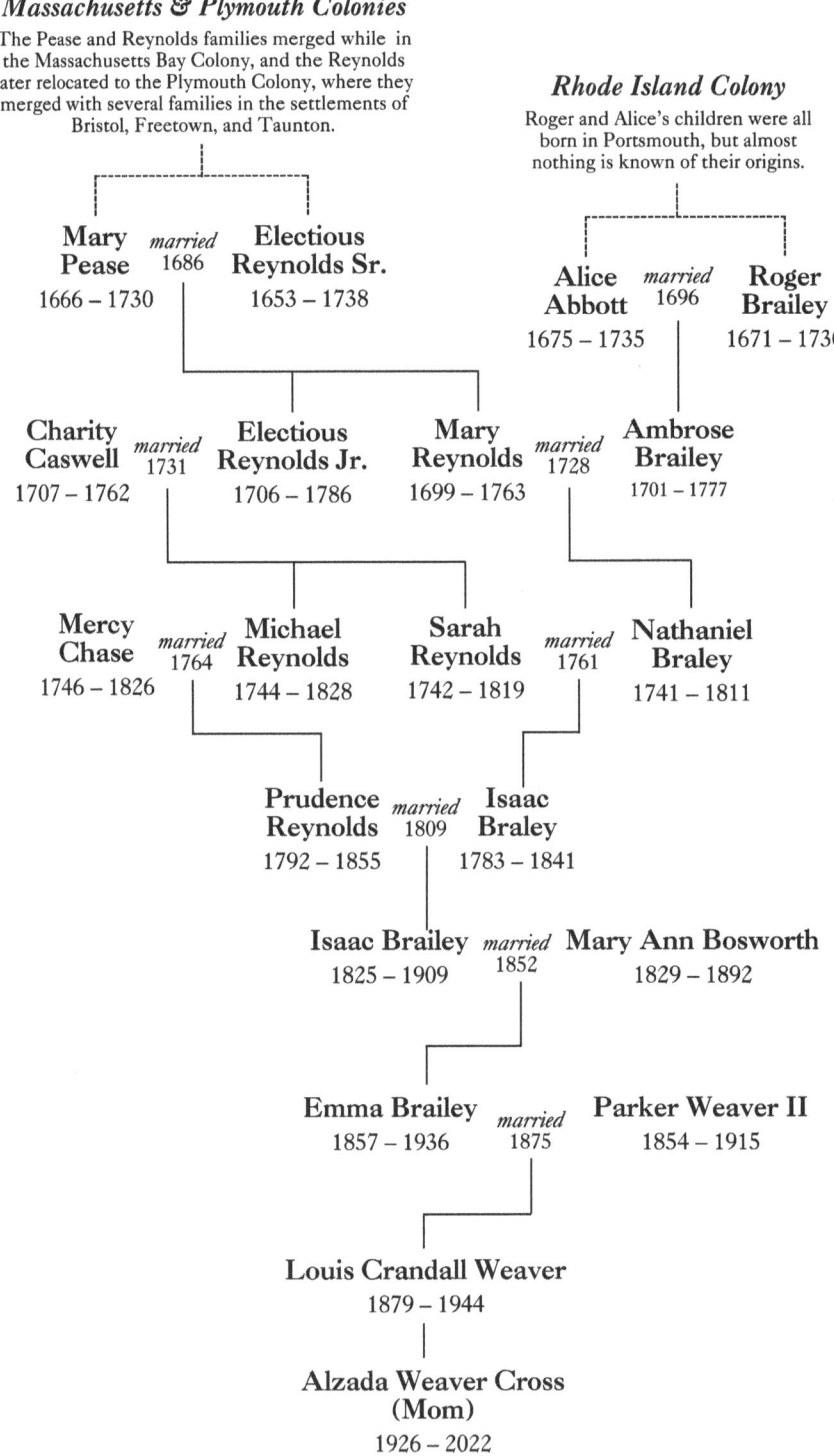

The Brailey Line

My Great-Grandmother, Emma Augusta Brailey, descends from deep Rhode Island and Massachusetts heritage, though there's a mystery surrounding exactly how and when the first Braileys crossed the Atlantic.

Modern researchers speculate they might have settled in Newport prior to 1640, but many family records were likely lost during the British occupation in 1776. Despite these gaps, the 1913 book, *Braley Genealogy: The Descendants of Roger Braley 1696-1913*, provides a starting point with a very simple entry – *"Roger Brailey: There is no other information to be found in regard to Roger other than the record of his and wife Alice's children births at Portsmouth, R.I., except that on the 6 July, 1696, he was a witness in a drowning inquest."*

There are no other details about the lives of Roger and Alice Brailey, but the book lists all of their children – including my direct ancestor, Ambrose Brailey – and continues for more than 300 pages cataloging descendants up to 1913. It's a dry read, but the introduction, written by a descendant named Abner Braley, provides a few refreshing tidbits.

For instance, regarding the confusing variety of surname spellings, Abner Braley wrote – *"Of the different spelling of these names we can only note the usual tendency of the 17th century to guess at a man's name when writing it. On the Portsmouth, R.I., records, Roger Braley, whom tradition calls the progenitor of the American family has his name spelled 'Brailey.'"*

Abner also highlights the family's *"tendency"* to join the Society of Friends, and recounts an old Brailey family legend about a trio of Welsh Quaker brothers who were forced into service of the warring English navy. Being pacifists, they decided to escape, which they did, surviving life on the lam by eating the soles of their shoes!

Whether it was one of these legendary brothers or a distant relative, my Brailey line begins to blossom with the 1728 marriage of Ambrose Brailey and Mary Reynolds, daughter of Electious Reynolds Sr. and Mary Pease. Like my Weaver connections to the Freeborns and Coggeshalls, my Brailey line intertwines multiple times with the extended Reynolds family.

And if you thought keeping track of Braileys was tough, here's a list of misspelled entries for Electious Reynolds Sr., compiled by genealogists from various colonial records ranging from 1674 to 1734: *Elodius Reynolds, Alexis Renolds, Alexius Reinolds, Eleckieas Ronalls, Alixious Reenolds, Elec Renalds, Allextius Rennalds, Allexander Renalds, Eleksha Renals, Ellexander Reynolds.* Baffling!

It's unclear if Electious Sr. was born in England or Massachusetts, but records suggest he fought in King Philip's War before settling in the village of Salem, where he married a woman named Mary Pease in 1686.

Mary's father, Robert Pease, arrived in New England as a little boy in 1634, sailing with his father and uncle aboard the *Francis* (the same ship that brought the Freeborn family). He became a weaver by trade, and in 1658, he married a woman named Sarah.

Sarah's birth date, family name, and origins are still a mystery to historians, but a tragic paper trail pops up in May of 1692 – when she was arrested and jailed for committing *"Sundry acts of Witchcraft."*

Puritan Salem was a tinderbox of political and religious tension, and in the winter months of early 1692, a group of girls sparked a witchcraft wildfire that quickly raged out of control. They feigned *"fits"* and claimed they were being *"afflicted"* by the *"specters"* of the accused – almost eighty percent of whom were women.

During the mass hysteria of the Salem Witch Trials, nearly 200 people were accused of witchcraft, the oldest being a man of eighty-one, and the youngest, a four-year-old girl, whose mother was eventually executed.

An illustration entitled, "Witchcraft at Salem Village," from the 1881 book, "Young Folks' History of Boston." The scene depicts a girl experiencing the "affliction" of a witch's specter while testifying in the Salem courthouse.

By 1693, twenty-four of the accused were dead: nineteen were executed by hanging, one was tortured to death as the sheriff tried to force a confession, and at least five died in prison.

Sarah Pease, who was in her late fifties (or early sixties), survived the appalling conditions, enduring the sweltering summer and freezing winter, until she was finally released an entire year after her arrest.

In the aftermath of the trials, Electious and Mary moved their family out of Salem and went south to Middleborough, a Plymouth Colony settlement established in the early 1660s.

In addition to Mary, the third child of Mary (Pease) and Electious Reynolds Sr., I also descend from one of their youngest – Electious Jr. This particular Reynolds branch connected with families from settlements along the northwestern edges of the expanding Plymouth Colony, places like Swansea and Freetown, the latter of which would later be incorporated into what would become – drum roll, please – Fall River!

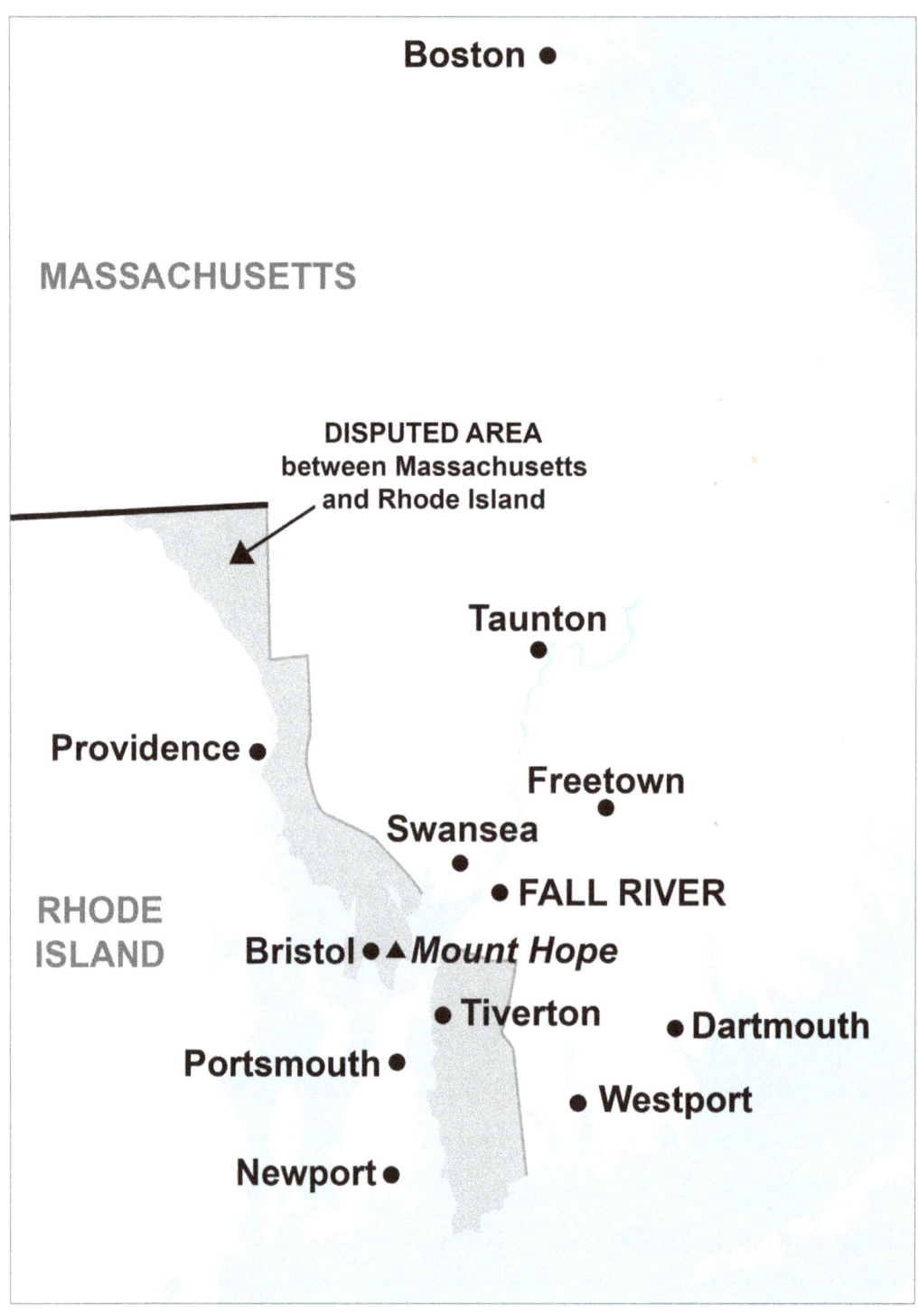

This map is for illustrative purposes only. As a reference for scale, Newport, Rhode Island is about 80 miles south of Boston. Aquidneck Island, where Newport and Portsmouth are located, is about 15 miles long and about 5 miles across at its widest point.

Bristol Counties

The marriage of Emma Brailey and Parker Weaver II was more than just a union of two people – it symbolized an epic intertwining of Rhode Island and Massachusetts lineages, each deeply rooted in their respective region's colonial history. And when Emma and Parker's son, my Grandfather Louis Weaver, married my Nana Susan Gifford, it further strengthened Alzada the Wonderful's close-knit constellation of Bristol County ancestors.

For readers unfamiliar with our "little neck" of New England, a brief geography lesson (and the map provided) might prove helpful. It's important to keep in mind that the boundaries of many modern New England towns and cities bear little resemblance to the settlements from which they grew, and, as such, the way people referred to these places has evolved over time, sometimes dramatically.

Bristol County, established in 1685, was named for the bustling Plymouth Colony shire town of Bristol (founded in 1676), and included settlements like Taunton (1639), Rehoboth (1644), Dartmouth (1664), Swansea (1667), Little Compton (1682), and Freetown (1683).

These places, now familiar names on modern maps, had humble beginnings, and their histories were often bloody, especially when we consider the colonial wars that carved their borders.

The Bristol settlement arose from the aftermath of King Philip's War, which had officially begun in 1675 when a small group of Pokanokets laid siege to the settlement of Swansea, where homesteads were destroyed and several colonists were killed. At the time, it was just another instance of the escalating violence between different factions of Wampanoag and encroaching colonists, but soon after the Swansea raid, a full eclipse of the moon cast a dark shadow over New England, and some Wampanoag interpreted it as a sign to broaden and intensify the attacks.

The Wampanoag sachem Metacomet, whom the English called King Philip, had tried to maintain the tense relations established by his father – Massasoit, the Pokanoket chieftain who feasted with the Pilgrims on the fabled first Thanksgiving – but everything was about to change.

Plymouth and Massachusetts Bay colony officials ordered swift retribution for the Swansea attacks and sent an expedition to destroy the nearby Wampanoag village at Mount Hope, the highest point in the area at 209 feet, overlooking modern-day Mount Hope Bay.

The colonists destroyed the village, and while what historians broadly refer to as King Philip's War encompassed many battles across many miles, Mount Hope is notable for two reasons. When the colonists destroyed the village at Mount Hope in 1675, it officially became all-out war for Metacomet – and then, just over a year later, it was on Mount Hope that Metacomet was killed.

By the end of the war, thousands were dead, maimed, or sold into slavery, and most of the devastation fell on the native people, including Metacomet, whose body was dismembered for trophies, and his wife and child sold into slavery in Bermuda.

The Wampanoag village at Mount Hope quickly became the English settlement of Bristol, and as more colonists acquired more and more land, border disputes became more and more common, from neighbors squabbling over fence lines to whole communities debating which settlements belonged to which colony.

In 1691, by order of a royal charter, the "Province of Massachusetts Bay" was formed from the Plymouth, Massachusetts, and Maine colonies, plus a little bit of Nova Scotia. But the border disputes continued, with

An illustration of Metacomet, from "History of Philip's War" by Thomas Church (1829).

little old Rhode Island typically the target of aggression from both Massachusetts to the east and Connecticut to the west.

In 1746, a royal decree redrew the borders of all the disputed towns in and around Narragansett Bay, splitting the original Bristol County into two – one part remaining with Massachusetts, and the other joining Rhode Island, including the town of Bristol itself, which had always been a part of modern-day Massachusetts.

Our Gifford ancestors, for the most part, never left Massachusetts. William Gifford stayed in Sandwich until his passing, but his son Robert (1660-1730) found his way to Dartmouth in Bristol County. There, the Giffords entwined with other old colonial families, like the Wrights and Petteys, and then spread to Westport, where Robert's grandson, Benjamin Gifford (1717-1807) became a wealthy landowner – Benjamin also had the dubious honor of losing much of his land to gambling debts.

But even without swathes of land to their name, the Giffords flourished, merging with members of the Fish and Lake families of nearby Tiverton, just west of Westport.

Tiverton, like many towns along Narragansett Bay, also changed hands in 1746, becoming part of the Rhode Island side of the new boundary. During the Revolutionary War, Tiverton was a refuge for colonists fleeing British occupation and a mustering point for militia forces, with men from Tiverton taking part in the Battle of Freetown, one of the many skirmishes that defined the war's chaotic front lines.

Meanwhile, over on the Massachusetts side, Benjamin Gifford's son, my great-great-great-great-grandfather Ichabod Gifford (1742-1801), was making his own mark in history. He joined Colonel William R. Lee's Additional Continental Army, and served as a drummer during some of the Revolutionary War's most pivotal battles, including the Battle of Monmouth and the Battle of Rhode Island.

Finally, we come to the star of the show, our beloved Fall River in Bristol County, Massachusetts. Incorporated in 1803 and originally written as "Fallriver," the town would become an industrial juggernaut, but the etymology of its name often causes confusion. It's not the Fall River that runs through Fall River, but the Quequechan River, and it was the Quequechan's mighty falls that powered the town's transformation into a world famous textile production hub.

In 1781, before Fallriver was formally established, the First Baptist Church was founded, and while the congregation had to move around at first, by 1850 they had constructed their new home on North Main Street in modern-day Fall River. Since the early 1900s, if not before, this place has been so meaningful to the lives of so many of my family members, both past and present, and in 1983, the church building was added to the National Register of Historic Places.

The name of Fallriver changed to Troy in 1804, then changed again to Fall River in 1834, and as the town expanded, the southern parts of Fall River began to merge with northern Tiverton.

In 1856, the townspeople of Tiverton voted to section off this industrialized northern area, and it was renamed Fall River, Rhode Island. Regardless, arguments over boundaries persisted until 1861, when the U.S. Supreme Court stepped in, officially moving Fall River, Massachusetts' former border at Columbia Street down to State Avenue, nearly three miles south, absorbing Fall River, Rhode Island.

If you're confused, don't worry; the only thing you really need to remember is Fall River's well-deserved nickname of "Spindle City," as it was the many cotton mills and booming textile industry that drew so many of my ancestors to bustling Fall River.

Alzada the Great's father Eli Gifford with a cat in his lap in an undated photo shared with me by my third cousin William Veselik. Beside Eli is either his wife Susan, who died in 1896, or a relative.

Alzada the Great's maternal grandparents in undated photos. At left is Elusana (Fish) Pettey, and at right, James Pettey. The photo of James was also found by William Veselik, who has done extensive research on both the Gifford and Pettey families.

The Parents of Alzada the Great

About ten miles southeast of Fall River lies the scenic town of Westport, where Alzada the Great's father, Eli Gifford, was born on October 7, 1832. His parents, Ichabod Gifford, also of Westport, and Diana Beedon Gifford of Dartmouth, were hardworking people deeply rooted in the land and the rhythms of farm life.

Eli was a middle child with six siblings, but in 1847, his elder brother, John, passed away from consumption, the dreaded widespread disease that, decades later, would also claim their mother Diana.

In 1859, Eli married Susan Pettey in Westport, and by 1863, they had two sons, John and James.

In the fall of 1863, at the age of thirty-one, Eli was mustered into the 3rd Massachusetts Heavy Artillery Regiment of the Union Army, forcing him to leave his growing family behind.

His regiment was initially stationed as part of the garrison guarding the forts in Boston Harbor and along the Massachusetts coastline, but by the spring of 1864, they were dispatched to guard Washington, D.C.

This critical maneuver freed up the more seasoned troops for frontline duties, and during Eli's time guarding the nation's capital, he was promoted to Corporal.

This is an enlarged detail from a much larger photo, another of my relative William Veselik's finds. It's likely Eli Gifford, taken between 1863 and 1864, when he was serving in the Union Army during the Civil War.

A disability, possibly epilepsy, led to Eli's discharge in August of 1864, and when he returned to his family, he settled into a peaceful life and a steady job as a hostler, caring for teams of horses and ensuring they were well-groomed and healthy.

For the last fifteen years of his life, Eli worked for the Fall River Provision Company, earning an impeccable reputation for his skill and dedication as a teamster – driving teams of horses to deliver goods throughout the area.

I'm certain Eli's love for animals ran deep, and there happens to be a very charming photo of Eli with a contented cat curled up in his lap; however, I'm uncertain who sits beside him – perhaps it's his wife Susan.

Susan Caroline Pettey was born September 13, 1840, in Bristol, Rhode Island, to James Pettey and Elusana Fish Pettey, the second of their six children. Like Eli, Susan came from a hardworking, close-knit family, and around 1850, the Petteys relocated to Westport, where their last two children were born.

It was in Westport where Susan likely first crossed paths with Eli, but it's possible they may have already been familiar with each other, as Eli's family tree also boasted Pettey lineage through one of his great-grandmothers – however, the spelling of the surname (Petty, Pettes, or Pettis) varies across branches.

Susan and Eli were married on December 10, 1859, in Westport by clergyman Philip Sanford. They had their first child, John, in 1861, just before Eli went off to war, and when Eli returned, they had three more boys – James in 1863, Frank in 1865, and George in 1869. Two years later, into this bustling household of four little boys, Susan and Eli celebrated the birth of their only daughter and last child – my great-grandmother, whom I have lovingly dubbed Alzada the Great.

Alzada the Great

Alzada Estes Gifford was born November 1, 1871, in Dartmouth, Massachusetts, and within a few years of her birth, the Giffords relocated to Fall River.

Though we don't have nearly enough family lore to draw conclusions from, according to contemporaneous records, there were a few other women named "Alzada Estes" in the region, including one born in nearby Tiverton in 1859, perhaps suggesting a nod to the prominent Estes family of Rhode Island, where Alzada's mother, Susan Pettey, was from.

Fun fact: The use of the name "Alzada" in New England might have been influenced by the early waves of Portuguese immigrants who came over to work in the area's thriving whaling industry; nearly half of all modern-day Fall River residents have Portuguese ancestry.

In 1878, an all too common tragedy struck the Gifford family when they lost their youngest boy, Frank. Alzada was just six when her brother, nearing his thirteenth birthday, passed away from *"Cerebral Softening"* – a common way at the time to describe a variety of conditions. We don't know much more about what happened to Frank, but it could have been the result of a sudden injury or stroke, or even a genetic condition, possibly inherited from his father.

Frank was laid to rest in Beech Grove Cemetery in Westport. A solemn reminder of how fragile life could be, this loss must have been terribly sad for the Giffords, and likely brought the family even closer. Their bonds were strong, and perhaps it was because of this early loss of Frank that Eli and Susan kept their children and grandchildren as close as possible for as long as possible.

Alzada the Great's early years were shaped by education and family togetherness. She was fortunate enough to attend school, at least for a little while, which meant she could read and write – skills we think of as basic necessities, but were rare among kids of her time, especially girls.

I like to imagine that, along with reading and writing, Alzada also had talent for arithmetic – numbers and math. Her love of learning no doubt later influenced her own children, especially Nana Susan's love of card games and Great-Aunt Carrie's love of reading.

We don't know if Alzada ever worked outside the home, but if she did, it was probably in the mills. Her father and brothers were always employed, and it's likely that young Alzada's job was to help her mother with household chores as soon as she was able.

In the early 1880s, the Gifford family made another move, this time to Gardners Neck in Swansea, a peaceful area with sweeping views of the Taunton River. It was here, in this tranquil countryside setting, that my research into Alzada's life took an unexpected and heartbreaking turn – imagine knowing almost nothing about an ancestor, and then suddenly discovering the most horrifying personal experience of their life in a century-old newspaper.

A Brutal Outrage

WARNING – This chapter contains a detailed account of the violent abduction and sexual assault of a child. Reader discretion is advised.

On August 4, 1884, when Alzada was twelve years old, as she and her friends were walking together, a man twice her age dragged her from the road and raped her. The horror of that day is unspeakable, and the events that followed only prolonged her trauma.

She had to identify her assailant – probably face to face, without the protection of the two-way mirrors they use nowadays – and then this young, innocent child was mercilessly pushed into the spotlight of all the local newspapers with zero regard for her privacy.

The day after the attack, reports ran in both the *Fall River Daily Herald* and the *Fall River Daily Evening News*, with the latter publishing a much more detailed account, which follows here in its entirety – and yes, they spelled Alzada's name wrong.

"A Brutal Outrage – Shocking Affair in Swansea – A brutal outrage was committed in Swansea, yesterday, by a tramp, the victim being a twelve-year-old girl, Alzadia Gifford. The girl lives on the David Anthony farm, at Gardner's Neck, with her parents, who recently removed from this city. Yesterday afternoon she was on her way, accompanied by two other girls of about her own age, from her house to Charles Anthony's new house on Gardner's Neck, when a tramp started up from some bushes by the road side, and inquired the way to Fall River. The Gifford girl told him to inquire of the men at work on Edmund Whitehead's new house. The man then seized the girl and dragged her, despite her screams and struggles, into a cornfield at the side of the road, where he brutally outraged her.

The other girls ran away and gave an alarm, and a farm hand named Samuel Braley started in pursuit of the tramp, who continued on the road to this city, and captured him before he reached Slade's Ferry Bridge. The tramp was then turned over to officer Shaw of the North Station. He gave his name as George Babcock, aged 25, and claimed to belong in Sag Harbor, L.I. [Long Island].

He was arraigned in the District Court this morning. The girl positively identified him, and he was also identified by witnesses who saw him come out of the cornfield. He made no defense, but claimed the witnesses were mistaken in the man. He was adjudged probably guilty and committed in default of $1,000 bail to await the action of the grand jury.

Babcock was arrested here for drunkenness about a year ago and then gave the name of Charles Albion."

There it was, for everyone to read, and while her family, friends, and neighbors no doubt sympathized with her, society was not kind to victims of such brutal crimes. Twelve-year-old Alzada's "reputation" was publicly ruined – in print – before she even reached her teens.

How tragically frightening, both the attack and the aftermath, for someone so young. And yet, keep in mind that at the time, the legal "age of consent" was abysmally low, ranging from ten to twelve in most states, except Delaware, where it was age seven – yes, really!

Massachusetts was more progressive, having raised its age of consent to sixteen just a few years before Alzada's assault – which may have played a pivotal role in the swift legal action taken upon her attacker.

About a month after the assault, on September 5, 1884, a newspaper item states – *"Charles E. Albion. Assault on Alzada E. Gifford, at Swansea, Aug. 4th, with intent to ravish. Pleaded not guilty"* – followed on September 9, 1884, by – *"Charles E. Albion of Swansea, convicted of assault with intent to commit the crime of rape on a little girl, was sentenced to the state prison for fifteen years."*

A BRUTAL OUTRAGE.

Shocking Affair in Swansea.

A brutal outrage was committed in Swansea, yesterday, by a tramp, the victim being a twelve-year-old girl, Alzadia Gifford. The girl lives on the David Anthony farm, at Gardner's Neck, with her parents, who recently removed from this city. Yesterday afternoon she was on her way, accompanied by two other girls of about her own age, from her house to Charles Anthony's new house on Gardner's Neck, when a tramp started up from some bushes by the road side, and inquired the way to Fall River. The Gifford girl told him to inquire of the men at work on Edmund Whitehead's new house. The man then seized the girl and dragged her, despite her screams and struggles, into a cornfield at the side of the road, where he brutally outraged her.

The other girls ran away and gave an alarm, and a farm hand named Samuel Braley started in pursuit of the tramp, who continued on the road to this city, and captured him before he reached Slade's Ferry Bridge. The tramp was then turned over to officer Shaw of the North Station. He gave his name as George Babcock, aged 25, and claimed to belong in Sag Harbor, L. I.

He was arraigned in the District Court this morning. The girl positively identified him, and he was also identified by witnesses who saw him come out of the corn field. He made no defense, but claimed the witnesses were mistaken in the man. He was adjudged probably guilty and committed in default of $1,000 bail to await the action of the grand jury.

Babcock was arrested here for drunkenness about a year ago and then gave the name of Charles Albion.

Article from the Tuesday, August 5, 1884, edition of the Fall River Daily Evening News.

Charles Albion served twelve years of his fifteen-year sentence, and immediately upon his release in 1896, he began actively and loudly proclaiming his innocence to anyone who would listen, insisting that while he was imprisoned, the actual culprit mailed him a full confession.

Naturally, the newspapers published some follow-up articles, one of which mentions a particularly gruesome new detail – that Albion held a pair of scissors to Alzada's throat and threatened to cut her as he dragged her into the field.

The legal outcome may have provided some small sense of justice for Alzada, but her attacker kept pulling her back into the headlines, back into the nightmare she fought so hard to escape, until Charles Albion was finally thrown back in jail for unrelated crimes – drunkenness, mostly.

But Alzada was resilient, and with grit and grace, she moved on with her life and began building a family.

The Children of Alzada the Great

I can't imagine what young Alzada went through during those years. Like the tragic loss of her brother Frank, I somehow feel certain that this traumatic attack was just another reason why her parents always wanted to keep her close and safe – and it made Alzada the Great always want to stay.

The first child of Alzada the Great, Frank Bradford Gifford, was born January 9, 1893, in Fall River. Frank was likely conceived around April of 1892, which means Alzada was probably just barely starting to show when a shocking crime occurred that would distract from even the most scandalous of pregnancies.

Coincidentally, it occurred eight years to the day after Alzada's attack, on August 4, 1892, in a little two-story house on Second Street, just a mile south of where the Giffords lived. On that hot summer morning, Andrew and Abby Borden were brutally murdered, and their "spinster" daughter Lizzie was the prime suspect.

Lizzie was arrested and imprisoned for almost a year, but after a twelve-day trial, she was acquitted and released, free to live out the rest of her life in Fall River. A morbidly fun fact: the "Lizzie Borden House" on Second Street is now a bed-and-breakfast and a very popular international attraction, drawing curious visitors of all kinds – from history lovers and true crime fanatics to thrill-seekers and paranormal investigators.

Alzada the Great probably named her son after her brother, Frank, who died when she just old enough to know, love, and remember him, and so it's her son's middle name, Bradford, that might be the best hint as to the identity of his biological father. Like the Bordens and the

Durfees, the Giffords had been proliferating throughout all of Bristol County for many generations, and so had the Bradfords. The name echoes through my family still, as my brother Dana's middle name is Bradford, and we also have a Bradford among my seven Reed cousins, brother to Carol and Matthew.

It's interesting to note that on Frank's official "Notice of Intention of Marriage," dated March 30, 1925, his father is named as "Frank B." (implying his father is named "Frank Bradford Gifford"), and his mother is named as "Alzada Estes" – implying that his mother's maiden name is Estes. For clarification, Frank was widowed in 1924, and this was his second marriage.

The notice of intention of marriage filed for Frank Bradford Gifford in 1925, three years after his mother Alzada passed away.

The record of Frank's birth doesn't help much either. No father is listed, and his mother is listed simply as "Alice," born in "Dartmouth, Mass." Next to the column that records the baby's name and "*color*" (but only "*if other than white*") is a column to record the baby's gender and "*Condition – as twins, illegitimate, &c.*" – and in Frank's row, next to the "m" for male, is "ille." for illegitimate.

Of the 2,821 births officially recorded in Fall River during 1893, very few have the "ille." notation, which isn't surprising. Consider how common it was for poor and unwed or widowed women to give birth and then report to work the next day, whether it was in the mills or taking care of her family. For some it was both, and to a single woman with even just one hungry, cold, crying baby in her arms, an officious piece of paper was the least of her concerns.

Frank's birth registration is clustered with several other "illegitimate" 1893 Fall River births.

What's most intriguing about Frank's birth record is that it's clustered together with five other babies, all with different birth dates just months apart, all in Fall River, all noted as illegitimate. Two of the children have the names of both parents listed, perhaps because they were unwed, and the other four have only the first name of the mother – Leontine, mother of Alfred Barnard; Mary, mother of John Shay; another Mary, mother of Annie Sullivan; and Alice, mother of Frank B. Gifford.

Because of this conspicuous grouping, it makes me wonder if the records came from Fall River Hospital, where a women's board was established in 1888, probably, in part, to provide care for the many "unfortunate" women of Fall River, who were likely hidden away from all the other patients, lest their immodesty offend.

Most births occurred in the home at this time, but maybe Alzada needed medical attention towards the end of her pregnancy and was admitted to the hospital, where she gave birth. Or, maybe Frank got very sick during his first year of life and Alzada, in a panic, rushed him to the hospital for help, and in doing so, was required to register his birth.

And, while it might just be a clerical error, or even a nickname, perhaps she gave her name as Alice to disguise her identity. With dozens of Gifford families in the area, she could be related to any or all of them; and Alice is similar to Alzada, but one is certainly more memorable than the other.

Alzada the Great gave birth to her second child, Caroline Elusana Gifford, on March 14, 1895. While I can surmise that she was named after Alzada's mother, Susan Caroline (Pettey) Gifford, and Alzada's grandmother, Elusana (Fish) Pettey, I haven't found a single record for Caroline's birth.

Mom's Aunt Carrie and her husband William never had children, and while it may have been by choice, there's also a possibility that she was unable to conceive or carry a pregnancy to term. As we now know, uterine, ovarian, and breast cancers have affected several generations of Gifford women, among them, Alzada the Great, and her mother, Susan, for whom she would name her third daughter, my Nana.

Ebb & Flow

From the very beginning, 1896 would be another year marked by tragedy for Alzada the Great. On January 29th, her beloved mother, Susan Pettey Gifford passed away from uterine cancer at just fifty-five years old. It had to have been one of the hardest moments in Alzada's life, but it was also an ominous foreshadowing of the fate she herself would later suffer.

It was in October of 1896 when, still grieving the loss of her mother and caring for her father and two young children, the demon from her past resurfaced – Charles Albion, her attacker, newly released from prison.

His showy proclamations of his innocence made Alzada, now in her early twenties, the talk of the town all over again. But, as mentioned, this once dangerous man who had terrorized a twelve-year-old girl was arrested for drunkenness – twice – and was soon back behind bars.

In the ebb and flow of Alzada the Great's life, a joyous new blessing was about to wash away some of her sorrow. A little over a year after she lost her mother, Alzada gave birth to Susan M.G. Gifford, my Nana Susan, on Valentine's Day.

There's no official birth registration for Susan, but in a very fitting traditional tribute, Alzada named her newborn after the grandmother Susan would never get to meet, carrying her legacy forward – and creating another heartbreaking precedent for Alzada the Great and her namesake, my mother.

Alzada never left her father Eli, and he never forced her out of the house, despite her having children "out of wedlock." All of Alzada's brothers had moved out and married in early adulthood, and all of them had children, too, but none of them ever moved back in with their parents. Of course, the boys never had to, because their little sister would always be there, dutifully caring for their parents.

Soon after Nana Susan was born, Alzada the Great moved with her father and three young children to 655 Durfee Street, where both Eli and Alzada would live out the rest of their lives.

In 1898, Alzada gave birth to another little girl whom she named Ardry L. Gifford, but she tragically passed away just sixteen days later from *"Cholera Infantum."* Ardry's death record lists her mother as "single," but her birth record lists a father, "Edward M.," an agent (his occupation), born in Bangor, Maine, as well as Alzada's address on Durfee. Sadly, it seems the only reason there is a record of Ardry's birth is because it was necessary to record her death.

One last joyful birth gave way to profound sorrow for Alzada in 1902, when her fifth and final child, Minnie E. Gifford, passed away six months later from *"marasmus,"* likely indicating she was too weak to thrive.

Minnie's birth record lists only her mother, "Alzada E. Gifford," but her death record, which gives the child's name as "Minnie E. Copenhaven," lists her parents as "Annie E. Gifford" at 655 Durfee in Fall River, and, surprisingly, her father, a "Rufus Copenhaven" of Westport. Though the father's name is quite distinct, I haven't been able to match it to existing records. Like baby Ardry, it seems we only have a record for Minnie's birth because she died so soon afterward.

Four years later, Alzada suffered another tragic loss when her father Eli passed away on July 12, 1908. Eli, who was still working at the age of seventy-five, had become ill on the job and quickly passed away at home.

Eli's obituary, which was published in the *Fall River Evening Herald* on July 14, 1908, gives his cause of death as *"general debility, old age"* and *"an affection of the heart, superinduced by the excessive heat."*

I'm not sure who wrote Eli's obituary, but it fails to mention his late wife Susan at all, and Alzada's name is misspelled as *"Alvada,"* while all three of his living sons are correctly named. The funeral coverage two days later mentions his grandson, Frank, as a pallbearer, but omits Alzada entirely.

Alzada the Great's name rarely appeared in newsprint, but when it did, no matter how it was spelled, it was never for good reasons – her attack in 1884, her attacker's release in 1896, her father's death, and her own.

In 1909, Alzada gets her first listing in the Fall River directory – never mind that it incorrectly lists her as her father's widow, because the mistake is rectified in the 1910 directory, listing her as "Gifford, Alzada E." residing at 655 Durfee. Alzada the Great was making her mark, however small, in the city where she was raising her three children all on her own.

In 1915, Alzada's son Frank married and moved out of the Durfee Street home where she would live out the rest of her life with her two daughters. In 1918, she got to meet her first grandchild – Susan's firstborn son Frank, but just a few weeks after her fifty-first birthday, on November 21, 1922, Alzada the Great passed away from ovarian cancer.

What a remarkable life she had. As her name suggests, Alzada the Great rose like a phoenix from the ashes of childhood violence and trauma, leading a life of quiet defiance and resilient strength. She nurtured her family, stood by her parents, and lived her life with a rare kind of independence – and there's certainly some ancestral precedent for that!

An undated postcard image of the first cotton mill built in "Fallriver" by Col. Joseph Durfee in 1811-13. From the Fall River Public Library's collection of historic postcards.

A 1910 postcard image of North Main Street in Fall River. From the Fall River Public Library's collection of historic postcards.

Spindles & Spinsters

In 1923, about a year after Alzada the Great passed away, Fall River's first wave of massive mill closures began, and Spindle City's once vibrant mill economy faded fast.

Fun Fact: A spindle is a rotating device used for spinning cotton, and also an indicator of a mill's production capacity – more spindles equal more output. In 1813, the first cotton mill was built in Fall River, and it contained fewer than 900 spindles. By the time Alzada the Great's parents were married in 1859, there were at least eight mills in Fall River, which contained a combined total of more than 32,000 spindles.

The outbreak and aftermath of the American Civil War in the 1860s made the Fall River mill economy boom even bigger and faster, and new jobs gave rise to new kinds of housing, particularly the three-story wood-frame "triple-decker" apartments typical of the area, the kind Alzada the Great and Nana Susan grew up in. By the time Alzada the Great was born in 1871, another twenty-two new mills had sprung up, and by 1880 there were as many as 120 mills with half a million spindles, officially earning Fall River the moniker of "Spindle City."

At the onset of the 1890s, which was fondly remembered by later generations as the "Gay Nineties," the Fall River of Alzada the Great's childhood was being swallowed up in the confluence of the Industrial Revolution, medical advancements, and widespread public education, just to name a few, and it all brought the turn of the century crashing in like a tidal wave.

The late nineteenth century was also the dawn of the "new woman" and the "bachelor girl" – women who stayed single by choice (or married progressive men), women who pursued careers outside the home, women who wanted to participate in business and politics as well as their church groups and ladies clubs – women who did what they wanted to do. This coincides with the rise of the term "Boston marriage," an arrangement in which two women – sometimes sisters or devoted companions, sometimes romantic partners, almost always wealthy – lived together.

A woman who never married was called a "spinster," a term which originally meant a working woman whose occupation was spinning thread, but over time the word was applied to any unmarried woman, rich or poor.

The term "spinster," like "Boston Marriage," was typically used pejoratively, and only by those who didn't approve of a grown woman, let alone two, finding success, happiness, and fulfillment independent of the control and contributions of a man – how dare they!

Lizzie Borden and her older sister Emma, for example, both lived out the remainder of their lives as relatively wealthy unmarried spinsters, and while legend says they didn't see or speak to each other in their final years, Emma passed away just one week after Lizzie in 1927.

For some women, like my widowed Great-Grandmother Emma (Brailey) Weaver, marriage – and remarriage – not only provided stability for a woman, it assured that members of polite society would maintain a positive opinion of her.

A few months after my Grandfather Louis and Nana Susan were wed, sixty-six-year-old Emma's engagement in September of 1923 made the headlines of three Fall River publications – the *Daily Herald*, the *Globe*, and the *Daily Evening News* – the best of which reads, *"Octogenarian to wed housekeeper."*

The octogenarian fiancé of Emma, the housekeeper, was William Joseph Burrows, born October 11, 1843, and he was *"not ashamed of his fourscore years."* He was a Union army veteran, wounded in the 1864 Battle of the Wilderness in Virginia and, while on leave for his injury, age twenty, he married his first wife Ida Weaver – coincidentally, the sister of Parker Weaver II, Emma's first husband – making William and Emma widowed in-laws through their Weaver spouses.

William and Ida had been married for fifty-seven years and had one daughter, Anna, who passed away at the age of forty-two in 1909. Ida passed away in 1922, shortly after William retired from his long career as chief engineer at the Grinnell Mill.

All this from just three articles, which basically say the same thing, and all of which barely mention anything about Emma, aside from her being a widowed housekeeper in her sixties.

On October 1, 1923, Emma and William were married at the home of Rev. Dr. E.C. Herrick, who had also married Louis and Susan just months prior. Mom once told me that Emma married Mr. Burrows just to be proper, so she could live with him and take care of him without raising eyebrows.

William passed away three years later at the age of eighty-three and was laid to rest in New Bedford. Emma passed away three years after him, aged seventy-nine, on November 24, 1936, in Fall River. She was laid to rest in Mount Hope Cemetery in Swansea, and while her headstone uses the surname Burrows (misspelled as Borrows), it also reads, "Wife of Parker Weaver," whom she rests beside.

In the decade before her untimely death, Alzada the Great experienced many momentous events. She probably read about the 1912 sinking of the Titanic in the newspaper, and witnessed the horrors of the 1918 influenza pandemic. She celebrated the end of World War I and the joyous arrival of her first grandchild, and she also lived to see the passing of the Nineteenth Amendment on August 18, 1920, at long last giving women the right to vote.

Like the "spinsters" and "bachelor girls" of yore, Alzada followed her own rules – if only she had lived to old age! If only Mom could have spent time with her namesake, being lovingly cared for by a devoted grandmother. If only I could have met her! If only I could connect with her somehow – if only.

The one photograph I have of Alzada the Great is a professional portrait and in decent condition, probably taken in the late 1890s. In it, the subtly smiling Alzada wears a mourning brooch with a portrait of her late mother Susan, who died in 1896.

This treasured image was almost forever lost to us, but in August of 1951 – just months before I was born – one Mrs. Palmer, an old friend and neighbor of Alzada the Great, mailed it to Nana Susan, enclosed with a letter.

Mrs. Palmer wrote, in part – *"Your mother gave me a picture of herself which I was very glad to have as I liked your mother very much. I am getting old, and I thought you would like to have it. Give Frank and Carrie my regards."*

She then adds, *"Your mother was a very pretty woman"* – and I couldn't agree more – Alzada the Great was absolutely beautiful!

Alzada Estes Gifford in her mid-twenties, about 1897, wearing a mourning brooch, which was fashionable at the time, and very likely a portrait of her late mother Susan, who died in 1896.

PART V

The Ancestors of Irving the Wonderful

1800s – 1930s & 2010s

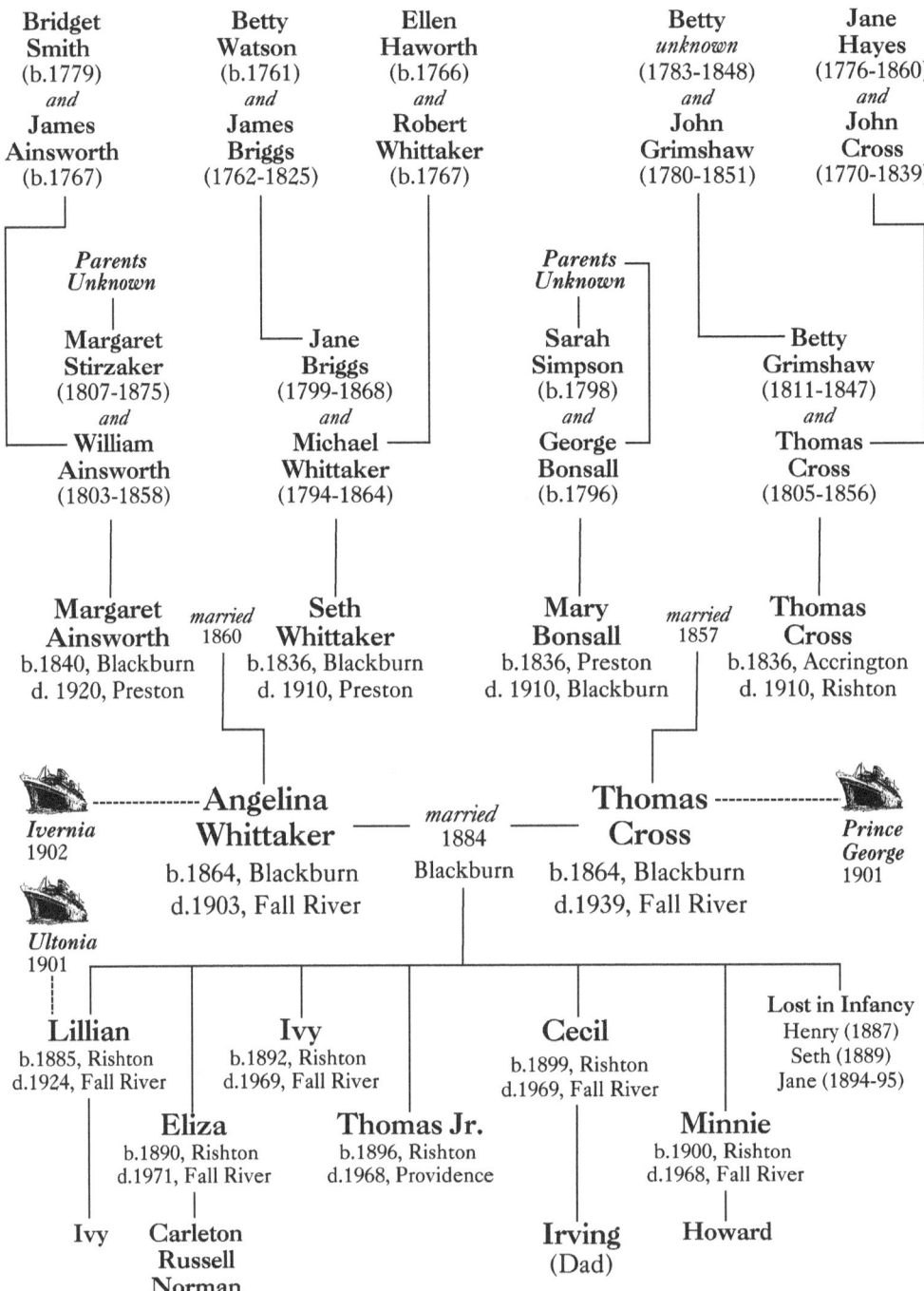

The Ancestors of Irving the Wonderful

YOU MIGHT THINK "Spindle City" was also the "Weaving Capital of the World," but that distinction belongs to Blackburn in Lancashire, England, where my paternal great-grandparents Angelina and Thomas were born and raised.

Along with the miracles of DNA matching, I am extremely lucky so many records are available for so many of my ancestors, both in the U.S. and the U.K. I've also been incredibly fortunate to connect with many wonderful people who have helped me piece together my ancestral puzzle – from newly discovered distant relatives to expert local historians and genealogists, and several kind strangers I may never cross paths with again.

It's an odd but exciting feeling when a stranger knows more about a direct relative of yours than you do. How could I not know these things? Why weren't these stories passed down? I've come to realize that everyone's connection to their past is different, and I've gained a greater sense – and appreciation – of how other people know and remember their own ancestors, whether they've met them or not.

Some families have countless tales that have floated down through the generations, and others have only secrets and mysteries drowned by time. I often found myself diving deeper and deeper into records and research, but to my occasional delight (and relief), there were also many big surprises drifting right there on the surface.

Take, for instance, the second wife of Reverend Thomas Cross, my step-great-grandmother Nettie Holmes – we didn't even know Thomas had remarried! On my research travels, I had the honor of meeting Nettie's niece Katherine, who shared so many memories of her beloved and fascinating

Aunt Nettie – the very same Nettie no one in my family had ever heard of! Granted, this might be because they married later in life – on the Canadian border – and likely never mingled with our Fall River family.

But stranger still, no one in my family had heard of Angelina either, not even her name, the person who gave birth to my grandfather Cecil and all his siblings – a person who, by many well-documented accounts, both from the time of her death and more than a century later, still makes her presence known among the living.

I was shocked when I stumbled upon Angelina's existence early on in my research, and her name – meaning both "guiding spirit" and "messenger of God" – seemed prophetic.

I'll never forget how I felt when I first read her name in the death record of my Grandpa Cecil. I knew I was meant to find her, and from that moment she has been alive within me. Her genes were always there, and now her spirit fills my heart – discovering "Angelina the Great" changed everything.

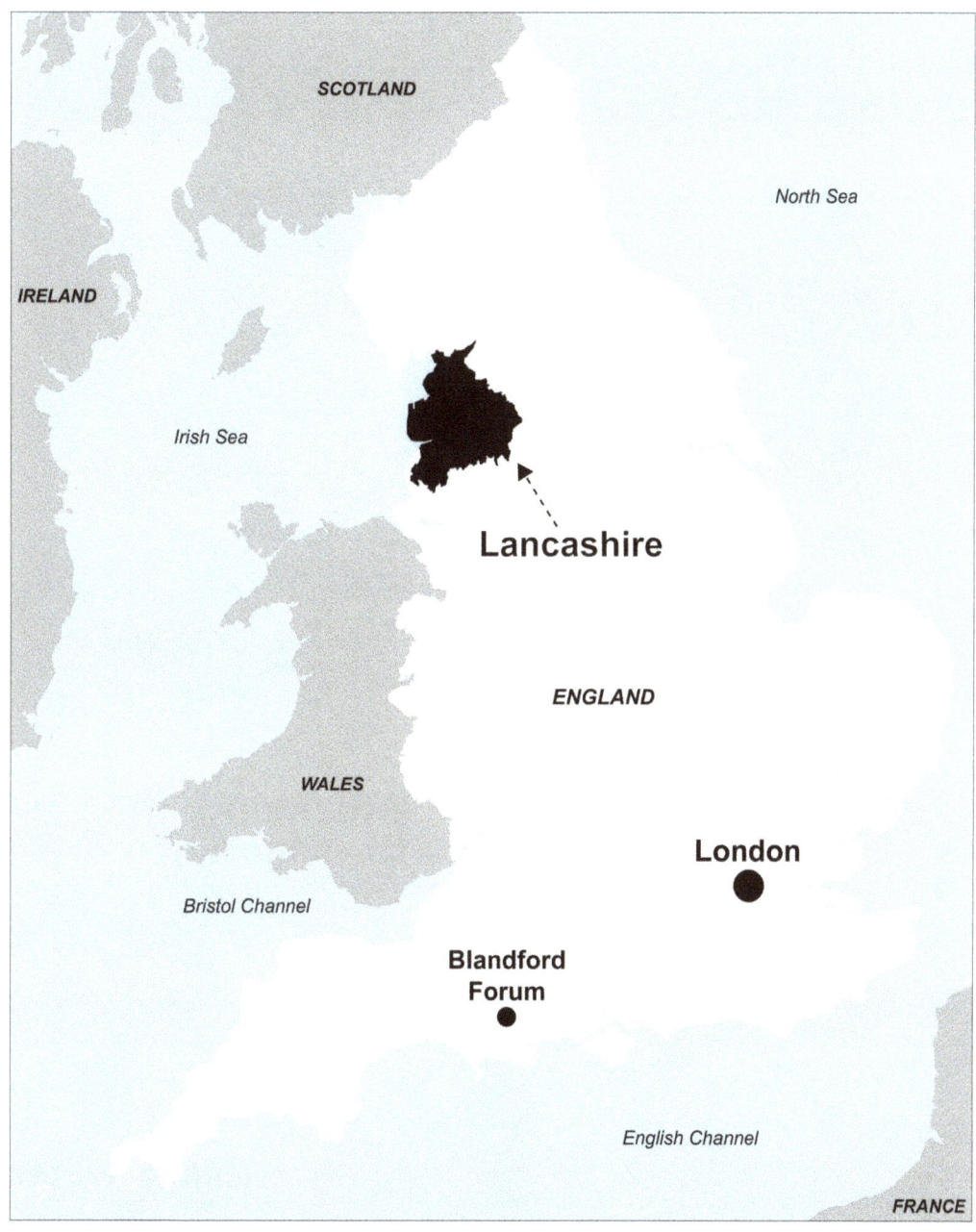

This map is for illustrative purposes only. The boundaries of Lancashire have shifted over time, but the above map shows its general location within England. The town of Blandford Forum in Dorset is marked because my great-grandparents lived there for a short time around 1891 while Thomas was working as a Temperance lecturer at a nearby boys school.

This map, which is for illustrative purposes only, shows the historic county of Lancashire. For reference, the distance between Preston and Rishton is about 11 miles. My Cross great-grandparents were predominantly from historic Blackburnshire, which includes the towns of Blackburn and Rishton. Also marked on the map is the major industrial city of Manchester; Pendle Hill, a natural landmark near where the Pendle witch trials took place in 1612; and the port city of Liverpool, where Thomas, Angelina, and all of their children were among the millions of people that departed for America.

Workshop of the World

Both Angelina Whittaker and Thomas Cross have deep Lancastrian roots, but, because their parents descended from peasantry instead of peerage, we must rely on simple church and census records. Fortunately, if there's one thing the English have always done exceptionally well, it's keeping excellent records, especially records of its citizens, noble or not.

The surname Cross is very common throughout parts of England and Ireland, originally denoting a person living at or near a road crossing or wayside crucifix, but the surname of Thomas' mother, Bonsall, and the surnames of Angelina's parents, Whittaker and Ainsworth, all harken back to very specific Anglo-Saxon habitational names of northern England.

Lancashire was officially established as a county in the twelfth century, but its history stretches thousands of years into the past, with indications of settlement in and around Blackburn dating back to bronze age urn burials and an iron age sacred spring.

The Romans came, saw, conquered, and were mostly gone from the area by the onset of the fifth century, leaving behind a military road and a temple dedicated to the sun god Serapis, followed by centuries of Christianization and an early "*Church of Blagbourne.*"

Twenty years after the Norman Conquest in 1066, "*Blacheburne*" is listed in the Domesday Book, which records two churches, five leagues of woodland, and not much else.

Blackburn's population grew over the next few centuries as the local wool weaving economy flourished, and in 1331, King Edward III invited dozens of expert Flemish weavers into the country to enhance the rapidly booming textile industry.

The Tudor dynasty brought monumental social, religious, and economic change to all of England, especially Lancashire, and in 1536, the region played a major role in the Pilgrimage of Grace, a widespread protest against King Henry VIII's break with Rome and his violent dissolution of the monasteries. The rebellion was crushed, its leaders tried and executed, yet the people of Lancashire kept a firm hold on their deeply held Christian beliefs and traditions, both Catholic and Nonconformist – along with a lot of folk medicine and a little magic.

This boiling cauldron of beliefs was bubbling over by the time the very Protestant King James I ascended to the English throne in the early 1600s. King James was well-educated and intelligent, but he was also obsessed with witches and demons, and in 1612, near Pendle Hill, about eighteen miles northeast of Blackburn, the king's fervent philosophies and mandates led to the horrific imprisonment of twelve people from three of rural Lancashire's most flagrantly Nonconformist families.

All three families were headed by unmarried older women – one a wealthy widowed landowner and a known Catholic, and the others, two extremely poor and extremely old "cunning women" – folk healers who could make traditional potions and cast Christian-based spells and charms, all things they'd learned from their mothers and grandmothers.

These two cunning women also happened to be rivals, and both were called "witches" (and worse) long before the trial. Of the twelve accused, only two were men. One of the cunning women died awaiting trial, and the rest were executed by hanging, all except one – a nine-year-old girl who testified against her entire family.

Thirty years after the Pendle trials, the English Civil War broke out in 1642, a series of bloody conflicts between pro-monarchy royalists and anti-monarchy parliamentarians. Throughout the course of the war, some major battles and smaller skirmishes took place in Lancashire, including the pivotal Battle of Preston in August 1648, just ten miles west of Blackburn, soon after which, King Charles I was charged with high treason and executed.

Lancashire, like many northern counties, was already politically and religiously tense. The wealthy landowners and aristocracy supported the king, but the average working citizen supported parliament, and all of this was further aggravated by the growing religious divides among Catholics, Anglicans, Puritans, and other Nonconformists.

By the 1700s, textile production was the leading industry of Blackburn, which was famous for its signature textile patterns – Blackburn Greys and Blackburn Checks – and in 1766, nearby Rishton earned the distinction of being the first place in Great Britain to mass produce calico fabric, which has a thickness somewhere between very thin muslin and very thick canvas.

After the 1760s, with the onset of what historians have termed the Industrial Revolution, Blackburn and Rishton were among the many little Lancashire communities that experienced explosive textile manufacturing growth, along with a major shift to weaving with imported cotton fibers instead of just local wool.

The invention of the cotton gin in 1794 sped up the processing of raw cotton, and soon it was Great Britain's largest import, almost all of it coming from the United States and passing through the ports of Liverpool. Factories in Lancashire's southern cities spun the cotton into thread, and the weaving of textiles happened in its northern factories, with Blackburn leading production.

But with the rapid advancement of spinning and weaving technology, more factories filled with more efficient machines sprung up, making work done the traditional handloom way obsolete, causing a precipitous drop in employment – in Blackburn, sixty percent of handloom weavers were out of work among an already poverty-stricken and malnourished population.

These dire circumstances launched the Lancashire Loom Breaking Riots of 1826, which began with a congregation of starving, unemployed, disgruntled weavers who'd assembled at nearby Enfield to discuss their plight. The crowd, which was well-riled before the meeting even began, was quickly whipped into a frenzy, fueled by immense desperation and with nothing left to lose but their lives.

With some participants armed, the rioters descended upon factories at Accrington, about five miles east of Blackburn, where they destroyed nearly 250 power looms in under an hour. Troops arrived on the scene and started arresting people before they could move on to Blackburn, but the riots continued in other Lancastrian towns for days.

But times were changing. The handloom weavers were forced into the new way, and by 1860, Lancashire was home to 2,650 cotton mills, in which 440,000 people produced half of the world's cotton textiles. By 1870 there were 2,500,000 spindles in Blackburn alone.

As Lancashire became known as the "Cradle of the Industrial Revolution" and "Workshop of the World," Blackburn earned the title of "Weaving Capital of the World."

It's against this backdrop, this ancestral tapestry woven with wool and cotton and whispers of witches – tattered and stained with blood, sweat, and tears – that my great-grandparents were born.

The Parents of Angelina the Great

My Great-Grandmother Angelina Whittaker was born in Blackburn on February 3, 1864, to Seth and Margaret (Ainsworth) Whittaker, their third daughter after Jane, born in 1860, and Eliza, born in 1863.

Both of her parents, Seth and Margaret, were born in Blackburn and died in Preston, and both descend from long lines of working class Lancashire families.

Angelina's father, Seth, was the son of Blackburn-born Michael Whittaker, but he also has a deep connection to the area of Darwen, just south of Blackburn, the birthplace of his mother Jane Briggs. Michael, an innkeeper, married Jane, a spinster, in September of 1826, and together they had seven children, including my great-great-grandfather Seth.

The parents of Angelina's mother were William Ainsworth and Margaret Stirzaker, two more very old Lancashire surnames, along with Whittaker and Briggs, with the Stirzaker family possibly coming from Rufford, several miles west of the Ainsworths in Blackburn.

It was in Blackburn, at the Anglican Church of St. Mary the Virgin, that William and Margaret intended to be married on May 19, 1823, but before they could even make it to the altar, they were asked to leave.

As per the records, when twenty-year-old William, a tailor, tried to marry Margaret, a sixteen-year-old spinster, they were turned away by the officiant, Vicar John William Whittaker, who refused to solemnize their union *"on account of one party being incapacitated due to intoxication."*

Happily, the records also show that William and Margaret were successful (and presumably sober) on their second try the following day, May 20, 1823 – and with a different officiant named R. Garnett.

Despite this initial nuptial hiccup, William and Margaret had several children, which brings us back to the parents of Angelina the Great: Margaret Ainsworth and Seth Whittaker.

When they got married in 1860 on the eighteenth of January – my birthday! – Margaret was nineteen, Seth was twenty, and they both had mill jobs as cotton power weavers.

Seth worked in the mills for the rest of his life, maybe even until his death in 1910 at the age of seventy-three, and both he and Margaret would outlive two of their adult children: Arthur, who died at twenty-seven in 1902, and Angelina, who died in 1903 at age thirty-nine.

Angelina's brother Arthur was the first to be buried in what would become the family plot, where Seth and Margaret were also laid to rest, in the historic Great Harwood Cemetery near Rishton.

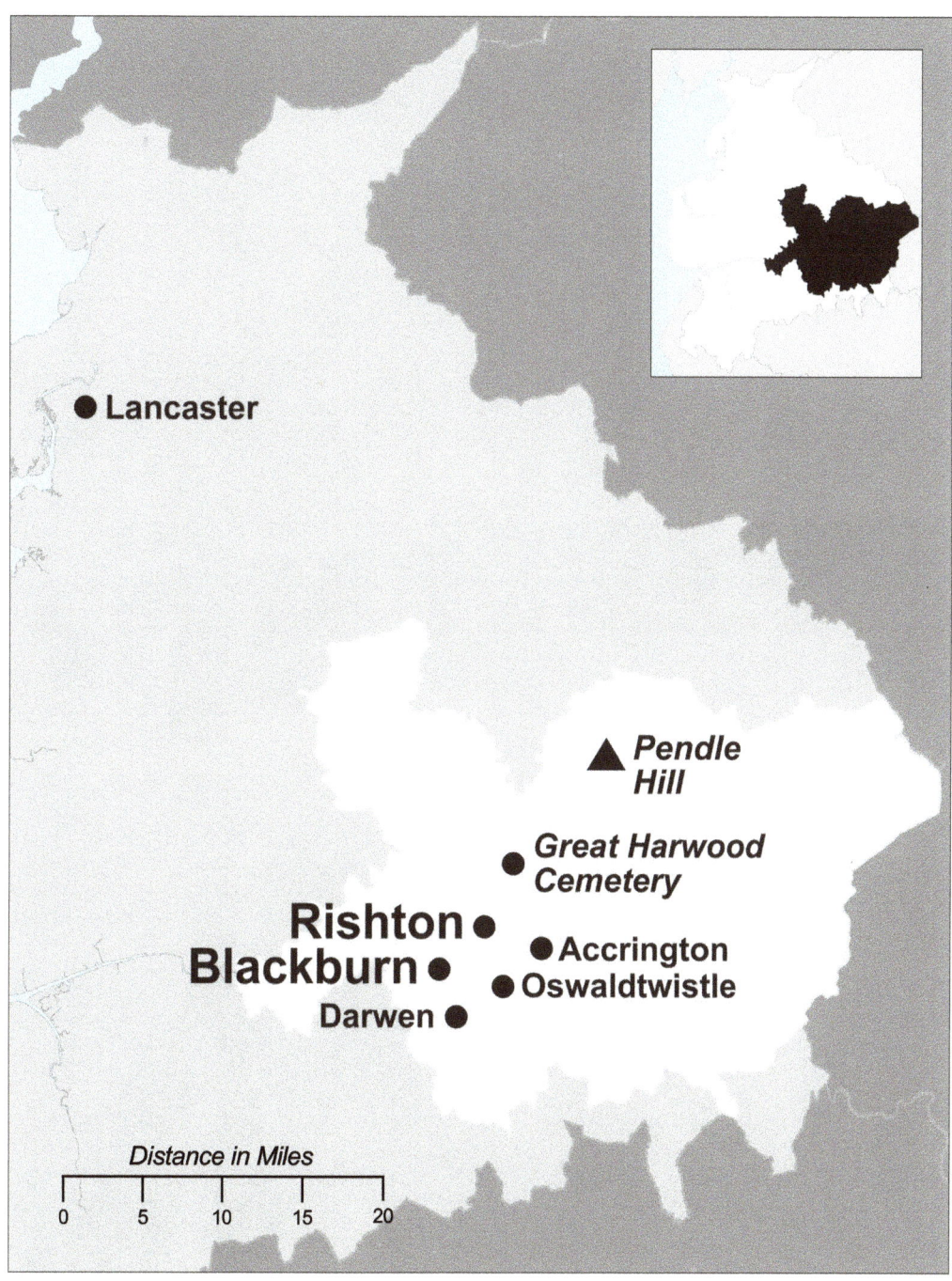

This map, which is for illustrative purposes only, shows the cluster of towns and villages where my Cross great-grandparents and their ancestors were born and raised. All of these places are located within historic Blackburnshire (highlighted in black in the inset above), previously known as the "Blackburn Hundred," with "hundred" being an archaic Anglo-Saxon term used to determine the taxation value of an area. Also indicated on the map is Great Harwood Cemetery, where several relatives of Thomas and Angelina are buried, including their three children lost in infancy.

Two 1862 newspaper illustrations of people in line, waiting for coal tickets and food to get them through the hardships of the Lancashire Cotton Famine.

Angelina the Great

Angelina was born during the Lancashire Cotton Famine, one of the international ripple effects of the American Civil War, which disrupted cotton exports and devastated the mill economy of northwestern England. As an industrial area totally dependent on American cotton harvested by enslaved people, thousands and thousands of people lost their jobs, including Angelina's father Seth, a mill overseer and loomfixer.

By July 1861, the Union had established blockades at all major ports in the southern United States, and the impacts were instantaneous. By December of 1861, widespread poverty and famine had paralyzed the region – and yet, even as the people starved and froze, even as they stood in line for hours every day, waiting to receive charitable assistance, they also stood in solidarity with the fight to abolish slavery.

In December of 1862, Angelina's family may have attended the Great Meeting in the major industrial city of Manchester, which was known as Cottonopolis, just south of Blackburn. During this meeting, thousands of millworkers came together to publicly support President Abraham Lincoln, even though it was his blockade that had caused their dire situation. Many also sent letters to Lincoln, and in his reply, the President acknowledged their suffering, while commending their commitment to human dignity, and to their heroism, *"which has not been surpassed in any age or in any country. It is indeed an energetic and re-inspiring assurance of the inherent power of truth, and of the ultimate and universal triumph of justice, humanity, and freedom."*

But not everyone felt the same way. Some mill owners, whose wealth depended on the cotton trade, sympathized with the Confederacy, and occasionally, small amounts of cotton did make it out of the American south – imagine Clark Gable as the blockade runner Rhett Butler in *Gone with the Wind*, smuggling cotton out to sea in the dark of night. But even if those little bits of cotton indeed made it to the ports of Liverpool, it was always immediately snapped up by the many mills of Manchester before any of it could reach smaller cities.

Soup kitchens fed the unemployed and their families, while churches provided charitable support and created public works projects. Relief committees were formed to raise donations and distribute the essentials of food, fuel, and clothing, and neighbors shared what little they had with each other.

After the American Civil War ended, the cotton started to flow across the ocean again, and the families of Blackburn returned to their looms and spindles. But the hardships were not easily forgotten, nor were they over, for in Victorian England, employment could be just as life-threatening as unemployment – especially for children.

In the 1871 census, both of Angelina's parents are back to work, along with her ten-year-old sister Jane. Her eight-year-old sister Eliza would soon leave school to join Jane, and Angelina would be right behind her. In those days, children as young as seven were expected to work or their families would starve, and for mill owners, children were an abundant and convenient source of cheap labor. Their days were long and grueling, and Angelina and her sisters would have been responsible for a variety of tasks in the mill, ranging from the mundane and menial, like sweeping floors and using their nimble little fingers to tie broken yarn together, to the death-defyingly dangerous, their small size making them ideal for scrambling up and squeezing under the roaring machinery.

It was dangerous for adults, too – in fact, simply breathing inside one of these mills was hazardous to human health. The common practice of "steaming," in which artificial heat and moisture was added to already poorly ventilated air with humidifiers, was thought to minimize thread breakage and dampen down dust, but it may have also facilitated the spread of disease among workers.

Still worse was the method of "kissing" the shuttle, the process of loading fresh bobbins of thread into containers, or shuttles, the threads of which then fed into the loom to be woven together – it's a bit like threading a needle from a spool of thread but on a much bigger scale. To do this, the worker would put their mouth on the eye of the shuttle and sharply inhale to draw the end of the thread through. In the process, not only were workers inhaling fibers, dust, chemicals, and other debris, they were picking up the bacteria of all the people who had kissed the shuttle before them – and they did this at least 300 times a day.

Consumption was a leading cause of death at this time, and it was especially high among mill workers. Once widely thought to be a hereditary disease, it wasn't until 1882, when the trailblazing microbiologist Robert Koch published his findings on *Mycobacterium tuberculosis*, that Tuberculosis, as it came to be called, was identified as an infectious disease.

Angelina's brother James arrived in 1872, then Arthur in 1875, and Minnie in 1879, and while the Whittakers moved from time to time, they always stayed close to Rishton, eventually settling in at 49 Hermitage Street, according to the 1881 census. Angelina, now seventeen, was working as a cotton weaver alongside her older sisters, their younger brothers were still in school, and their little sister Minnie was a toddler.

Not far from Angelina's home, just a quarter mile west on High Street, lived a young loom worker by the name of Thomas Cross. They were practically neighbors, linked by the Rishton Bridge, which spanned the Leeds and Liverpool Canal, but it's possible they first met at church or working in the mills. Though the provenance of their romance is unknown, one thing is for sure – destiny was weaving something special for these two.

The top illustration depicts a room of power looms with mostly women working (except the one male overseer), and below, a man and woman (both barefoot) setting machines in a spinning room, with a boy (also barefoot) in the bottom right corner, underneath the yarn, cleaning up debris. From "History of the Cotton Manufacture in Great Britain" by Sir Edward Baines, 1835. Drawings by T. Allom, engravings by J.W. Lowry.

The Parents of Thomas the Great

My Great-Grandfather Thomas Cross was also born in Blackburn, just three weeks after Angelina, on February 24, 1864, to Thomas Cross and Mary Simpson Bonsall Cross, the fourth of their seven children, two of whom – the first and the last – were lost in infancy.

Thomas' mother Mary was born in Preston, a daughter of my Manchester-born great-great-great-grandparents, George Bonsall and Sarah Simpson. We don't know much about their lives, except for some small but fascinating traces found in the early records of the 1820 migration of thousands of people to the British Cape Colony in South Africa.

In one group of colonists, led by a man called George Smith, were George Bonsall (24), a schoolmaster, his wife Sarah (21), and their two young children, Henry (2) and Ann (1). All seventy-one settlers in Smith's party embarked the *Stentor* at Liverpool on Christmas Eve 1819, and after several months at sea, on May 15, 1820, they finally reached Algoa Bay in the Cape of Good Hope, settling in an area called George Vale.

It was here that George and Sarah's third child Jane was born, but within a year of their arrival, things became dire for the Bonsalls, and on May 31, 1821, we find a brief entry in the records which reads – "*George Bonsall of George Vale was now incurably ill. His wife, Sarah, begged permission for their return to England. They were entirely without subsistence.*"

Like the Bonsall family, at least a third of these nearly 5,000 Cape Colony settlers did not have any agricultural experience, and those that did were only familiar with the land, climate, and crops of England, Scotland, Wales, or Ireland. Some settlers claimed they didn't have enough land to work with, and even if they did, farming conditions were so bad that the crops were constantly failing. By 1823, fewer than 500 settlers remained, and the Bonsalls were among those that returned to their homeland of England, where George recovered and they had their fourth child, John, in 1824. John and his final four siblings were all born in Lancashire – that's a total of eight children, six of whom survived to adulthood, including my great-great-grandmother, Mary Elizabeth Simpson Bonsall, Thomas the Great's mother.

Thomas the Great's father, Thomas Cross – whom we'll call Thomas the Elder to avoid confusion – was born in Accrington, east of Blackburn, to parents Thomas Cross and Betty Grimshaw. Their first daughter, Betty, passed away when she was two, but they then had three more children – Thomas the Elder, Ellen, and William.

Setting another sad family precedent, in 1847, when Thomas the Elder was eleven, his mother Betty, a mill worker, passed away at the age of thirty-six.

He had already been working in the mills for well over a year when he lost his mother, and in 1851, the census lists fifteen-year-old Thomas, a power loom weaver, and his eleven-year-old sister Ellen, a card loom hand, living in Blackburn with their uncle John Cross, their father's brother.

In the same 1851 census, their father, a laborer, is listed as living with another of his Cross brothers, Richard, in nearby Oswaldtwistle, south of Rishton, along with his son, Thomas the Elder's eight-year-old brother William, who's still in school.

The ebb and flow of Thomas the Elder's childhood and early adult life is a spin-cycle of ups and downs, and in 1856, twenty-year-old Thomas' father passes away.

Happily, a year later, in June of 1857, Thomas weds Mary Bonsall in Blackburn, and by 1858 they have their first son, George. Sadly, George passes away six months later, and in 1860, Thomas' sister Ellen passes away aged just twenty-one. In 1861, as they celebrate the birth of their next child, John, the Lancashire Cotton Famine begins, putting Thomas the Elder, a weaver, out of work. But then came their next daughter Sarah, followed by Thomas the Great, and then Mary.

At some point in the 1860s, Thomas the Elder became a green grocer, and by the 1871 census, he has moved his wife and four children to Rishton, where their last two daughters are born – Emma and Miriam.

Thomas the Elder opened a grocery shop across from their High Street home, where his wife Mary devoted herself to keeping house and caring for the children, who all went to school until they were old enough to work in the mills. But for young Thomas the Great, his education never stopped, and there were still plenty of lessons to be learned on the factory floors, in the streets of Rishton, and beyond.

Thomas Cross in an undated photo.

Graduate of the Cotton Mills

Growing up under the daily grind of mill work in a small industrial town with so many layers of history, the intelligent and inquisitive young Thomas the Great would have been familiar with the many social, political, and spiritual upheavals that had shaped his community.

Like Angelina, Thomas would have also been all too familiar with the brutal everyday hardships of his time, and as he came of age, his heart and mind were drawn to the social causes that would define his life's work.

By his twenties, he was a dedicated advocate of the Temperance movement, which warned of the dangers of alcohol and the damage it does to both body and soul. Following his unwavering belief in the power of change, Thomas traveled from town to town, passionately lecturing on the devastating effects of alcoholism, which was rampant in the overcrowded industrial cities of England. So many families ruined, so many lives lost to drink, and at a time when addiction was misunderstood as a personal failing rather than an illness. The consequences were mostly among the poorest, but anyone, even the wealthiest nobles and the most pious churchgoers, could fall prey to this ruthless affliction.

His message was both bold and compassionate, and likely a reflection of his parents'– and their parents'– Methodist beliefs. With a long history of religious reform and political activism in the region, it's no surprise that Thomas the Great found a role model in the legendary John Wesley, the founder of Methodism.

John Wesley (1703-1791) was a visionary English Biblical scholar known for bringing the teachings of Christ to the everyday lives of the common people. His words and works inspired generations of reformers, among them my great-grandfather, especially in regards to education, labor, and prison reform, as well as his stand against slavery, and his early influence on the Temperance movement. Thomas the Great was following right in his footsteps!

My early research hinted at this Wesleyan connection, and with the kind help of a Rishton librarian, I discovered that Thomas the Great was indeed a member of his local Wesleyan Church, a branch of the Methodist denomination. I now have no doubt that John Wesley's teachings and philosophies inspired Thomas the Great's spiritual and social activism.

As I delved deeper into researching Thomas' life, I connected with my second cousin, Barbara Ashworth, who is also a great-granddaughter of Thomas and Angelina, through their daughter Eliza's son Russell.

Barbara, who is also an ancestry enthusiast, has provided me with an abundance of family memories and insights into the personality of our shared great-grandfather, including family photographs given to her by her uncle, Norman Ashworth, Russell's brother, accompanied by Norman's hand-written notes.

Norman's description of Thomas the Great paints a vivid picture of a remarkable man who led his life with courage and conviction –

"This is Thomas Cross, whom I consider a quite remarkable man. Completely self-educated, he started working in the cotton mills of England at about nine years of age, and eventually became an ordained minister in the Universalist Church.

"He was a labor organizer in England in the early days of the Industrial Revolution. As a result, he was blackballed by employers. He was offered a job by his brother-in-law, Thomas Aspin, if he stopped his union activities.

"Because of his principles, he refused and eventually came to America with his oldest daughter, Lillian, for work. He sent for his wife and his five younger children after he got settled.

"Thomas Cross worked in the U.S. in the cotton mills and was a public speaker on Sundays, in the days when public speaking was a form of entertainment, speaking mostly on socialist and labor matters. He made as much money speaking as working, and liked to be introduced as 'Thomas Cross, Graduate of the Cotton Mills.'"

In my favorite photo of Thomas, he stands outdoors among clusters of leafy, sun-drenched bushes, his hat pushed back, and an umbrella slung jauntily over his shoulder, forming a halo around his smiling face. It's a most befitting image for man who lived his life with dignity and purpose, a bright man, a kind man, a man of faith and fairness, a man who wanted to make the world a better place.

Thomas Cross in an undated photo, enjoying a sunny day.

The Progressive Crosses of Rishton

When they were both twenty, Angelina and Thomas were married in Blackburn on November 1, 1884, witnessed by Angelina's sister Eliza Whittaker and Eliza's husband John Aspin. Just six months later, their first child, Lillian, was born on May 16, 1885.

Their son Henry arrived in May of 1887, but he passed away a few months later, and they would once more endure this profound sorrow when their next son, Seth, born in January of 1889, also passed away in infancy.

Angelina and Thomas welcomed their daughter Eliza in 1890, then Ivy in 1892, and then Jane in 1894, who passed away the following year. Thomas Jr. arrived in 1896, then Cecil, my grandfather, in 1899, and lastly Minnie, born in 1900. Nine joyous births and three tragic losses in just fifteen years.

It was a Rishton historian, the marvelous Pamela Edgar – whom I met by placing an "advert" in the local paper – that made the touching discovery of the final resting places of Henry, Seth, and Jane in the Great Harwood Cemetery of Rishton. It's hard to imagine the emotional toll these losses took on Angelina and Thomas, but child mortality rates were tragically high in those days.

At the same time, poverty, like alcoholism, was also thought to be caused by a personal defect, which is why the poor were treated like criminals – which is why both Thomas the Great and Thomas the Elder did what they could to shift this cultural mindset. Sometimes they got really creative! Take, for instance, the time the two Thomases put on a performance at their local workhouse, a public institution where the poorest of society lived and worked to pay for their food and lodgings.

Thomas the Elder was serving as the elected board guardian of the Blackburn Workhouse, and in May of 1898, according to a newspaper article, he arranged a special concert for the *"inmates"* – a telling term that refers to the workhouse residents. The Rishton Wesleyan Choir sang several religious anthems, and a secular cantata titled "Sherwood's Queen." And guess who conducted the choir – none other than Thomas the Great! Not surprisingly, Thomas the Elder was re-elected as board guardian later that year.

Along with his Wesleyan values and beliefs, it's clear that Thomas the Great was also deeply inspired by his father from a young age, and it's probably why he got such an early start in public speaking – if Thomas were a young man today, he would no doubt be an "influencer" with thousands of followers!

In his early adult years, Thomas worked during the weekdays and spoke to social clubs and church groups on nights and weekends, all around Blackburnshire and beyond. And people wanted to listen to him – he was just like them, a mill worker, a husband and father, a son of Blackburn.

By 1891, however, twenty-seven-year-old Thomas the Great had taken his show – and his little family – on the road, to Blandford Forum in Dorset, some 250 miles south of Blackburn, where the census lists his profession as *"Temperance Lecturer."* But scribbled with it in a similar but lighter hand are the words *"School"* and *"Author"* – intriguing!

As it turns out, with Angelina and their two young daughters, Lillian and Eliza, by his side, Thomas was living his passion for helping, educating, and inspiring others. In this case, he was enriching the lives of young men and boys from underserved communities as a lecturer at the nearby Dorset County Industrial School for Boys. The school used to be the Dorset Boys Reformatory, and was established in the 1850s as a detention home for boys under sixteen who had been sentenced by the court, many of whom were just unfortunate victims of poverty and neglect, not young criminals in the making. As social and scientific opinions evolved, so did the reformatory, and by the 1880s, it had officially become a school, which, according to records, had its own fully functional farm – and a band!

That explains the *"School"* – but what about that other word scribbled in with Thomas the Great's 1891 census profession – *"Author."*

Well, anyone who attended one of his Temperance lectures would have probably received an informational flyer or pamphlet related to the topic of discussion – like the many physical, mental, and spiritual benefits of abstaining from alcohol – and who else would pen the contents of his own socially conscious collateral?

Perhaps the school position was only temporary, because in 1892, Thomas and Angelina returned to Rishton, where their next five children would be born. Thomas went back to working in the mills full-time, but he never gave up lecturing, and over the years his topics grew to include much more than just the tenets of Temperance.

The socialist movement had been steadily gaining momentum in England, with trade unions pushing for workers' rights, improved working conditions, and higher wages, and still more pushing for sweeping social reform, including better education and improved living conditions for all.

To better understand the social and spiritual influences that shaped Thomas and Angelina, let's refer to a 1977 scholarly article by Alan Ainsworth entitled, "Religion in the Working Class Community, and the Evolution of Socialism in Late Nineteenth Century Lancashire."

As the working poor and merchant classes stratified even further during the nineteenth century, Ainsworth writes, the term "Nonconformist" took on distinctly upper-class connotations, perhaps even Puritanical by some standards, denoting more respectable and well-off members of society – and typically, the owners of the mills.

Ainsworth aptly quotes the Irish-born and Quaker-educated Samuel Hobson, a socialist activist in late 19th-century Manchester – *"The Nonconformist manufacturers of Lancashire and Yorkshire prayed for and generally with us on Sundays, and preyed on us for the rest of the week."*

Traditional – even superstitious – practices had survived among the working classes, particularly in the countryside, but in the industrial towns and cities, religion had to provide more than just a place to sit on Sunday morning, and leadership had to do more than just chastise once a week from the pulpit – they had to practice what they preached.

With the introduction of the workhouses, the working poor had no need of charitable church handouts, nor was there any reason to attend and abide by the fussy rules of formal Sunday service, though many still attended.

But why go to a big fancy church where you may get disapproving looks from both clergy and fellow congregants, when you could meet up with your friends and neighbors and coworkers to pray and sing or listen to uplifting sermons and fascinating lectures?

Ainsworth also writes – *"It was not unusual for members of the same family to belong to different churches. It mattered more that they found a congenial atmosphere there, rather than this or that interpretation of the scriptures. Well might one working class woman recall her mother's spiritual predilections as 'creedless and pewless.' Expressed religious opinions tended to be not simply dogmatic, but also fluid, and often varied depending upon the social context in which it was offered."*

Caught in the swift current of spiritual and social fluidity, Thomas and Angelina likely drifted from meeting to meeting, from lecture to lecture, learning about different non-Nonconformist philosophies, while still attending the Wesleyan church on High Street. They probably picked up pamphlets and read the weekly newspapers, and it's probably through a meeting or article that they discovered the Spiritualist movement.

"Bridge House, Rishton" by Alexander P. Kapp. This image of the former Wesleyan Church on High Street in Rishton, which has since been converted into apartments, was taken from the Rishton Bridge.

"Rishton Bridge No 108A" by Mat Fascione. This image, taken north of the bridge looking south, shows the canal below, and the back of the former church (the taller structure behind the building to the far right).

These are the three oldest daughters of Angelina and Thomas, pictured in Rishton, Lancashire, England, circa 1894. At left is Lillian, the oldest of their children, with her baby sister Ivy, and on the right, Eliza, the middle sister of Lillian and Ivy.

The Spiritualist Crosses of Rishton

As the dawn of the twentieth century approached, wave after wave of social and spiritual change washed over the smoggy industrial cities of Blackburnshire, and we find more and more people tapping into a profound yearning to connect and commune with both God and nature – and the great beyond.

The Spiritualist surge had begun almost fifty years earlier in 1848 with the Fox Sisters, daughters of a Methodist family in Hydesville, New York. The girls, ages fifteen and eleven, quickly became very famous for their ability to "talk" with spirits, interpreting the mysterious knocking, cracking, and tapping sounds that manifested at their command into messages for the living. It was eventually revealed that they were faking everything – all the taps and spirit talking – but it was already too late.

The Spiritualist movement spread rapidly across the Atlantic, igniting imaginations all over Europe, and especially in England, and by the 1860s, it was said that more than two million people in the United States embraced Spiritualist beliefs.

Among those millions were, supposedly, President Lincoln, who was known to attend séances – some of them in the White House – albeit at the behest of his grief-stricken wife, Mary Todd Lincoln, who was desperate to speak to their departed children: Edward, who died at age four in 1850, and William, who died at age eleven in 1862.

Several years after President Lincoln was assassinated on April 14, 1865, their youngest son, Tad, died at the age of eighteen. Only their first-born son, Robert Todd Lincoln, survived to adulthood, living to the age of eighty-two.

A large part of Spiritualism's appeal was the hopeful belief in a hereafter, with a greater value placed on the potential immortality of the soul rather than its innate immorality. Few dedicated Spiritualists questioned or doubted the presence of a higher power, and many were devout Christians of varying denominations as well as devout Spiritualists. It was like joining a Temperance league or literary society, and meetings were more than séance circles and "trance talking" – there was fun and friendship, discourse, debate, and the Spiritualists' membership was mostly comprised of curious, churchgoing, civic-minded citizens who shared common questions about life and death.

The Blackburn Spiritualists' Society held meetings that explored a vast range of topics, from spirituality and religion to social theory and reform, as well as how all the above intersect. Here are some of the lectures listed in the papers for the Blackburn Spiritualists weekly meetings:

- *The Aim of Spirit Communion*
- *Children in the Spirit World*
- *Death, and What Then?*
- *Faith or Fact – Which?*
- *Heaven Here and Hereafter*
- *If Christ came to Blackburn*
- *Intemperance, Poverty, Disease and Crime*
- *Is Spiritualism a Religion*
- *Nature's Uncrowned Kings*
- *Peeps into Paradise*
- *The Philosophy of Human Fellowship*
- *Priests, Principalities and Powers v. The People*
- *Remedies for our Street Children*
- *Salvation through Faith and Salvation by Works*
- *The Social and Moral aspects of the Labour Movement*
- *Spiritualism: Fact or Fancy* (given by a Wesleyan preacher)

There were also scientific lectures *(The History of Medicine)* and trendier themes *(The Language of Flowers)*, and while the subject matter could be somber, the meetings were anything but. Between lectures they hosted fortnightly social events and parties featuring string bands, dancing, choral concerts, comedy shows, and *"Potato Pie and Pudding Suppers"* – and there were Christmas celebrations, harvest and flower festivals, workshops and classes – even christenings!

Some meetings and lectures were for women only *(What Women Ought to Know)* and, in fact, most clairvoyants, mediums, and trance speakers – however they labeled their specialty – were women, some quite young. Twelve-year-old Janet Bailey became well-known all over Blackburnshire for "giving Clairvoyance," and remained a fixture of local Spiritualist societies for many years, eventually becoming a teacher.

> THE SPIRITUALISTS' HALL, late Grammar School, Freckleton-street.—TO-NIGHT, 7-30, Lecturer, Mr C. MPI N, Leeds, 20 years Wesleyan Preacher. Subject, "Spiritualism, Fact or Fancy." Questions allowed. SUNDAY AFTERNOON, 2-70; EVENING, 6 30; Lecturer, Mr. G. H. EDWARDS; Clairvoyant, Miss BAILEY, 12 years old. MONDAY EVENING, 7-30, Lecturer, Mr. WM. WARD; Clairvoyant, Darwen friend. Collection each evening.

> SPIRITUAL HALL, NORTHGATE.—TO-MORROW (SUNDAY)—HARVEST FESTIVAL,—the Platform will be occupied by Mr. GEORGE EDWARDS and Miss JANET BAILEY, both of Blackburn; in the afternoon, at 2.30, there will be a Public Circle, when Miss Janet Bailey will give Clairvoyance; Lecture at 6.30 by Mr. Edwards, and Clairvoyance by Miss Bailey. On Monday evening, at 7.30, Fruit Banquet, Social, and Dance; tickets 6d. each. Public Circles on Sundays at 11, and Wednesdays 7.45 p.m. Monthly Committee.

Two newspaper notices in the Blackburn Standard and Weekly Express that mention the young clairvoyant, Miss Janet Bailey. At the top (and hard to read), the Blackburn Spiritualists' Hall notice from February 22, 1890 – also note the featured lecturer, a "Wesleyan Preacher." At the bottom, a much more legible clipping of the Northgate Spiritual Hall's notice from September 8, 1894.

But Spiritualist gatherings were not just about séances, in which people like Miss Bailey channeled the voices of the dead – it gave living voices that had long been silent a chance to be heard. These meetings were one of the rare spaces that gave women a platform for public speaking. Women weren't allowed to be ministers or politicians, and while it wasn't technically illegal for them to address crowds of people, it was certainly frowned upon – unless they were a teacher, and their audience made up of children, and even then, they had to remain unmarried to teach.

No matter what the topic of discussion was, questions from the audience, even if disbelieving, were encouraged, with one meeting notice proclaiming – *"Come, hear, and judge for yourselves, whether Spiritualism is unscientific, unscriptural, untruthful, and immoral."*

And there were plenty of skeptics and critics. Both the movement and its more open adherents were often prime targets for contempt and ridicule from both the pulpits and the public halls, and because of this, many people downplayed – or flat out denied – their Spiritualist affiliations, especially more prominent members of society. But anyone with any kind of reputation to uphold was at risk.

In 1886, even a young Blackburn police constable by the name of Dibdin was forced to resign his position when it was discovered he was attending Spiritualist meetings, with his superiors claiming that it made him mentally unfit to do his job – besides, according to the police chief, *"there were plenty of churches and chapels in the town, and also the Police Christian Association."*

In P.C. Dibdin's case, this was pure prejudice, but not all criticism of the Spiritualist movement was unfounded. By then, both law-abiding mediums and garden variety con-artists were being prosecuted on charges of fraud and theft, for taking advantage of people made vulnerable by grief or ignorance, and granted, not all those accused were innocent.

But greed has no creed, and all the highly publicized debates and trials and controversies did not deter people from showing up to secretive séances in search of their lost loved ones and a deeper significance to their suffering, a sign of hope from the other side.

In the early days of the Blackburn Spiritualist Society, members gathered in the parlors of private homes and rarely spoke about their meetings in public, but in 1889, they began promoting their newly founded Spiritualists' Hall, which was established in a vacant grammar school.

The Blackburn society celebrated their sixteen-year anniversary in 1894, and in 1896, the first Rishton Spiritualists Church was officially established, giving the Crosses a dedicated place in their very own town to explore the mysteries of life and death and everything in between.

The Spiritualists were often jumbled up with other movements that were, at the time, perceived as zany protosciences – like that outrageous new concept called "psychology," for example. Or how about that wacky "wireless telegraphy" thing?

Now known as radio, wireless telegraphy was the brainchild of Italian inventor Guglielmo Marconi, who, in 1896, first successfully demonstrated his new technology, which allowed invisible but audible transmissions to be sent from one location to another through the air – only four miles, at first, then all the way across the English Channel, and then an astounding 2,100 miles across the Atlantic!

If sounds and messages could travel through thin air via radio waves, why couldn't the voices and words of spirits from the afterlife reach the living? Perhaps sounds from the other side were transmitted at a frequency only audible to those psychically sensitive enough to receive it, like a medium. The more scientific-minded Spiritualists hypothesized and experimented and compared findings, but like any belief system, the most important variable was immeasurable – faith.

By the late 1890s, Thomas and Angelina had been devout members of the Spiritualist movement for many years, as well as lifelong churchgoing Wesleyans. Thomas was a registered voter, but Angelina, as a woman, was not allowed to vote, and I wouldn't be surprised if they were both staunch suffragists – another controversial movement at the time.

In 1898, Thomas was still working and lecturing, often as a featured speaker for local Spiritualist meetings, but he had also developed a solid reputation as a labor reform activist, and it was because of his many progressive beliefs and actions that he became known to every mill owner in the area as utterly unemployable.

Thomas and Angelina's last child, Minnie, was born in September of 1900, but within a year of holding his newborn daughter in his arms, Thomas would be an ocean away from his beloved family, starting a whole new life for them – a new life in a new place in a new century!

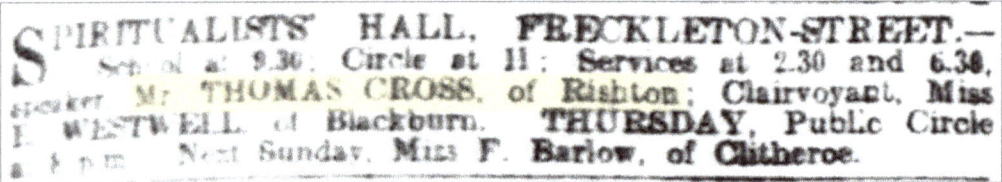

The Blackburn Spiritualists' Hall notice in the August 13, 1898, issue of the Blackburn Standard and Weekly Express. The notice reads, "School at 9:30; Circle at 11; Services at 2:30 and 6:30, speaker Mr. Thomas Cross of Rishton; Clairvoyant, Miss E. Westwell of Blackburn. Thursday, Public Circle at 8 p.m. Next Sunday, Miss F. Barlow of Clitheroe."

The Crosses Cross the Atlantic

The dawn of the twentieth century would bring massive changes for everyone, not just the Crosses. A couple of weeks after New Year's Day 1901, Queen Victoria passed away, ending her reign of sixty-four years. News of her death sent shock waves throughout the British empire, as most people – anyone under seventy – had known no other monarch but her.

Queen Victoria's death was a sign of hope for some, a chance for things to change for the better. The British empire was bigger than ever before, but life in little towns like Rishton was getting worse.

The area's once thriving weaving industry had been withering away for years, eaten up by competitors in bigger cities, and the little local mills that had once employed generations of families were closing.

With opportunities already scarce, Thomas' labor crusading was going to send his family to the workhouse, but he wasn't going to sacrifice his principles for a paycheck.

By 1901, the Crosses had likely already heard of a place called Fall River in America, where there were dozens and dozens and dozens of mills that were always hiring, especially workers with experience, of which the Crosses had plenty – and there were already boatloads of English people there, some they likely knew, or whose relatives they might have known back in Lancashire.

For the Crosses, Fall River represented more than opportunity, it was a lifeline in a tempest of uncertainty, and crossing the Atlantic wasn't just a physical journey, it was a leap of faith. Spiritualists of the time often used water as a metaphor for crossing over from one realm to the next, with hymns like "The Angel Boatman," "The Ship of Life," and

"That Land Beyond the River," and I doubt the symbolism was lost on my great-grandparents as they prepared to leave everything they knew behind and dive headfirst into the unknown.

As was often the case with emigrating families, the head of household would venture over first to set up their new life. So, Thomas made the trip to Liverpool, where he boarded the *Prince George*, and after about twelve days, he arrived in Halifax, Nova Scotia. From Halifax he continued to the Port of Boston, arriving on August 29, 1901, and from Boston he made his way to Fall River, where he set about finding a job and a new home for his family.

A notable aside (as opposed to a fun fact): One week after Thomas arrived in America, President William McKinley was assassinated in Buffalo, New York; he was six months into his second term and succeeded by his vice president – Theodore Roosevelt.

About a month after Thomas the Great's arrival, the eldest child of the family, Lillian – just sixteen years old – boarded the *SS Ultonia* in Liverpool and set off to join her father. It seems like an unthinkable journey for one so young to make, but she was no doubt already quite responsible, and she was also accompanied by a friend her age, Clara Hendel. The two teens arrived in America on October 24, 1901, and would soon find work together as weavers in one of Fall River's many mills.

Though they had to spend the Christmas holiday apart, once the weather warmed, Angelina the Great settled their affairs, packed their bags, and made her heart-wrenching goodbyes to family and friends.

She traveled to Liverpool with five children in tow – Eliza (11), Ivy (9), Tom (6), Cecil (3), Minnie (1) – and on May 13, 1902, they all boarded the *Ivernia*, Cunard's new 600-foot transatlantic ocean liner.

There were dining saloons and promenade decks, and just a few months earlier, *Ivernia* had one of those new-fangled Marconi radio systems installed.

Teen Thomas Jr. (or possibly preteen Cecil) with his oldest sister Lillian (Cross) Haworth, probably around 1911-12. Perhaps this was taken at the 1911 wedding of their sister Eliza – which means Lillian was in her late twenties and had already given birth to her only daughter, Ivy Haworth.

The SS Ultonia was the ship that brought Lillian to America in 1901. Ultonia – the Latin name for Ulster, one of Ireland's four traditional provinces – was 500 feet long, and originally built in 1898 to move cargo and cattle, but in 1899 it was updated to carry passengers, with more and more accommodations being added and upgraded over the years. In 1917, Ultonia sunk about 200 miles off the coast of Ireland after it was torpedoed by an Imperial German submarine.

This photo of Cecil with his second-oldest sister, Eliza (center), and youngest sister, Minnie, was probably taken about three or four years after they lost their mother Angelina. It's possible that it was taken on the day they all became American citizens – September 16, 1907. If so, that would mean Cecil is eight in the photo, Eliza is newly seventeen (with her birthday falling on September 13th), and Minnie is newly seven (her birthday being September 14th).

It sounds like smooth sailing, and for first class passengers perhaps it was, but Angelina and her children were traveling third class with hundreds of other families all crowded together in communal dormitories – for ten days! Ventilation was poor, sanitation facilities inadequate, seasickness rampant, and, if you could keep them down, meals were basic rations of bread and bland porridge.

Angelina the Great's steely determination and hope for a new life in America carried her through, and on May 22, 1902, she and her five little Crosses arrived in Boston. They traveled to Fall River to be reunited with Thomas and Lillian, and just like the more than 120,000 other English immigrants to the United States that year, their family was finally together again, weaving their American dream.

Thomas spent long hours as a twister six days a week in the Hargraves Mill on Quarry Street, but every Saturday, after completing a full shift, he would go home, clean up, pack his bag, and take off for Sunday speaking engagements all over New England. He was often featured by the Worcester Association of Spiritualists at the Bull Mansion in Worcester, Massachusetts, and announcements of upcoming lectures in the *Worcester Daily Spy* would draw hundreds of people to hear *"Thomas Cross of England"* speak.

Angelina settled into her new apartment in her new neighborhood on Reeves Street, and was preparing to join Thomas and Lillian in the mills, but just as the family was starting to feel at home, tragedy struck – less than two years after her arrival in America, Angelina the Great passed away on September 6, 1903. She was just thirty-nine years old.

Her death certificate lists diarrhea as the cause, which was very common at the time, but it's more likely that the diarrhea was caused by her body finally shutting down after a long battle with tuberculosis, one of the other leading causes of death at the time, especially for women and children – and cotton mill workers.

Angelina had been gravely ill for months and was bedridden when she died, but her faith and family comforted her all the way to her final moments. Her funeral and burial were conducted with full Spiritualist rites, and she was laid to rest in Oak Grove Cemetery, her grave marked only by a small, numbered plaque.

Their happy new home was shattered, but Thomas believed that his wife's spirit would continue on, having departed for that most distant of shores. According to the Crosses' neighbors, however, Angelina the Great's spirit never left Reeves Street.

The Specters of Angelina

On the afternoon of Sunday, September 6, 1903, Thomas was returning home to Fall River after giving a lecture, and when he finally walked through his front door, he was met by the solemn, tear-stained faces of his oldest children, and the bewildered whimpers of his youngest. Although Angelina had been ill and confined to bed for a while, no one expected her to pass so soon, but it was obvious her time was near.

She was gone before dusk, and just moments after taking her last breath, an inexplicable phenomenon occurred, the first in a series of supernatural events that would soon captivate all of eastern Massachusetts.

The Crosses lived in one of four small apartments in their Reeves Street tenement building, and it was the family next door that first reported something strange. As they were sitting down to Sunday supper on the sixth of September, *"a thick white mist"* suddenly filled the room that shared a wall with the Crosses' apartment.

The family sprang up in a panic, fearing a fire, and the mother flailed her arms around to disperse what she thought was smoke. But there was no smoke, there was no fire, and the white mist vanished as quickly as it appeared – and when the neighbors learned of Angelina's passing minutes later, they determined that the mist must have been her spirit.

A few days later, a close friend of Angelina experienced something even more extraordinary. As she was retrieving a jar of preserves from her cellar, she was overcome by an inexplicable feeling, and when she looked around, the spirit of Angelina appeared before her. The woman didn't scream or feel frightened, describing the lifelike apparition as gentle and serene, smiling as it softly swayed, and with no trace of the sickness that had ravaged her body. The friend shared her strange story with the family, but despite Thomas' dedication to Spiritualism, he doubted it was really the specter of his beloved Angelina.

But, whether Thomas believed it or not, several weeks after the family laid their matriarch to rest, the Crosses of Fall River would discover that no one really cared what they believed, least of all their neighbors – or the press.

We don't know the precise timeline of events, only what was reported in the newspapers, but sometime in late October of 1903, as ten-year-old Eliza – whom the reporters call the *"little mother"* of the house – was caring for the children and cleaning, she came across a handprint on a pane of glass while washing the kitchen windows.

Eliza used plenty of soap and water on both sides of the glass, but it still wouldn't come off. She showed her father Thomas and sister Lillian when they got home from work, but no matter what they did, the handprint, allegedly – *"defied all attempts to remove it."*

Helpful neighbors tried wiping it away, and as they marveled, a nosy neighbor nonchalantly inquired as to what the fuss was about, followed by another, and then another, which drew the attention of passersby, spreading *"the story of the strange spectre,"* and *"soon it became noised about through the neighborhood."*

The news carried so fast and far that on October 29, 1903, reporters started showing up in front of the Crosses' Reeves Street home. The family tried to downplay the situation, with Thomas vehemently maintaining that, as a devoted Spiritualist, he had personally witnessed signs from the spirit world – and could indeed communicate with his late wife – but he did not believe the handprint was hers.

Their neighbors, however, were providing a much more interesting storyline, and they were all very willing to give their very detailed descriptions of personally witnessing the specter of Angelina back in September.

FALL RIVER HAS A MYSTERY

Woman's Hand Imprinted on Window Pane.

Spiritualists Excited by "Message From Mother."

Humble Home of Thomas Cross, Enthusiastic Believer in Cult, Center of Attraction for Believers and Nonbelievers.

FALL RIVER, Oct 29 — The humble home of Thomas Cross in the tenement section of the South End was visited today by hundreds of people to see what many hold to be a striking Spiritualistic manifestation.

On a pane of glass in a kitchen window can be plainly seen what appears to be the imprint of a woman's hand, the palm, the fingers and thumb, and even the lines of the palm being distinctly visible. All efforts to remove the imprint have failed.

Mr Cross is a Spiritualist. He is employed in one of the cotton mills, but on Sundays and when other occasions permit, preaches his doctrines.

Mrs Cross died two months ago. She too was an ardent Spiritualist, but the children, of whom there are six, three boys and three girls, know little of the doctrine. The oldest, a girl of 10 years named Eliza, is skeptical of the faith of her parents, and Spiritualists interpret the appearance of the hand on the windowglass as a sign to the doubting daughter from the mother.

The hand was discovered by the girl as she was washing the window, and repeated efforts have failed to erase the imprint. Hot water and soaps, acids and muscular effort have so far served only to make the hand stand out more plainly.

The fingers are spread wide apart, and the knuckles are large as though the hand had been used to hard work. The more enthusiastic among the believers in Spiritualism who have witnessed the phenomena do not hesitate to say that they detect the mark on the third finger showing where the wedding ring was long worn.

The merely curious who have visited the place have bent their energies to finding an explanation of the mystery, and have even gone so far as to remove the window from its place to permit a more thorough examination. One after another have given up the puzzle.

Mr Cross does not attach great importance to the matter, as he says he is accustomed to receiving still more wonderful communications from the departed.

From the front page of the Boston Globe on Friday, October 30, 1903.

A SPIRIT HAND

Imprinted on Window Pane in Reeves Street Tenement.

NEIGHBORHOOD IS MYSTIFIED

Some Believe It Manifestation of Spirit of Mrs. Cross.

The impression of a spectral hand on an ordinary window pane, which impression steadily refuses to be removed, has caused considerable talk among the residents of Reeves street, which is a short street running northerly from the eastern extremity of East Grinnell street. The impression is believed by many to be the imprint of the hand of a dead woman, who, with her husband, was a firm believer in the principles of Spiritualism, up to the minute of her death.

Excerpt from the lengthy front page article in the Fall River Herald on Oct. 30, 1903.

Some onlookers agreed they could clearly make out the impression of a wedding band on the handprint's ring finger, and another theory suggested that, because little Eliza was skeptical of her parents' faith, the handprint was surely a sign from Angelina to her *"doubting"* daughter.

On the morning of October 30th, the day before Halloween – or Mischief Night, as some call it – the front page of the *Fall River Daily Herald* ran its reportage in a lengthy article entitled – *"A Spirit Hand – Neighborhood is Mystified – Some Believe it Manifestation of Spirit of Mrs. Cross."*

Even the venerable *Boston Globe* placed the story on their front page, the headline screaming – *"Fall River has a Mystery: Spiritualists Excited by 'Message from Mother.'"*

But what began as an intriguing paranormal mystery was already unfolding into a tragic farce, and as tens of thousands of people were reading and talking about the Spiritualist Crosses of Fall River, hundreds of believers and skeptics – including *"an army of kodak fiends, artists, and newspaper reporters from near and far"* – were rushing to Reeves Street to see for themselves, only to be met with crushing disappointment.

On the night of October 29th, hours before the October 30th papers were printed, Eliza had already managed to successfully remove the handprint from the window pane.

But it was too late, and with Thomas and Lillian away at work again, as the crowd continued to swell, little Eliza was forced to face down a mob of strangers peppering her with questions.

In the *Boston Globe's* October 31st follow-up article, we get Eliza's heartbreakingly simple answer – *"The baby put [her] dirty fingers on the window, and I washed out the marks as soon as I had time."*

She then apologized to the crowd for allowing the window to remain dirty – *"But mother was sick so long, and then she died, and I haven't had any one to help me since."*

That Halloween night, there were no decorations and parlor games for the Crosses, just a messy yard to clean up and curious stragglers to ward off. It was a time of mourning for them, and it must have been very upsetting to have no control, to watch helplessly as the safety of their home suddenly became a public spectacle for gawking and gossip.

Still, how fascinatingly strange to think that my great-grandparents were once the talk of New England – from the busy mill floors to the Halloween feasts, from Sunday church services to social club gatherings, everyone was buzzing about the Spiritualist Crosses of Fall River that autumn of 1903.

After all, maybe the handprint vanished on its own, having successfully delivered the message its sender intended.

> *Beckoning hands at the gateway tonight,*
> *Faces a 'shining with radiant light,*
> *Eyes looking down from yon heavenly home,*
> *Beautiful hands they are beckoning, "come."*
> *Beautiful hands, beckoning hands,*
> *Calling the dear ones to heavenly lands;*
> *Beautiful hands, beckoning hands,*
> *Beautiful, beautiful, beckoning hands.*
>
> – Excerpt from the Spiritualist hymn,
> "Beautiful, Beckoning Hands" (1888)

A Gathering of Spirits

Since I first learned about the Cross family's deep Spiritualist connections and the sightings of Angelina the Great, I've felt an undeniable pull to learn more about her – a spectral hand beckoning me closer.

It was so much more than curiosity – I was completely enchanted by her story – and it led me to attend my first séance on a bitterly cold January night in 2015. Eager to uncover more about the lives and beliefs of Angelina and Thomas, I approached the séance like any research project – with an open mind, a sprinkle of skepticism, and a genuine desire to learn.

I've seen enough movies and TV to know the more sensational side of Spiritualism – those fraudulent, dramatic displays of ventriloquism dripping with so-called "ectoplasm" – but much to my relief, modern everyday Spiritualists don't believe any of that stuff was real either.

I searched for Spiritualist churches in New York City, where my husband Clarel and I lived and worked, and sure enough, I came across the Spiritualist Church of NYC on East 35th street. It was a typical church in a lovely neighborhood, with a regular schedule of evening Sunday services and twice-monthly "Spiritualist Message Circles" – the modern terminology for a séance, which comes from the French word for "session."

The only requirements were to be on time and bring twenty dollars cash, so I marked my calendar for the upcoming Sunday session, and when it finally arrived, Clarel walked me through the cold night air into the warmth of the church.

Congregants were milling around as they waited for the service to begin. It was nothing out of the ordinary, or so it seemed to me, but Clarel was feeling uneasy, and though he'd planned to accompany me to the service and session, he decided to wait for me at his office a few blocks away instead. So I ventured in alone.

Once inside, I kept to myself and quietly sat in an empty pew, and while I remember the service and sermon being very peaceful, the details are a blur, as my thoughts were already drifting to what would come next – the séance upstairs.

I wasn't quite sure what to expect, but I was ready, and after the service, I paid my twenty dollars and climbed the stairs. I entered a softly lit room with twelve chairs arranged in a circle, at the center of which was a small table with an aluminum trumpet cone set upon it, meant for channeling spiritual energy.

Our group consisted of three certified mediums, two women and one man, and nine guests – three young women, three men, two middle-aged women, and one senior citizen – that would be me. We seemed like just regular folks, each with our own reasons for being there, all of us looking for something – answers, comfort, connection.

The first medium quietly began the session by welcoming us and inviting any spirits who wished to communicate, saying, "We are here to receive communication from those who have crossed over, those now living on in another dimension called the Spirit World."

The second medium asked us to give our first names, and as we went around the circle, I felt a small shiver when I quietly said "Deborah."

The séance continued with prayers for protection and peace, followed by a simple meditation, and as I sensed our group settling into a state of calm reflection, the mediums began to receive messages.

The first spirit who visited was the uncle of one of the young women; she was studying medicine, and he encouraged her to stick with it. Then came messages from departed grandparents, parents, siblings, and friends.

At no point did any of our number giggle or daydream; they demanded nothing and graciously accepted whatever came. Some shed tears of relief, like the young woman whose brother had been killed in a motorcycle accident. Through one of the mediums, the spirit of the brother communicated that he was fine, and that she needed to move on with her life. There were no scary or ominous warnings, only messages of comfort and hope for the bereaved, assurances that those we love who have crossed over were not suffering.

As the session went on, I sat in quiet observation, silently listening to every message with a mix of hope and anticipation, hanging on every word, waiting, wishing there was someone in this gathering of spirits who wanted to speak to me. Time was ticking away...and then...it happened.

"Deborah..."

My heart raced at the sound of the medium saying my name.

"There are two people here for you," the medium said, her face soft and serene.

Two...but who? – I thought, holding my breath.

"Two women," the medium said, her gaze anchored far beyond where I sat, as if drawn by a lighthouse on a distant shore. "They look old – but they died young. Could they be aunts, grandmothers, or great-grandmothers?"

I was stunned, unable to move or speak, and then her gaze drifted back and locked on mine.

"Deborah, are you a writer?"

Not thinking clearly, I blurted out – "No! No, certainly not..."

The medium's gaze shifted back to that faraway beacon, and, as if she were just reading off a telegram, she confidently continued – "Because the message I'm getting from both spirits that have come here for you is one of encouragement. They want you to know that you are loved, and they are encouraging you to keep on writing."

She waited patiently while I mulled things over, and I realized the truth was complicated, so, I confessed – "Well, actually, I have been writing a family history for some time now…"

"Yes…" she said, "There are two women encouraging you to keep writing." Full stop, end of telegram – and it hit me like a radiant sunbeam of pure warmth and light!

Could it really be Angelina and Alzada, my two great-grandmothers, reaching out to me? Was Angelina my "guiding spirit," a messenger from God? Was Alzada my "dawn," raising her voice from the darkness?

The connection was so strong, and I felt so certain – it was as if their love had traveled through time and space to find me in that little room.

The session ended with a prayer of gratitude, and I silently left the circle and slipped back down the stairs. I pushed through the ornate doors into the bitter cold, and as I crossed the threshold, the past and present rushed together – and I felt transformed.

Clarel, my lighthouse, was waiting for me in the car at the curb, guiding me back to a warm, familiar space, and when he asked how it went, as I tried to explain, the tears filling my eyes were enough to convey the power of what happened.

In the days and weeks that followed, I reflected deeply on the experience, and it only strengthened my resolve to continue the search for my ancestors – and to keep on writing.

A Trip to England

It was that gathering of spirits in New York City that sparked my eight-day journey to England in May of 2016. I was joined by my newly discovered second-cousin, Barbara Ashworth, who came all the way from Vermont, and Pamela Edgar, the wonderful historian who quickly became my dear friend.

We three wise women set off on an adventure to explore the homeland of Angelina and Thomas Cross, and from the moment we arrived, we found the people of Rishton and all of Lancashire to be exceedingly friendly and welcoming – elders are treated with great respect, so we felt like honored guests wherever we went.

When I first thought about visiting Rishton, I pictured an industrial relic, worn down by the weight of its past, but what a delightful surprise it was to find nature reclaiming the abandoned mills with vibrant greenery.

I wanted to experience the world of my great-grandparents, and as I wandered through town, I imagined Thomas and Angelina walking the very same streets, passing the places where they lived and worshiped and grieved and celebrated. I stood on the Rishton Bridge over the Leeds and Liverpool Canal, right next to the Wesleyan church they attended, which has since been converted into apartments.

I sought out the remnants of the mills where they might have worked together, and I imagined Thomas stealing glances at beautiful Angelina as she concentrated on her job, pretending not to notice him noticing, oblivious to the blush creeping up her cheeks. Or maybe it was Angelina who first noticed Thomas – an instant attraction to the magnetic charm and eloquence of this young minister in the making.

The older residents of Rishton were an absolute joy. Full of life and eager to share their stories, they welcomed me warmly – even when I knocked on doors as an uninvited guest!

All I had to say in my American accent was, "My great-grandparents lived here," and I was invited in without hesitation, sipping tea in no time.

Every conversation was a gift, with tales of love, hardship, and joy, always told with wit – and talk about charming accents! One delightful lady who lived close to the house where Angelina and Thomas once resided was out walking her dog when I approached. She was kind and lived quite modestly, but she had a wealth of stories to share from her childhood and fifty-five-year marriage.

Another neighbor suggested we stop by the local pub, the Roebuck, for a bite to eat. We were starved from all that walking and talking, so we went right over, only to find out the Roebuck doesn't serve food – just alcohol.

We were too hungry to drink our lunch, so the friendly owner chatted with us for a bit, and then walked us over to a nearby restaurant, but he insisted we return to the pub after we had properly dined. It was an invitation that was hard to resist – but what would Temperance-minded Thomas the Great have to say!?

Every day of our trip was like this – an adventure filled with friendly faces, lively conversations, and lots of walking, much of it in graveyards, seeing where our many ancestors were laid to rest. But what really stands out in my memory was our trip to see where my great-grandparents made their final stop before heading to America.

As I traveled by modern train to Liverpool, I tried to imagine what it was like for them, especially Angelina, to set sail on a long and possibly dangerous voyage. Angelina had recently been to the Port of Liverpool at least twice – once to bid her husband goodbye, and then her daughter – but that third time would be very different.

My traveling companions. From left to right are my second-cousin Barbara Ashworth, my friend and Rishton historian Pamela Edgar, and me!

When I arrived at the Port of Liverpool, I boarded a little ferry, imagining thirty-eight-year-old Angelina embarking the massive *Ivernia*, and as I sailed, I thought about her final moments in England.

I wondered what went through her mind as she stood on the deck with her five young children, waving goodbye to loved ones, her heart filled with hope and anxiety, knowing she might never see her big family or little Rishton ever again.

Then, as Thomas and Lillian had done so bravely before her, she took one last look at her homeland, and led her children down to the dormitory to settle in for their journey to an unknown shore – the end of one life, the beginning of another.

Dad's Maternal Irish Family Tree Branch

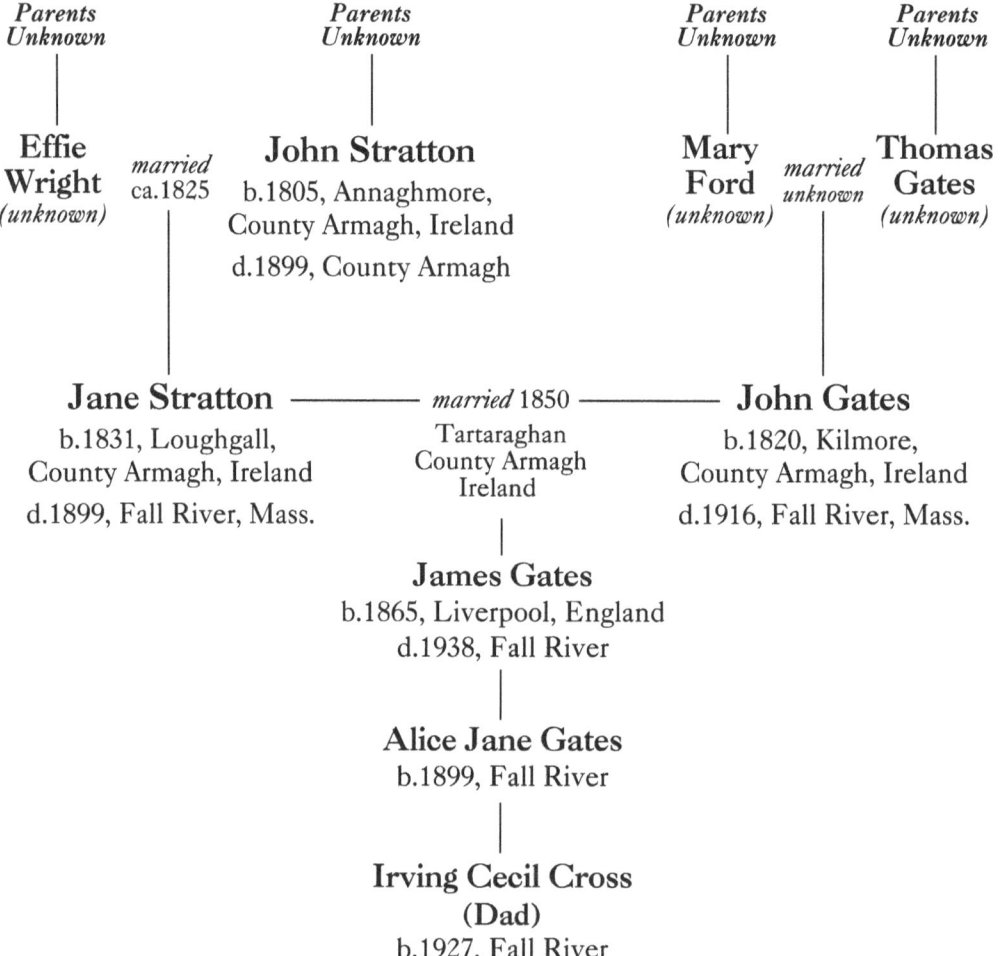

Irving's Irish Ancestors

Although this part of the book is devoted to the ancestry and lives of Dad's paternal Cross grandparents, his maternal grandparents, James and Lottie Gates, were also English immigrants. Learning of Lottie's Lancashire (and Yorkshire) lineage was nice, but not surprising, so imagine my delight when I discovered that her husband, my great-grandfather James Gates, is my only ancestral connection to the Emerald Isle!

Records are scarce for my Irish-born branches, but the documents we do have only include birthplaces within a cluster of little villages, all in County Armagh, about forty miles southwest of Belfast.

County Armagh is located in the historic province of Ulster, modern-day Northern Ireland, but in the time of my Great-Grandparents, it was only referred to as Ireland, albeit still under colonial control of the United Kingdom, especially throughout Ulster.

James Gates' parents – Jane Stratton and John Gates – were born, raised, and married in County Armagh, and it's likely that all of their parents were, too – maybe even their parents before them, maybe even generations more.

But what about the very English surnames on this branch – Ford, Gates, Stratton, Wright? Not even a wee bit Irish! The answer lies in Ireland's tragic and bloody history as one of England's oldest colonies – and, more officially, as the Kingdom of England's very first "overseas possession."

In 1169, a century after England was conquered by the Normans, Anglo-Norman King Henry II invaded Ireland for the first time – with the endorsement of the pope – and for more than 800 years, at least some part of Ireland has been under English control.

There's a whole lot more to it than that, of course, but I'm guessing my ancestors must have been among the many waves of English colonists that flowed west across the Irish Sea at some point in the past several centuries.

Perhaps it was during the establishment of the Ulster Plantation, a 1600s "British" endeavor enacted by King James I of England – who was also James VI of Scotland – which sent thousands of English and Scottish protestant "planters" to six Ulster counties, including Armagh, to cultivate land taken from the native Irish.

If we look at my paternal family patterns, perhaps my ancestors were also among the early English-Irish followers of John Wesley, who visited Ireland numerous times throughout his life, including County Armagh, where he spoke at least nine times from 1767 to 1789.

According to the Armagh Methodist Circuit, during his fourth visit to the town of Armagh, which took place June 4-6, 1773, Wesley noted in his journal entry from June 6th – *"I explained the great text of St John to an exceeding large congregation. We had at church an anthem which I know not that I have heard these last 50 years, 'Praise the Lord, o my soul' (written by Robert Okeland c1560); and sung in a manner that would not have disgraced any of our English Cathedrals. The congregation was the largest I have seen in Ulster; and I believe, for the present, all were convinced that nothing will avail without humble, gentle, patient love."*

All four of my great-grandfather James' older siblings were born in County Armagh, Ireland, but according to the records, James was actually born in Liverpool, England – which isn't so strange, as the Irish have been shaping the language and cultural landscape of Liverpool for centuries.

But it was during the Great Famine (1845-1852) that hundreds of thousands of Irish moved to Liverpool – nearly 300,000 in 1847 – many of whom only stayed long enough to secure passage on a ship to America. This would also be the destiny of my great-grandfather James, who was only

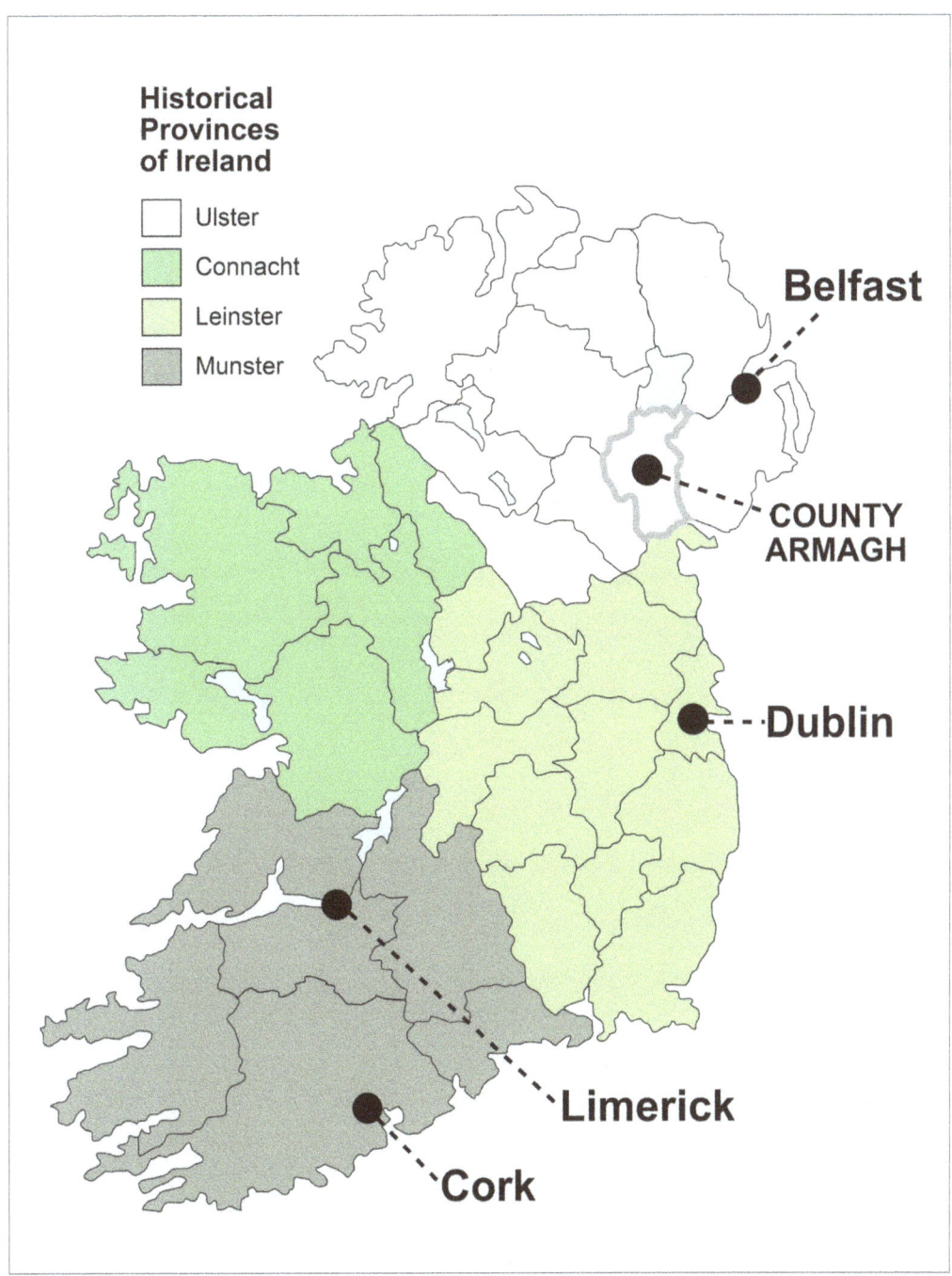

This map is for illustrative purposes only, and shows the historic locations of the four traditional provinces of Ireland. Dad's maternal great-grandfather, James Gates was the son of Irish-born parents that descended from at least a few generations based in County Armagh, which is in historic Ulster, now part of the country of Northern Ireland.

two when his family set sail from Liverpool for Fall River, and it's likely he never even laid eyes on the homeland of his parents.

My Grandpa Cecil, like his father-in-law James, was born in England and taken to America before he was old enough to really remember, and, while we can only speculate, I wonder if this shared commonality in their early life stories influenced their relationship.

One thing is for sure – the ONLY thing beer-drinking cigar-smoking anti-union anti-social Cecil had in common with his Temperance-activist labor-organizing preacher father Thomas was one of the few things he had in common with his only son Irving – their passion for music.

Reverend Cross

Thomas and Angelina were married for eighteen years before her passing in 1903, and just six months after Thomas lost his wife, in March of 1904, his father Thomas the Elder passed away back in Rishton.

It must have been crushing to lose two of the most important people in his life in such a short time frame, but Thomas remained steadfast and resilient, and unlike other men of his time who might have remarried quickly or sent the children off to live with relatives – which is what happened to his own father – Thomas kept his family close, raising his children while balancing his work in the mills and his passion for inspirational speaking.

Like countless immigrants who found their way to America, Thomas was also counting down the five years of residence required to become a citizen of the United States, and the time finally arrived on September 16, 1907. Thomas was forty-four and living at 127 Penn Street in Fall River, and in his citizenship petition, he's described as 5-feet-2-inches tall – a small man with a big voice! – with brown hair, gray eyes, and a light complexion. His six children, who ranged in age from seven to twenty-one, were also granted "derivative citizenship" through their father's naturalization.

Lillian (21), however, six months earlier, had gotten married to John Drudy Haworth (1878-1955). Another Lancashire-born immigrant, John Drudy was an orphan who grew up in a workhouse and was adopted by a couple named Haworth by the time he was thirteen.

In 1893, at age fifteen, John arrived in Boston with his adoptive parents aboard the *Cephalonia*, and they settled in Fall River, where he met and married Lillian, with whom he had one daughter, Ivy Haworth (1909-1978) – Thomas the Great's first granddaughter!

Thomas Cross Jr. with his niece, Ivy Haworth, taken circa 1913. Ivy was the daughter of his oldest sister, Lillian, and her husband, John Haworth. Ivy Haworth was Rev. Thomas Cross' first granddaughter.

Thomas continued his lecturing, and though his travels took him all over New England, he eventually connected with Reverend Henry Arnold of the Bogle Street Christian Church, right there in Fall River. The two formed a strong bond, and before long, Thomas began traveling with Rev. Arnold to Albion, Maine, for the Maine Christian Conference, for which Arnold served as secretary.

Thomas the Great's dream of becoming a preacher finally came true on September 9, 1912, when he was officially ordained as a minister by the Maine Christian Conference.

The Rev. Henry Arnold presided and delivered the ordination sermon, and the Rev. T.J. Humphrey, conference president, signed the ordination certificate. The Rev. Thomas Cross, after much experience as an itinerant pastor, had now earned his place as the resident reverend of the Christian Church in Eastport, Maine.

Curiously, just four years later, Rev. Cross stepped down from his position, giving his last service on the second Sunday in October of 1916. Thomas's departure was described as a *"distinct loss to our cause"* in the *Herald of Gospel Liberty*, and it's clear the church community greatly valued his contributions, with vestry clerk William Howes capturing the sentiment in the minutes from one the church meetings – *"We are fortunate to have such a leader as Minister Cross. His sermons are helpful and inspiring and ought to stimulate us to be more helpful to others.*

"In his remarks he impressed us with the statement that he had no fault to find, and only wished us to use our conscience in all matters and act up to what we believed to be for the best interest of the church. We shall do well to live up to his wishes and requirements."

But I wondered why – why had he stepped down? My cousin Cathy, my Aunt Joan's daughter, was also interested, and we both wanted to uncover more about our great-grandfather Thomas's life in Maine.

Cecil (right) with his older siblings, Ivy and Thomas, circa 1909. Ivy never married, and cared for their father Thomas until he passed away in 1939. Thomas Jr. married Elaine Marshall of Rhode Island, and though he worked his whole life, first in the mills and then as a machinist for Brown and Sharpe Manufacturing Co., Thomas' obituary remembers him as a "well-known singer and singing teacher," along with being a local radio singer in the 1930s, and as a soloist for several churches, including the Central Congregational Church in Providence.

Before long, Cathy had developed a theory that something had changed in the Rev. Thomas Cross life around 1916, and it turned out to be a major detail that no one in our family ever knew – that Thomas the Great had married again!

> Albion Maine September 9th 1912
>
> Maine Christian Conference
>
> This is to certify that Thomas Cross pastor of the Christian Church Eastport Maine, was ordained a minister of the gospel at Albion Maine September 8th 1912, Ordination sermon by the Rev Henry Arnold, prayer Rev Geo H Kent. Charge to candidate. Rev Albert Coucks. Right hand of fellowship Rev T P Humphrey President of the conference
>
> Attest { T P Humphrey President
>   Rev. Henry Arnold secy.

Rev. Thomas Cross' ordination letter from 1912.

The front (top) and back of the postcard Thomas Cross sent to Nettie Holmes Hawkins, his soon-to-be second wife, in April of 1912, shortly after the death of her second husband. Rev. Cross' message to Nettie has been lost to time.

Following Footsteps

Determined to know more about the life of Thomas the Great, to understand the Christian path he walked more than a century ago, and to find out more about this unknown second marriage, my husband Clarel and I set off on a road trip to Eastport, Maine – the easternmost city in the United States, from where you can practically toss a coin to Deer Island on the Canadian shore.

It's a charming place, with a small population of fewer than 1,000 residents, and an even smaller footprint, with a land area of over just three miles. We stayed at a quaint bed-and-breakfast, wandering the streets, and meeting the locals, and much to our delight, the rumor around town was that we were making a movie. While untrue, what we discovered would certainly make for a great flick – a period piece / romantic comedy about a widowed English minister wooing a twice-widowed Canadian dressmaker in picturesque coastal Maine.

The most exciting part of our trip came when we visited the Fort Sullivan Barracks Museum, where we met Cory Critchley, a volunteer at the Peavey Memorial Library. We asked if she knew anything about the longtime resident Nettie Holmes – the name of the woman that Thomas married, as discovered by my cousin Cathy – and sure enough, Cory had a whole file!

Cory explained that sometimes loved ones dropped things off at the library after relatives had passed away, and the same was true for my newly discovered step-great-grandmother Nettie Holmes. The most exciting part – in the file were two postcards, addressed to Nettie at her home in Beaver Harbor, Maine, written by Thomas the Great himself!

The front of the first card features artwork that says, "Welcome Easter Morning," and is postmarked April 8, 1912, three days after Nellie's second husband, William Hawkins, died of pneumonia. Thomas likely met Nettie in one of the congregations he ministered to, or maybe they belonged to the same lecture groups – perhaps both – and it's probable that he sent this postcard simply to console her on the loss of her husband.

However, six months later, on October 11, 1912, Thomas sent a much more risqué postcard, the front of which reads – "Which is Sweetest Flowers or Kisses?" – and has a picture of young lovers smooching in a field of flowers, no doubt suggesting a blossoming romantic relationship between Thomas and Nettie.

After the museum, Clarel and I went to Nettie's final resting place in Hillside Cemetery, where the exceptionally helpful caretaker directed us to Winchester Field, Section J, lot 1 – and there was the headstone of Nettie Holmes Cross.

With her resting place confirmed, we made our way to Eastport City Hall, where Deputy Clerk Mary Jane Summers greeted us with a smile, an authentic Maine accent, and a refreshing sense of humor. After searching in the back room, she returned and excitedly announced her first find – the original marriage certificate of Thomas and Nettie.

It was exactly what we were looking for – Thomas, a minister, living in Oakland, Maine, his second marriage; and Nettie, a dressmaker in Eastport, Maine, her third marriage; they were wed in Eastport on June 28, 1916, by Clergyman Herbert L. Packard.

Clarel and I also visited the library to search the *Eastport Sentinel* newspaper, hoping to find a social item about Nettie and Thomas. At that point, in the 2010s, the papers weren't digitized yet, so we had to search each edition by hand – and only while wearing the white cotton gloves provided to us.

The front of the postcard Thomas sent to Nettie on October 11, 1912 – unfortunately, like the Easter postcard, the back of this card is no longer legible.

Rev. Thomas Cross in later years.

We silently searched page after page, and after a long while, I suddenly heard Clarel's exclamation of discovery, a dramatic disruption to the calm quietude of the library – he'd found a notice of marriage!

"*Rev. Thomas Cross and Mrs. Nettie Hawkins were married at the home of the bride's parents, Mr. and Mrs. Nelson Holmes, in this city last Wednesday afternoon, Rev. H.L. Packard officiating. The happy couple left at once for Lubec, and they will visit also at Penfield, New Brunswick, and Boston before returning here to spend the remainder of Mr. Cross's vacation. Their residence will be Oakland, Maine, where Mr. Cross has a pastoral charge.*" (*The Eastport Sentinel*, July 5, 1916, No. 28.)

That's pretty much where the paper trail ends for Thomas and Nettie's married life. They never divorced, but it seems highly unlikely they lived together for more than just a few years, because by 1919, Thomas was called to be the minister of the First Universalist Church in Orleans, back in Massachusetts, another of the United States' easternmost coastal communities – and Nettie stayed in Maine.

A few years after my Maine research expedition, Mom joined me on my journey to learn more, and we took a road trip to follow Thomas the Great's footsteps in Cape Cod.

At the Orleans Historical Society, an extremely helpful volunteer named Bonnie Snow guided us to the vestry records of the Orleans Universalist Church, which included Thomas the Great's tenure from 1919 to 1930. Mom and I read through record after record, and it was obvious that Rev. Thomas Cross was held in the highest regard by all his parishioners – he was a part of their lives, officiating baptisms, marriages, and funerals.

Rev. Cross also officiated two very important ceremonies for his own family – my family – the wedding of his son, my grandfather Cecil, in 1924, and the baptism of his grandson, my father Irving, in 1928.

Tragically, Thomas the Great's oldest daughter, Lillian, passed away on December 13, 1924, from "valvular heart disease." Like her mother, Angelina the Great, Lillian was only thirty-nine years old. Along with her father and five grieving siblings, Lillian left behind her husband, John Haworth, and her fourteen-year-old daughter, Ivy, and she was buried with her mother at Oak Grove Cemetery.

Thomas the Great's mother passed away in 1911, his elder sister Sarah in 1919, and his elder brother John in 1923, and in September of 1938, he returned to his homeland aboard the *SS Samaria* to visit his surviving younger sisters, Mary and Emma. I like to imagine they all spent a very happy Christmas together, reminiscing about good times and long gone loved ones, because when Thomas arrived back in Boston on February 17, 1939, he passed away just four days later, aged seventy-four.

Rev. Thomas Cross was interred at Oak Grove Cemetery in Fall River, our final stop in following the footsteps of this legendary man, whose legacy of faith, fairness, and love lives on, not just in the pages of this book, but in the hearts and minds of all who read about him.

Nettie the Great

I was eager to learn more about the step-great-grandmother I never knew I had, so when someone suggested I call Mrs. Marie Holmes, I did – and what a treat that turned out to be!

Mrs. Marie Holmes was an effervescent, loquacious storyteller, and at the age of ninety-five she was still working as the senior editor for the *Quoddy Times*, where she'd been since 1958. She was also the widow of Oliver Wendell Holmes, Jr., the son of the famous justice, Oliver Wendell Holmes – and an exquisite hostess.

Mrs. Holmes invited Clarel and me to her home for tea, where she regaled us with story after story, and gave us a precious parting gift – a book by her late brother-in-law, Theodore Holmes, subtitled *The Descendants and Related Families of John Holmes, beginning in 1776*, in which she had made careful notations wherever Nettie was mentioned.

Nettie Eliza Holmes was born on March 9, 1869, at Black's Harbour, New Brunswick, Canada, to Nelson Holmes and Emeline Scott Holmes, the eldest and only daughter of their four children. When she was nineteen, her grandfather, Captain Angus Holmes, tragically passed away when he was swept overboard, as described in the *Eastport Sentinel* on October 3, 1888 –

"A telegram was received here last Thursday from Boston, conveying the sad intelligence that the schooner Eddie Pierce was lost in the gale of the day before, and that Capt. Angus Holmes, master of the vessel, has been washed overboard and drowned. The vessel sailed from here for New York, having for cargo 4,000 cases of sardines and a few thousand boxes of smoked herring. When 14 miles off Cape Cod on Wednesday, they were caught in the heavy gale of the day, and at noon the vessel's sails were blown away and a plank sprung from the stern.

> "After trying to lighten the vessel by throwing over cargo and steady work at the pumps, the water gained on them so fast that all hopes of keeping the vessel afloat were soon abandoned. Fortunately, a steamer was sighted, and a signal of distress was run up. It was just before the Bavaria reached them, about 4 o'clock, that Capt. Holmes was washed overboard by one of the heavy seas that swept the vessel's deck.
>
> "Capt. Angus Holmes was a man fifty years of age and he leaves a wife and large family, part of whom are grown up. He was a steady, industrious man, respected by all who knew him, and his sudden death is a hard blow to the sorrowing family in whose love and welfare he had always taken his greatest pleasure in life."

This was not the last tragedy that would befall young Nettie. In 1891, at the age of twenty-two, she moved to Lynn, Massachusetts, where, five years later, on June 4, 1896, she married Canadian-born Albert Gillison, the son of Scottish-born Catholic parents. We don't have the exact details, but soon after their marriage, Albert drowned, likely at sea, just like her beloved grandfather.

Nettie was a creative person and a skilled dressmaker, and apparently quite the adventurer and businesswoman. Her obituary states that, in 1900, Nettie owned a dress shop that employed about twenty people in Durango, Colorado. But perhaps this lifelong Atlantic-coaster grew homesick in the rocky deserts of southwestern Colorado, because by 1902, records indicate that she's moved back to New England.

It's in Eastport, Maine, in November of 1902, that Nettie marries her second husband, English-born Canadian William Hawkins, the son of a Baptist farmer. William, too, met an untimely end, passing away from tuberculosis in 1912 at age forty-six, which is when Rev. Thomas the Great sent her that Easter postcard. Four years later, Thomas and Nettie were married.

Providing a very human view of this thrice-married woman is her niece, Katherine Snell – "Aunt Nettie was an aunt any child would dream of having. I have so many fond memories. She spent so much time with me – teaching me how to make kites of newspapers, sticks, and paste, and how to dry them in the oven, and how to make beads of colored paper and of salt and flour. She made me boxes of doll clothes every Christmas – I could go on and on!"

What a warm remembrance! I'm so grateful to have memories of my step-great-grandmother, even if they're not exactly my memories.

Nettie passed away at ninety-one on November 24, 1960. During our trip to Maine, when Clarel and I went to Hillside Cemetery in Eastport to see her final resting place, we found a large headstone that read HOLMES. The headstone listed the names and dates of Nettie's parents and her second husband William, but Nettie's name had no dates, so I wasn't sure if she was really buried there. Cemetery caretaker Mark Cook graciously looked up the record for us, and, sure enough, Nettie Holmes Cross is buried right where she's supposed to be.

According to the burial record, the Holmes had six plots. Three of them are indeed occupied by her parents and second husband, and Nettie is buried lengthwise across the three remaining burial compartments – *"so that no one else may be buried there or the plots resold"* – a fitting memorialization of her larger-than-life presence, still claiming her space long after her death.

Mom in 2016 at the Gifford family burial plot in Beech Grove Cemetery in Westport, Massachusetts. She is standing next to the newly-dedicated headstone of her grandmother, Alzada Estes Gifford.

The new headstones I commissioned for Alzada the Great (left) in Westport, and for Angelina the Great and my great-aunt Lillian Cross Haworth in Fall River. The stones are about the same size, but the photo on the right is "zoomed out" to show the numbered plaque that used to be her only gravemarker.

Death is Nothing at All

I've visited the final resting places of all my great-grandmothers: Alzada in Westport, Emma in Swansea, Lottie and Angelina in Fall River, and Nettie in Eastport.

Emma and Lottie, who were both laid to rest beside their husbands, have headstones that mark their places on earth, as does Nettie, but Alzada had only a modest nameplate peeking out of the grass, and Angelina's grave was marked by nothing more than a small sorrowful number.

These two great women, who loom large in my heart and soul, deserved a memorial befitting their extraordinary spirits, and I simply could not allow their legacies to be reduced to such humble tokens.

So, with love and admiration, and in honor of the profound impacts they both made on my life, I commissioned two beautiful headstones to properly honor Alzada and Angelina – and Lillian, who is buried alongside her mother. In 2016, shortly after I returned from England, the headstones were finally placed. It took nearly a century to properly commemorate them, but better late than never, I say.

I wish I had the time and resources to research and detail the lives of all my ancestors and relatives. The travel is fun, the discoveries thrilling, and I find myself daydreaming about their lives, wondering what I'll stumble across next – and make no mistake, there's a lot of stumbling, but that's part of the fun, too, I suppose.

And yet, I can't imagine devoting every moment of my life to endless research – always stuck in the past among the dead, constantly clicking or flipping from page to page, record to record, comparing and cross-comparing, fact-checking and backtracking, because that's what the bulk of the job requires. Besides, not every story can be traced, and some records are irretrievably lost to time – or never existed at all – but that's part of the journey too, resigning yourself to the unavoidable fact that you will never be able to know everything about all of your ancestors.

I've been blessed by the kindness and generosity of many people throughout my research, people like my second-cousin Barbara, who, in addition to being a fantastic traveling companion, has shared everything she's gathered on our great-grandfather Thomas Cross – and, most precious of all, the only known photo of Angelina the Great.

It was taken circa 1895 – and yes, Angelina was beautiful, with a well-defined narrow jaw, prominent yet gracile cheekbones, and fine wavy hair swept back from her high forehead, possibly a shade of light brown or auburn (though that might be the sepia tone of the photo).

Angelina's slender arm is confidently perched on her hip, and she stands with her three daughters – Lillian, Eliza, and Ivy, each of them looking well-fed, clean, and nicely dressed. She has just a hint of a smile, and her eyes gaze directly into the camera with a knowing look, as if she's aware of her place in time.

I grieve for her as if I'd known her. Had she lived to old age, she would have been eighty-eight when I was born. But Angelina's life, her courage, and her deep connection to something greater than this world, resonates in my heart.

Her Spiritualist beliefs demystify death by replacing sadness and dread with comfort and understanding, because death is nothing at all – just the end of one journey, and the beginning of another.

Angelina with her three oldest daughters – Lillian (left), Ivy (center), and Eliza (right) – circa 1894 in Rishton, Lancashire, England.

PART VI

The Happily Ever After

1970s – 2022

Mom and Dad on their motorcycle.

The Happily Ever After

MOM AND DAD were both blessed with remarkable longevity, and as the years passed, even though their bodies slowed down, their minds stayed fast and sharp – and their love only grew stronger.

Mom always hoped Dad wouldn't work past sixty-two, which he didn't (well, sort of), but her reasoning was sound – she wanted to spend as much time as possible with the love of her life, and she definitely did!

For any child who loves and admires their parents, watching the onset of new health problems is difficult, especially when there's nothing you can do. It's just a part of life. The extraordinary thing was that Dad and Mom made all those hard times so much easier for me and my siblings.

They were our lighthouses, guiding us through the fog of sadness and confusion. They made jokes instead of complaints, offered words of comfort to others in their own moments of suffering, and if things were getting too glum or grim, it was time to turn up the fun.

Time flies when you're having fun, and when you've lived a life as good as they did, death is nothing to fear.

Dad in the 1970s.

Irving's Affirmations

My father wasn't afraid of death – unenthusiastic, perhaps, but never afraid. And while he was undoubtedly the most accepting, fun-loving, outgoing person I have ever known, he had a much quieter private side, too.

Dad was far more self-aware than we ever realized as kids, and it wasn't until I was an adult that I discovered our father was dealing with occasional bouts of anxiety and mania at the same time we were running wild through our wonderfully carefree childhood.

We now know that Dad actively tried to cope with intrusive thoughts and frantic feelings by repeating positive affirmations, seventeen of which we have a copy of, written in Dad's hand on the front and back of an envelope, which I found while going through boxes of old files and keepsakes. He may have written them down during one of his visits to Butler, perhaps in group therapy, or maybe they were copied from a book. Dad certainly had a way with words, and these affirmations offer a rare glimpse into his inner being – a more intimate extension of the Dadisms we've always loved.

And now, here are Dad's seventeen *Taking Charge Affirmations for Building Self-Esteem* – which includes a short preface on how to use them.

"Positive Self-Talk – Your mind creates your stress. As you think, so you become! The extent to which we love and respect ourselves has a lot to do with how well we relate to the world around us and, consequently, with how much stress there is in our lives. The way to use aspirations is to repeat them to yourself so frequently that you start believing them and living with them. Consider taping this list to your bathroom mirror, or taping it over your desk so it's handy all day. Or you can take an affirmation each day, memorize it, and repeat it to yourself during spare moments – so it really sinks in."

Dad's 17 Affirmations

1. I am a valuable and unique individual, and I am worthy of the respect of others.

2. I look at life optimistically and I am eager to accept new challenges.

3. I am (learning to be) kind, truthful, patient, and compassionate.

4. I am (learning to be) optimistic about reaching my goals. I look at temporary setbacks as steppingstones to strengthened character and resolve.

5. I (am learning to) enjoy receiving compliments, and I enjoy helping others get recognition and credit for the work they do.

6. I (am learning to) feel warm, loving, and good about myself.

7. I am not affected by the negative opinion of others; I enjoy giving my best, growing in awareness, and striving to live up to my own high standards.

8. I am successful to the extent that I feel loving toward myself.

9. There is no one in the world who is more important than I am; there is no one that is less important.

10. Every day I make time to count my blessings.

11. I am productive and efficient; I divide big jobs to be manageable (bite size) tasks, and I do one thing at a time.

12. I am (learning to be) gentle, forgiving and kind to myself.

13. I do not / I am learning not to worry. If something can be done about a problem here and now, I do it: otherwise, I let it go.

14. I (am learning to) appreciate every moment of my life. I don't dwell on the dead past or the imagined future.

15. I (am learning to) love everyone unconditionally, including myself.

16. I (am learning to) understand everyone and everything around me as my teacher.

17. I understand that to be upset over what I don't have is to waste what I do have.

I saw some of these affirmations in action, although I didn't know it at the time. One perfect example involves affirmations #6 and #15, which occurred during an overnight visit to Grammy and Grandpa's house with my then two-year-old daughter Jessica, the first Cross grandchild.

Grandpa Irving carefully helped little Jessica get up onto a step ladder in front of the bathroom sink to brush her teeth before bedtime and, as she looked at herself in the mirror, with such innocence and earnestness, as if speaking to someone else, she said, "I love you, Jessica."

Grandpa, standing behind her, smiled tenderly at her reflection, and then looked at his own and said, "And I love you, Irving."

Thanksgiving 1977 – Front row – Karen Napier, my husband Bob, me, Steve holding baby Jessica, Mom, and Pam; Middle row – Uncle George, Dad, Dave, Aunt Irene, Marcia (Steve's wife), Uncle Ed, Aunt Joan, Grandma Alice; Back center – my cousin Cathy.

Grammy and Grandpa with Jessica during Grandparents Day at school.

Grandpa & Grammy Wonderful

We were aboard Big Mamie with Mom and Dad when my husband Bob and I shared the exciting news – they were going to be grandparents! Just shy of fifty years old, Mom and Dad were radiant with joy, and, having given birth six times – and by all accounts, easily – Mom was my role model throughout my pregnancy.

I ended up past my due date – which never happened to Mom – and the night before I was scheduled to be induced, we stayed in a small bedroom in their Swansea home. I went into labor in the middle of the night, and Mom was immediately up and at 'em, bustling around, getting us ready, and sending us off.

Just a few hours later, both she and Dad were at the hospital in Fall River to meet their #1 grandchild – Jessica Elizabeth Gale MacFarlane! From the moment Jessica arrived, Grandpa and Grammy jumped into their new roles with boundless enthusiasm. They participated in everything; from tennis practice to the swimming pool, from Grandparent's Day at school to the orthodontist – whatever it was, they were there.

Fast forward to Jessica's teen years – Grandpa even guaranteed the loan on her first car, with Grammy playfully nudging him to "just sign here." Ever machinery-minded, Dad encouraged her to get a stick shift, and taught her how to drive it on the way home from the dealership.

After Jessica, Grammy and Grandpa Cross welcomed Rebekah, Allan, Sarah, Alexandra, Benjamin, Cody, Brian, Dylan, and Kayla – ten wonderful grandchildren to cherish, and they were active in every one of their lives. Besides their participation in the kids' sporting and social activities, they had a special talent for turning the most mundane tasks, like homework or chores, into something super fun and meaningful – like the time Grandpa helped Rebekah make an alarm clock out of a lunchbox for a science fair project. Even raking leaves could be a blast!

Grandpa and Grammy were always ready to entertain or enlighten or encourage, and that meant the fun times were extra fun – the bicycle rides, the singing and dancing, the adventures, the holidays.

Oh, the holidays! Halloween was always a whirlwind of excitement, with Grandpa sharing in the scare tactics – and candy! Christmases were always spent together, of course, and Grammy was always unforgettable during our annual Easter egg hunts, eagerly helping the little ones search. In her later years, she insisted on a head start, and would giggle like a little girl as she hobbled along trying to keep up with the grandkids!

Grammy and Grandpa got a head start at retirement too – officially retiring at sixty-one and sixty, respectively – a brilliant move by Mom, who wanted to enjoy life with Dad. But, in all the best ways, retirement made them more active than ever, because they suddenly had all the time in the world to lavish even more love and attention upon their blossoming brood of adoring grandchildren – and each other.

Grandpa with my girls – and a goat!

At left, Jessica and Grandpa, ready to go trick-or-treating, and at right, Grandpa and Rebekah.

At left, Allie with Grandpa, and at right, Jessica, Rebekah, and Allie skating on Lily Pond, Newport.

Mom and Dad in Riverdale, New York.

A Wonderful Retirement

For the first several years of their retirement, Mom and Dad lived with us in Riverdale, New York. Mom helped care for our three daughters – Jessica, Rebekah, and Allie – and Dad, never one to stay on a "loose pulley" for long, eased into his retired life by working as the manager of our luxury home-building company.

Both he and Mom happily pitched in with caring for the girls, from helping with schoolwork and extracurriculars to making delicious meals – and making us all laugh – and so much more. It was truly a blessing to have them with us. Grammy even (reluctantly) became the official driver for the girls. She had to physically and mentally brace herself for the twice daily trips into Manhattan, but after a while, she became a real pro – a fearless (and expletive-free) NYC driver!

My kids describe the time that Mom and Dad were living with us as "heavenly." Once, when Allie was asked why she thought her Grammy and Grandpa got along so well, as if it were obvious, she simply said, "Grammy is the cooker and Grandpa is the fixer."

We were spoiled by all the cooking and the fixing, but eventually it was time for them to return to their beloved Swansea home for the remainder of their retirement years, where they lived in harmony and happiness, never becoming those stereotypical bored and bickering retirees.

To be clear – my parents never bickered – but oh, how they bantered! Their playful exchanges, the back-and-forth bandying of jabs and jokes, were always light-hearted and full of love and laughter, and they were both so down-to-earth, so instinctively nurturing, and so effortlessly endearing in the art of banter, that they never needed to bicker.

As Dad and Mom aged, they kept doing whatever made them happy: square dancing, camping, zipping around on a motorcycle well into their seventies. We Cross kids, as their adult children, many of us with spouses and young children of our own, leapt at any opportunity to take care of them the way they took care of us, mostly by having even more everyday kind of fun!

Beyond the simple things, I also had the privilege of treating my parents to some indulgent adventures. Mom and Dad rarely (or maybe never) splurged on anything extravagant for themselves. They had no appetite for expensive cars, designer clothing, or exclusive fine dining, and though they never craved luxury, traveling the world together brought all of us joy.

My husband, Bob, grew up with an elderly aunt, Matante Metivier, and he'd always longed to have two parents in his life – it's no wonder he connected so well with his parents-in-law!

Mom and Dad welcomed Bob into the Crazy Crosses with open arms, and Bob loved them back, relishing their time together – as well as generously picking up the tab for some once-in-a lifetime experiences.

Our first odyssey almost didn't happen. Mom swore she would never fly, and since we certainly couldn't go without her, it took some persistent persuasion to get her to go. She finally agreed, and with that, we – Mom, Dad, a few of my siblings, Bob, me, and baby Jessica – were off to the Bahamas!

We stopped in Miami first, where we boarded a small private plane to a tiny private island in Eleuthera – another perilous moment when Mom almost refused to go. We have a photo from this trip with Mom holding Jessica on her lap – her face is smiling, but on the inside she was petrified! But, all in all, our brave Mom had a blast, even though food shopping meant a boat ride across St. George's Cay to Spanish Wells, a small fishing village.

Mom and baby Jessica on the way to the Bahamas.

Bob and I loved the Bahamian spiny lobsters and octopus, but Mom (and my siblings) didn't even like seafood! With such slim pickings, thank goodness Mom, ever the frugal foodie, had the forethought to bring a full suitcase of frozen food.

Mom enjoyed drifting over the warm coastal waters on her inflatable float – but once my father alerted her to a barracuda swimming around, that was the end of that.

Mom and Dad went to Florida with us many times, as well as Washington D.C., Toronto, and London; and of course we'll never forget our rafting trip to Colorado, where Mom took a tumble into the river.

We also went to Switzerland, where Dad got to ski the Alps, and where we accidentally abandoned him on the slopes one day – a story that still gets plenty of laughs.

We even toured the Greek Isles on a chartered yacht, complete with captain and cook, and while cruising the Aegean Sea, we encountered the most horrendous experience of our lives – a "medicane" – a Mediterranean hurricane, which caused life-threatening waves and torrential rain.

We finally reached safe harbor coming into Siphnos – and yet, despite our near brush with death, all Mom could do was chastise Dad for binocular-gazing at the topless windsurfers. Dad swore that he was watching the fisherman.

But, while titillating vistas and sumptuous accommodations were nice, it wasn't all that important to Dad and Mom, and, despite that one Swiss Alps oopsie, what mattered most of all was being together.

Dana, me, and Dad skiing in the Swiss Alps.

Mom and Dad on the tennis court, at the pool, at Pam's wedding, and ready to go square dancing.

Adventure director Bob during our trip to Greece. No matter where we were, he could always fit right in.

In a cave in Greece. Mom, me, and Pam, and in front of us, Rebekah, Jessica, and Bob.

Mom on a scooter in Greece.

Dad and Mom in Greece.

At left, Dad in Zürich, Switzerland, and at right, Dad at Pam's wedding.

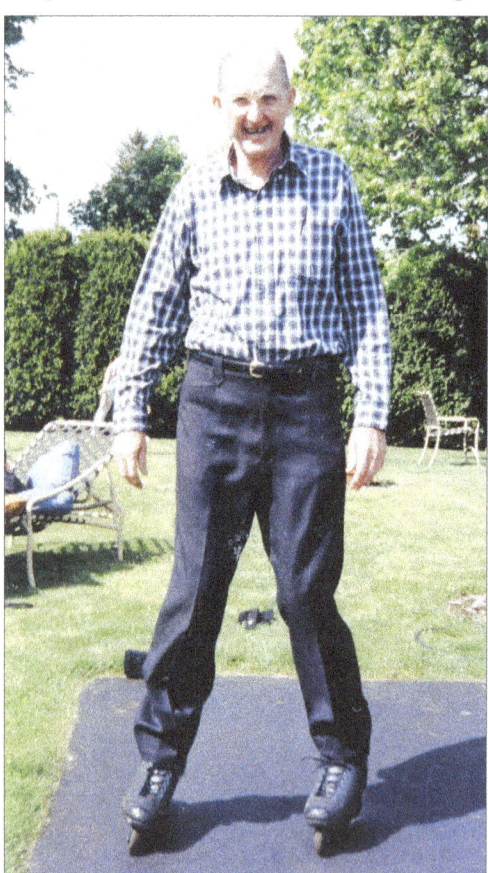

At left, Dad on inline skates, and at right, in his tennis stance.

Sir, You're Having a Heart Attack

Dad was diagnosed with diabetes later in life, but he always managed it well, and it wasn't until 1993 that our happy family had to face what would become the gradual decline of our beloved patriarch.

The day before his first heart attack, Dad was in Newport with Mom, watching the Tennis Hall of Fame championships; they made the twenty-five-mile trip on their motorcycle, with Dad driving and Mom holding on tight behind him.

My daughter Rebekah was a ball girl for the grass court event, and though it was unpaid, she got to meet lots of players, including her favorite, Brian Shelton. She also earned a free food voucher every day – however, as a dedicated vegetarian from a young age (and with no vegetarian options available), she gave all her vouchers to Grandpa, who immediately traded them in for hot dogs.

That night, when Dad started feeling unwell, he was convinced it was just heartburn from the hot dogs, but by morning it was worse, and Dad, never a complainer, debated with Mom as to whether he needed medical attention.

She won, thankfully, and drove him straight to the hospital, where she frantically searched for a wheelchair, which Dad refused, insisting he could walk, which he did, right into the emergency room. He described his symptoms to the doctor, and after an examination and some testing, a nurse placed an ID bracelet on his wrist.

Dad, in disbelief, asked, "Does that mean I'm being admitted?"

The doctor, concerned but perfectly composed, replied, "Sir… you're having a heart attack."

Word spread quickly and all six of us Cross kids rushed to the hospital in Fall River. He had to be transferred to Brigham and Women's Hospital in Boston for a balloon angioplasty, and because we couldn't ride with Dad inside the ambulance, we followed closely behind all the way to Boston – a caravan of Crosses.

We headquartered ourselves in the waiting room, playing cards to pass the time and distract our worried minds, until Dad's surgeon came to the waiting room to give us an update – after careful examination, they determined Dad needed open-heart surgery.

This news was met with a chorus of concern – "What?" – "Oh, my God!" – "When?"

The answer – "Right now."

What started as a straightforward procedure had suddenly become major surgery, so we were given the opportunity to immediately go see Dad as they were prepping him in the operating room.

It was terrifying to see our strong, invincible, fix-everything-and-do-anything-for-anyone-at-anytime Superman of a father looking so vulnerable, but each of us were fortunate to have a special moment with him that day, starting with the youngest, Dana.

Steve, as the oldest, went in last, and just before sedation, Dad whispered something unintelligible. Steve leaned in closer, and then Dad's raspy voice kicked in with full clarity – "Hey, Stevie, I've got a few hundred dollars rolled up in a pair of old green socks. Make sure your mother doesn't throw it out."

Dad was referring to his secret stash of casino cash, which he had stowed in his sock drawer back at home, and his sense of humor was a relief – he had plans to pull through, and we knew he could. But for Steve, it was an overwhelming and devastating realization. Just before he went in to see Dad, he had collapsed in the hospital corridor, sobbing.

"For the first time in my life I curled up against the wall in a fetal position and cried like a little boy," Steve recalled. "My wife Marcia consoled me and suggested I go tell Dad that I loved him," which he did, which brought about another realization – that at forty years old, Steve couldn't remember ever actually telling Dad that he loved him.

From that day on, Steve made sure to tell him at every opportunity, and while we all knew and felt the profound love we shared with Dad, we all started saying it out loud to him a lot more often.

Dad's surgery went well, and his doctors confirmed what we already knew – that our Dad had the biggest heart on the planet – metaphorically, of course. Physically, however, Dad's heart function would continue to weaken over the years. First it was working a fifty percent, then thirty percent, then twenty percent, but even as his heart's physical capacity diminished, his doctor always liked to say that Dad's heart was still bigger than all of ours combined.

Two photos from the 1990s – one of me and Mom, and one of Pam, me, and Mom.

1994

If there's one year that's especially hard for me to look back on, it's 1994. Mom was sixty-seven and in her prime – dancing, adventuring, and playing a mean game of pitch – and Dad, having bounced back from his heart attack the year before, was doing really well.

Then Mom found a lump in her breast, and the diagnosis was devastating – it was cancer, and her doctor recommended a mastectomy.

"Mrs. Cross, we have excellent post-operative reconstructive surgery," the doctor added, hoping to ease concerns about her appearance.

Without missing a beat, Mom looked over at Dad and asked, "Irving, would it be OK if I had just one breast?"

Dad's reply – "Of course, Alzada. I love you any way you are."

That was their love, unconditional and unwavering, both for each other and for all six of their children, and as their children, we supported Mom however we could, sometimes without even knowing it.

Take, for example, the day that Mom, while on her way to a doctor's appointment, was pulled over by a Providence police officer after rolling through a stop sign. She apologized, explaining that she was a bit lost, and then added – "Would it make a difference if I told you my son was a police officer?"

When the officer heard it was Detective Steve Cross, he immediately asked where she needed to go and gave her a police escort straight to the front entrance of the medical building – a small reminder that even in life's difficult moments, humility and humor can go a long way.

Mom's surgery was scheduled for May 24, 1994, at Miriam Hospital in Providence. We gathered around her bedside and tried to be strong, but it was Mom – the one awaiting major life-saving surgery – who was the bravest and strongest of us all.

When we were told the surgery would take at least five hours, I half-jokingly suggested we head to Foxwoods Casino to pass the time, and that is exactly what we did. Even Dad came along, and for a few hours, we distracted ourselves from the nerve-wracking wait.

The surgery went well, and a few days later, Reverend Don Mier from First Baptist Church came by to visit Mom in the hospital. Steve happened to be visiting, and when the Reverend commented on how lucky she was to have such a supportive family, Mom just couldn't resist a little sarcasm – "Oh, yes! They were really concerned! So concerned, they all took off to Foxwoods!"

We all had a good laugh, but in truth, it wasn't our finest moment; it certainly wasn't mine. As much as we all tried to keep things lighthearted, 1994 was a year that weighed heavily on me in many ways, and at forty-two, I was facing the most stressful period of my life.

My marriage was unraveling, and as I watched my parents' strong partnership continue to flourish, I found myself questioning why I couldn't create the same fairy tale marriage they seemed to have.

Bob and I separated and I moved with the kids – ages seventeen, fifteen, and nine, at the time – into a rental home in Irvington, New York, where they had to start over in new schools and make new friends, forever leaving behind their beloved childhood home, Bridlepath in Newport. Leaving felt like losing a part of ourselves, because Bridlepath wasn't just a place, it was the major centerpiece of so many happy memories.

At the same time, I was also transitioning from a decade of volunteer work as CEO of the HOPE Program to a full-time job as Senior VP at the South Bronx Economic Development Corporation. It was a whirlwind of change, and the financial strain of my soon-to-be ex-husband's real estate ventures was only making things more difficult. Eventually I was forced to file for bankruptcy due to debt associated with a few commercial developments going bad, including a high-rise in Texas that went into default during the oil market collapse of the 1980s.

But leave it to Dad to find the bright side. In an attempt to lighten my somber mood as we left the courthouse, he pulled my bankruptcy discharge papers out of his pocket and said – "You know, sweetheart, you really have to be somebody to owe fourteen million dollars."

He had a way of reminding me that perspective is everything. It was a waste of time and energy to keep pitying myself, especially when I'd just witnessed another woman actually lose everything in bankruptcy court over an unpaid JCPenney bill.

So, when we received the news of Mom's cancer, it was a pain I just couldn't bear, and I became a ghost of myself for weeks after her diagnosis, gliding through the days as best I could, trying to maintain a graceful façade, suffocating the anxiety that was building within me. I just didn't want to feel it, which is probably the same reason we all ended up at the casino during Mom's mastectomy.

Looking back from a distance of decades, I now see that whenever life felt unbearably heavy in the moment, the loving light of our family always shone through the gloom in one way or another, an inexhaustible flame of strength, resilience, and of course, humor.

Mom and Dad dancing at their 50th anniversary celebration.

Grammy and Grandpa with their ten grandchildren on their 50th wedding anniversary. Standing, from left to right: Jessica, Allan, Mom, Benjamin, Dad, Sarah, and Alexandra. Seated, from left to right: Cody, Dylan, Kayla, Rebekah, and Brian.

Fifty Wonderful Years

Dad's health improved for a while, and as the world anxiously anticipated the arrival of the chaos "Y2K" was rumored to bring, the Crosses were counting down to a different sort of once-in-a-lifetime occasion – Mr. and Mrs. Wonderful's fiftieth wedding anniversary!

In February of 2000, more than 100 family members and friends gathered in Swansea at the legendary Venus de Milo restaurant and banquet hall for a beautiful and very elegant affair *a la* Cross. Dad looked downright dashing in his dapper tuxedo, with a big white rose pinned to his lapel, and Mom was a vision of elegance in an exquisite ivory ensemble.

The celebration of their golden anniversary featured live music by the Bobby Justin Band, whose eponymous bandleader got his start at Durfee High in Fall River. Mom, also a Durfee High alumna, performed a touchingly beautiful solo rendition of "Love Me Tender," and Dad stole the show with an uproariously funny speech and a few tunes of his own.

Mom and Dad danced to one of their songs, "Could I Have this Dance," and they pulled out all of their tricks, which kept us, their audience, on the verge of both laughter and tears at every turn. They were both in their seventies and could still really cut a rug!

There was lots of dancing, love, and laughter, and, best of all, lots of memories, home movies, and photographs from that special celebration. One of my favorite photos shows Mom and Dad surrounded by all ten of their grandchildren – Mom is absolutely beaming with what I can only describe as pure happiness, the afterglow of fifty wonderful years.

Mom singing with Bobby Justin at her 50th anniversary celebration.

Dad with his four sons on his 50th wedding anniversary. From left, Dana, Steve, Dave, Dad, and Brian.

The summer after Mom and Dad's 50th anniversary in February 2000, we celebrated the wedding of Jessica and Abdessalam.

A photo of Mom (and me, behind her) from a trip to New York City. While the unspeakable horror and tragedy of September 11, 2001, was two decades into the future from when this was taken, I've included this photo because I've heard that, when collecting photos of the thousands of souls lost that day, to be displayed in the museum at Ground Zero, the curators intentionally chose photos of people smiling – living people pictured in moments of joy, memorializing their passing by celebrating their lives.

September 11th

That fateful Tuesday in 2001 began with an extraordinarily beautiful morning, and just an hour or two before the world changed, I was doing what I did every weekday morning – going to work.

At the time I was CEO of the nonprofit organization Per Scholas, and our office was actually more like a warehouse – a 100,000 square foot facility in the American Banknote Building in the South Bronx – where our main focus was recycling and refurbishing old computers for local schools and families in need. Our Chief Operating Officer, Plinio Ayala, and I always got in early to greet our team of forty employees, but we were also expecting a visit from our board chairman, John Stookey, first thing that morning.

As John, Plinio, and I got started with our meeting, a consultant we were expecting to join us called the office and told us she couldn't make it from Brooklyn to the Bronx because a plane had just struck the North Tower of the World Trade Center. Shocked, we immediately told our team, and then gathered at the windows by the freight elevators, where we had a clear line of sight down the East River.

Some of us remembered the bombing of the World Trade Center back in 1993, but as we observed the smoke billowing out of the North Tower, none of us could be certain if it was another attack or just a horrible accident. But then we witnessed the explosion of the second plane striking the South Tower, and as we looked on in total disbelief, some of us held hands, some prayed.

And then, as we waited by the window, and as millions more were watching on TV screens across the country and around the world, the South Tower collapsed, followed a half hour later by the collapse of the North Tower. There was tremendous confusion and fear, and everyone was immediately dismissed from work. Plinio and I scrambled to find ways to get our employees and students home, and then I set about checking in with my own children.

My son-in-law, Abdessalam, was working in the city that morning. I later learned, after many hours walking several miles, he finally made it safely home to my daughter Jessica in Yonkers – but, as a Muslim American, Ab would soon face the evils of prejudice and xenophobia that ensued.

My youngest daughter, Allie, was in boarding school in New Lebanon, New York, so I tried calling her, but because the landline and cellular networks were overwhelmed by the high volume of people all trying to do exactly what I was trying to do, I kept getting an "all circuits are busy" message. I couldn't reach her by phone, so I jumped in the car and made the three-hour 150-mile drive to get to her – and there she was, waiting in the lobby, hoping I would come! We embraced a long while, and then we went to a local church, where we sat quietly and prayed. I then withdrew her from school, and we drove home.

My middle daughter, Rebekah, who was studying at the University of North Carolina Charlotte, was getting ready for class when she heard the news – and she immediately panicked when she remembered that her father was supposed to be taking a flight that morning.

Bob recalls being on the runway at JFK, about to take off, when the pilot informed the passengers that there was a big fire at the World Trade Center. Minutes later, as they were taking off, Bob was looking out the window as the second plane hit the South Tower.

All flights across the country were grounded soon after, and his plane was forced to land in Raleigh, North Carolina – which is, coincidentally, only about 160 miles northeast of where Rebekah was in Charlotte.

Rebekah was relieved her father was safe, but she soon heard the devastating news that one of her high school friends, Tara, had lost her father, Robert Speisman, who was a passenger on the plane that struck the Pentagon in Washington, D.C. A few days later, we all went to his memorial service at Matthiessen Park in Irvington, where hundreds of people had gathered to mourn his passing and celebrate his life.

His wife was unable to speak, but the oldest of his three daughters, Tara – who just months ago had delivered her valedictorian speech at her high school graduation – went to the microphone. After a few moments, struggling for air between sobs, she said, "Dad, I know you are here with us. I feel you, and I hear you saying the same comforting words you've always said – 'Breathe, baby, breathe.'"

A Dadism if I've ever heard one, which is probably why I've never forgotten. Her words – and her father's words – meant so much to me then, and have only grown more meaningful to me over time.

In the days that followed, I soon heard from my dear friend and mentor, Father Rand Frew, who is also Allie's godfather. A loving and vibrant person and a wise influence on me and all my children, Father Frew was also a great date – and dancer – and accompanied me to many a social or charitable event in Newport and New York.

I first met Father Frew when he invited me to serve at the soup kitchen he founded at Holy Apostles Church in 1983, where he was the rector. Father Frew became my inspiration for forming the HOPE Program, which provided job training and support for people experiencing chronic homelessness, and he was also the founder of AIDS Action International, for which I had the honor to serve as a board member.

He spent much of his time in Thailand, but whenever he was stateside, we would get together for lunch, and he would reverently open his photo journal and tell me about each person in the book, all of them suffering from complications caused by AIDS. He comforted them in the last days of their lives, and these people, some quite young, shamed and shunned by their families and friends, who would have otherwise died alone, passed from life to death in the warm, loving company of Father Frew.

On 9/11, Father Frew was in New York, and he went straight to Ground Zero, where he provided the same loving support, care, and spiritual guidance to the first responders and volunteers working around the clock in extremely hazardous conditions to clear debris and search for remains.

Nearby St. Paul's Chapel became a symbol of resilience and hope during recovery efforts, and Father Frew was there for nine straight months – serving meals, lending a compassionate ear, and praying with the many who were traumatized by the horrors of that day and its aftermath.

A true hero, a person of faith and action, Father Frew passed away at the age of seventy-five in December of 2022, after twenty-one years of respiratory challenges related to his service at Ground Zero.

When I learned of Father Frew's passing in January 2023, I was still so absorbed in the grief of losing Mom two months prior that I didn't fully mourn his loss, something I didn't even realize until 2024, nearly two years after he was gone.

He called me in October of 2022, remembering Mom's birthday, and he said he wasn't doing very well, but he was comfortable. That would be the last time we spoke.

Not everyone gets to have two wonderful "fathers" in their life, but I did, and there will always be a special place in my heart for my dearest of friends, Father Frew.

Father Frew, Jess, Ab, and me in 2008, the night before Jess gave birth to my twin granddaughters.

Me and my dear friend, Father Rand Frew.

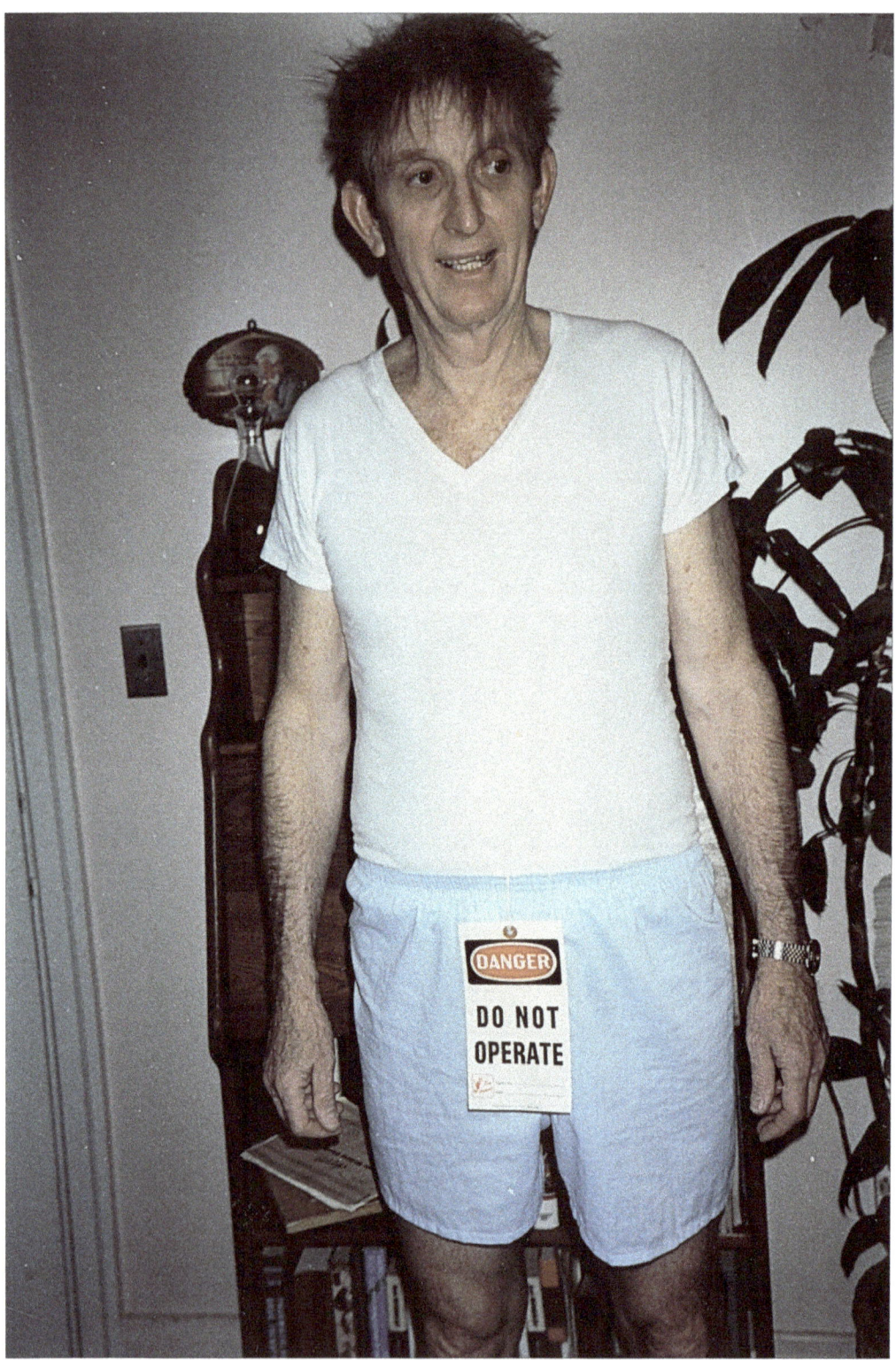

Dad doing what he did best – making us (and the hospital team) laugh!

Everybody Called Him Mr. Wonderful

Dad was living life with gusto after recovering from his open-heart surgery, until complications from his diabetes started affecting his feet.

As I've mentioned, while Dad was in the military, he learned how to properly care for his feet – and about the horrors of trench foot in World War I. Ever since then, he'd taken meticulous care of his positively beautiful feet, and taught all of us to do the same.

But in 2002, a mysterious sore appeared on one of Dad's toes, and when it refused to heal, his doctors decided the toe had to be amputated to prevent the infection from spreading. But then, on the same foot, another even worse sore appeared on a different toe, and it quickly became a deepening hole, which also required amputation.

Despite the medical team's every effort, the removal of the two toes didn't resolve the problem, and the doctors had no choice but to amputate Dad's foot to save his leg – and his life.

We were distraught. Our father losing his whole foot? It was so gruesome, so extreme. How could he lose something he depended on so much? What would become of our active, able-bodied father? How would he dance – how would he even walk?

But Dad, always the optimist, was courageous, believing there was life as long as you have breath. And if he was ever afraid – of his decline, of losing his foot, of his eventual death – he never showed it.

When surgery day came, we all gathered in the waiting room at St. Anne's Hospital, where our sister Pam was a nurse. There we waited, heartsick and solemn, and when Dad was finally wheeled into his room, we asked him how the surgery went.

"Piece of cake…" he said, smiling, still groggy from the anesthesia.

The medical team had hoped that amputating his foot would both stop the infection from spreading and improve Dad's blood flow, but his circulation continued to deteriorate, and his doctors later delivered more bad news – they would have to amputate Dad's leg below the knee.

Once again, we were all terrified, but not Dad, who was bewilderingly positive as they wheeled him into the operating room. We all cheered and applauded when we saw him come out of recovery with the biggest smile on his face, and he gave us a thumbs up, showing off his bandaged leg as he passed. He was feeling triumphant for beating back the disease – and ready to face the grueling physical therapy which awaited him.

No matter how hard it was for him, Dad never missed physical therapy, and he made it his duty to keep the atmosphere light-hearted – and this made Dad everyone's favorite patient, earning him the nickname of "Mr. Wonderful."

The nurses, the doctors, everybody called him Mr. Wonderful, and everybody loved him. Instead of complaining, he would make everyone laugh by cracking jokes. For instance, when a doctor once asked him if, should the need arise, he would want to be resuscitated, Dad quipped, "Maybe a little bit…if you think it would help."

And that was Dad, always offering a little light in the darkest of times, and perhaps that's why we never knew if he was worried or scared; perhaps that's how he kept the dark thoughts at bay – with light and laughter.

I had to avert my eyes from the fleshy overlap where his leg abruptly ended, but I got used to it, and eventually he was fitted with a prosthesis. It was a hassle to put on and uncomfortable to wear, but essential for maintaining his active lifestyle, and it was both heart-wrenching and inspirational to witness his resolve.

Dad persisted no matter what, always the epitome of positivity, but his heart was growing weaker by the day, and eventually his other leg had to be amputated. We gathered again in his hospital room, where there was just enough space for all six of us kids to sleep overnight, and early the next morning, a gift arrived from the nursing team – fresh coffee, juice, and pastries. I cried then, and still tear up when I remember the thoughtful generosity and support they showed our family – and Mr. Wonderful.

Our sister, our Nurse Pam, helped care for Dad, a profound blessing to all us siblings, and as our brother Steve has said, "No matter what the doctors told Dad, he would always say that he wanted to talk with Pammy before making any decisions."

With Pam's help, Mom cared for Dad at home after every surgery, and despite the obstacles, Dad was determined to keep living. He made a promise to spend every precious second with his family, and Dad always kept his promises, including the final one he made to me.

He was in home hospice care at the time, and as we were talking, he said to me, only sort of seriously – "Well, you know, sweetheart, I'm thinking of checking out."

I implored Dad to extend his stay long enough to hold his first two grandchildren, and he promised me that he would live to meet them – and he did! Jessica gave birth to Leila and Meriem on May 29, 2008. Anxious to see her ailing Grandpa, Jessica then traveled with her two-week-old twins from New York to Massachusetts for Father's Day weekend.

True to his word, when they arrived on Saturday, June 14th, Dad was propped up with pillows in bed, Mom snuggled close beside him, and together, for the first time, they joyously held their new great-grandchildren in their arms.

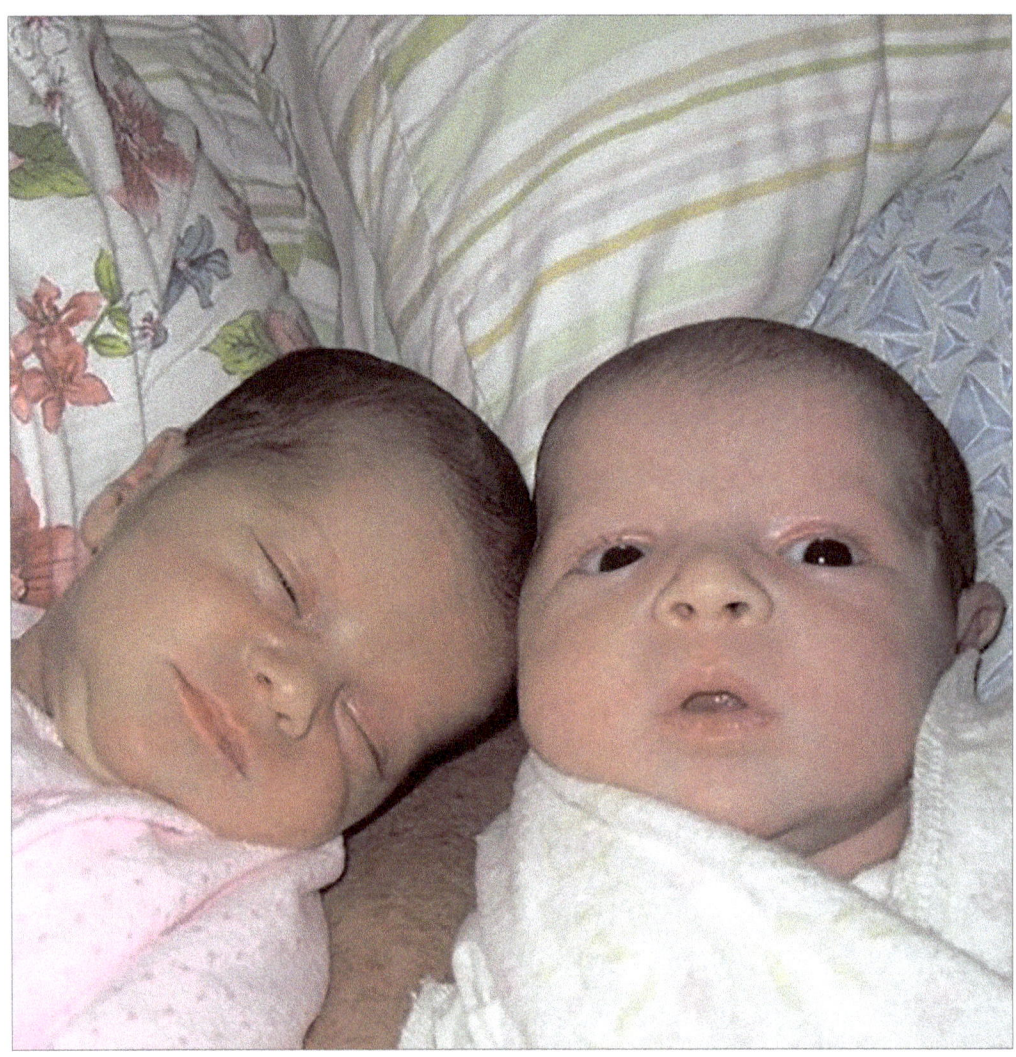

Newborn twins Leila and Meriem, my first grandchildren – and the first Cross great-grandchildren, pictured here in the arms of their loving great-grandparents, just hours before Mr. Wonderful passed away on Father's Day, June 15, 2008.

Father's Day

Early the next morning, Father's Day, June 15, 2008, my sister Pam and I were taking turns looking in on Dad as he slept in Mom's loving arms, the same position he slept in throughout their married life. On my last pre-dawn visit to their bedroom, I discovered Dad still nestled in Mom's arms, but gone. He was eighty-one.

It was the most profound sadness that had ever befallen us, and all six of us gathered with Mom in our parents' bedroom, where we cried together and sang "Angel Flying Too Close to the Ground" by Willie Nelson, a favorite song of Dad's that he always used to sing to Mom.

Mom then pulled out a letter Steve sent Dad after his first heart surgery some fifteen years earlier, and asked him to read it. Steve, surprised and touched that Dad had saved it, cried as he read the letter, the last paragraph of which made it into Dad's eulogy:

"After surgery, I saw you in the very fragile balance of life itself. After being with you for a short time, I began to stroke your forehead and to hold and squeeze your hand. I don't know why I did this. I think I did it because it was what you did to me as a young child. It was soothing to hold your hand and to talk to you by whispering in your ear that I loved you. Our hand contact triggered all my childhood memories of us together.

"Although I know death is inevitable for all of us, when that exact moment comes, I will pray that I will be holding your hand and stroking your hair, and yes, I will still be a confused and angry little boy who is heartbroken that my daddy is no longer with me. After my grief, I will be an elderly man who has found great inner peace within me knowing that I had such a beautiful and loving relationship with you and Mom. You are my hero. You are my best friend."

Steve's prayer was answered, and our entire family was with Dad, holding his hand, stroking his hair, kissing him, and telling him we loved him until the very end.

We were hesitant to have his physical body leave us, and as he was finally carried out, departing our family home for the last time, I forced myself to watch as the attendants, with the greatest care and respect, lifted his body into the hearse.

Life would go on, but first we had to put together the perfect funeral. Nothing was prepared in advance because none of us wanted to admit Dad was dying, so the next few days we were unified in the task of planning a memorial that would honor the extraordinary man we called Mr. Wonderful.

Making arrangements gave us all something to do while we were otherwise too grief-stricken to function – phone calls, obituary, photos, casket, flowers, calling hours, catering – and more importantly, the funeral service itself – the readings, the music selections, and the eulogy, to be delivered by Steve, Dad's oldest child, with input from all the rest of us.

We distracted ourselves from our sorrow with the details of Dad's funeral, and as all the happy memories of Dad flooded our minds, we often found ourselves laughing through the tears. As you can imagine, we were hearing "I'm sorry" a lot – sorriness for the loss of this man who would be mourned and missed by so many – and it reminds me of one of my favorite Dadisms.

If someone said, "I'm sorry" to Dad, he would reply, always with a grin – *"Well, you're sorry and I'm Cross!"*

This ironic Dadism was particularly funny because our Dad was NEVER cross, and he deserved a commemoration befitting a life that was neither sorry nor cross, only wonderful – and it was!

L'Chaim!

Dad's funeral was held on June 18, 2008. For me, with a birthday on the eighteenth of January, the number eighteen has always been special to me, but it wasn't until we lost Dad that I delved into the number's deep cultural significance, especially in the Jewish faith.

Each letter in the Hebrew alphabet has a corresponding numerical value, and the two letters, *Chet*, with a value of eight, and *Bud*, with a value of ten, make up the Hebrew word *Chai*, which means "living."

The number eighteen, symbolized by *Chai*, also influences the tradition of giving charity, or "giving *chai*" in multiples of eighteen, as well as the expression *"L'Chaim!"* – which is often heard on special occasions as a celebratory toast meaning, "to life!"

Giving and living to the fullest – that was Dad, our Mr. Wonderful. More than 200 people attended the funeral – the guestbook entries were eleven pages long – and all of these people who knew and loved him came to celebrate his extraordinary spirit and his remarkable life. Even his cardiologist was there.

Steve's eulogy beautifully reflected our father's legacy – his kindness, his generosity, his radiant spirit – and what follows are condensed excerpts from Steve's loving tribute.

"Dad never complained about his situation at any time. Come to think of it, Dad never complained about anything. He loved to make his family laugh. Whether it was reading funny telephone numbers, lying on the kitchen table as Frankenstein with a sheet over him, or joking around with the garden hose, spraying whoever was in his path – even if you were in the house you were not safe. By the way, it didn't have to be Halloween for him to lie on the kitchen table as Frankenstein.

"Dad's zest for life was contagious and permeated all our lives. He didn't think about helping people, he just did it, and he never expected anything in return. He knew that doing the right thing was reward enough. Dad led by example, and his children and those around him admired him for his integrity, kindness, and generosity, and especially for his big wide smile.

"I asked Dad recently if there was anything he wanted me to do when he passed away. He told me there were only a few things for me to do – take care of Mom; make sure all the children and grandchildren spend as much time as they can with each other; and the last thing he told me to do is tell the children and grandchildren that he loved them with all his heart."

Steve ended with, *"Dad, thanks for everything – and save a place for all of us at the heavenly card table."*

I remember thinking – *Let the games begin, Dad!* – and as the emotional service ended, our family members were the last to leave. The grandchildren who were big enough helped carry Dad's casket out to the hearse and, quite appropriately, a police honor guard on motorcycle led the procession to Mount Hope cemetery.

The song "Angel Flying Too Close to the Ground" inspired the design etched on his headstone – two gliding angels on mahogany granite, and a pair of intertwined wedding bands with the date of his and Mom's anniversary. And as we laid him to rest, we sang…

I knew someday that you would fly away,
For love's the greatest healer to be found,
So, leave me if you need to, I will still remember,
Angel flying too close to the ground.

Grammy Alzada, surrounded by her ten grandchildren and newborn twin great-grandchildren, on the day of Dad's celebration of life.

Dad's headstone in Mount Hope Cemetery, Swansea.

Mom in her early nineties – hair and makeup by me!

The Golden Years

We worried how Mom was going to manage her grief after Dad passed away. She was approaching her eighty-second birthday and still healthy, but emotionally exhausted. Luckily, Pam was with her several days a week, taking her to appointments, running errands, and doing things around the house. You can take Nurse Pam out of the hospital, but you can't take the nurse out of Pam, and all her siblings are so grateful for the dedicated care she gave both our parents over the years.

True to form, our resilient and spirited mother didn't just survive, she thrived – living another fourteen fruitful years, all because of her active social schedule and family life – a whole new chapter of glorious golden years which included many new adventures and celebrations.

Mom was always bright and very intelligent, as well as a crafty cruciverbalist and champion card player, and she was still beating us by a mile on tough crossword puzzles and at the card table well into her eighties. But it was always her family that interested her most, and she was so happy when "all six" of us siblings were present. The worst offense we could commit was not showing up, especially to a planned event, such as Sunday suppers in Swansea, a tradition which continues to this day. But we never skipped an opportunity for quality time with Mom, because we loved being with her.

During this golden era, Grammy Alzada – the albatross – had five more wonderful great-grandchildren, one every two years: Luke (2014); Noah (2016); Madeline (2018); Rylee (2020); and Juliette (2022). She was also part of five more weddings: my brother Dana and Sawako (2010); Clarel and I (2010); my daughter Rebekah and Jeff (2014); my daughter Allie and JP (2019); and my niece Sarah and Matthew (2019).

There were countless family birthdays and holidays, and while the memories are happy, one of these Christmas celebrations stands out because of an incident that was particularly harrowing – and later humorous, of course.

We were all gathered at Steve's house, and after we had feasted, it was time for games. Everyone broke into teams for charades, and during Mom's turn, as she was acting out *The Lion King*, she made an enthusiastic feline leap – and fell to the floor, roly-poly style, with her head landing just inches away from the crackling fireplace. An admirable dramatic effort, but not good for a woman in her nineties on blood-thinning medication. As a precaution, we took her to her doctor, who, of course, asked how she fell.

Mom chuckled a bit as she began to explain – "Well, I was playing charades with the kids, and I was acting out *The Lion King*…"

The doctor roared with laughter, but advised her to "Please, just be a little more careful next time."

As Mom's mobility decreased and her medical needs increased, none of us wanted to even think about her being in a nursing home, and that's when, in 2017, our brother Brian made the heroic decision to move in with Mom and take care of her.

And then there was COVID. Every day, thousands of people were dying – especially the elderly – and we did all we could to keep Mom safe. Just before Christmas in 2020, Brian and I drove Mom 1,500 miles from Swansea to my home in Florida so that we could take advantage of the governor's plan for all seniors to be first in line for the vaccine.

As soon as it was available, we put Mom in a wheelchair and joined the long winding line, where we waited for more than eight hours. We witnessed heartwarming camaraderie while in line, with folks donating water and snacks, as well as blankets for the cooler morning temperatures, and fans in the late afternoon when the temperature was, like Mom, well over ninety. But, oh, the joy when it was our turn!

The Happily Ever After

Four generations in the pool, from left to right – my daughter Jessica, my granddaughter Meriem, me (Zizza), my brother Brian, Grammy, my daughter Allie, and my granddaughter Leila.

Great-Grammy Alzada, looking fabulous in her sun hat.

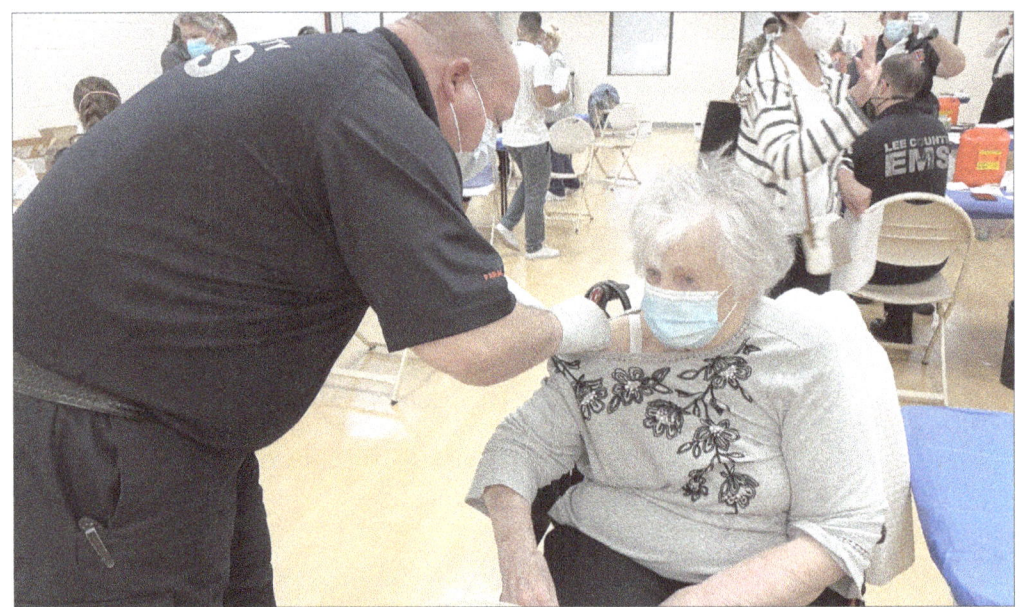

At top, Mom getting her COVID vaccine. Below, Puzzlemaster Mom.

We have a photo from that day, and although Mom has her mask on, rest assured that getting a shot in the arm never felt so good!

We affectionately referred to Mom as "the package" whenever she was in transit between siblings – our precious cargo – and after spending the 2020 holidays in Florida, we transported her back to Massachusetts, where she and Steve resumed their weekly ritual of dinner and cards at the club every Wednesday night.

Of course, Mom also had Brian taking care of her every need, from appointments and medications to her nutrition and exercise – and most importantly, her entertainment! They would play cards together for hours at a time, which no doubt helped keep her mind active and engaged, along with all her puzzles.

Pam, who was still working full time at the hospital, would come over almost every day to help her bathe, do her laundry, and make her favorite tapioca pudding. Dave and Dana, who lived nearby, would also visit often, and every month I would visit for a few days from New York.

Because I lived the farthest away from Mom, I was the child who got to sashay into Swansea and whisk her away for special day trips and exciting excursions – like getting her hair and nails done, or going out to lunch – and to Macy's, the only place she liked to shop, and always for Alfred Dunner, her favorite clothing brand – and always with coupons.

But, like always, no matter what we were doing, the most important thing was simply being together, because, while I knew we were always going to have fun, I also knew that Alzada the Wonderful's golden age couldn't last forever.

Mom gets ready to blow out the candles at her 90th birthday celebration in October of 2016. From left to right are me, Steve, Brian, Mom, Pam, and Clarel.

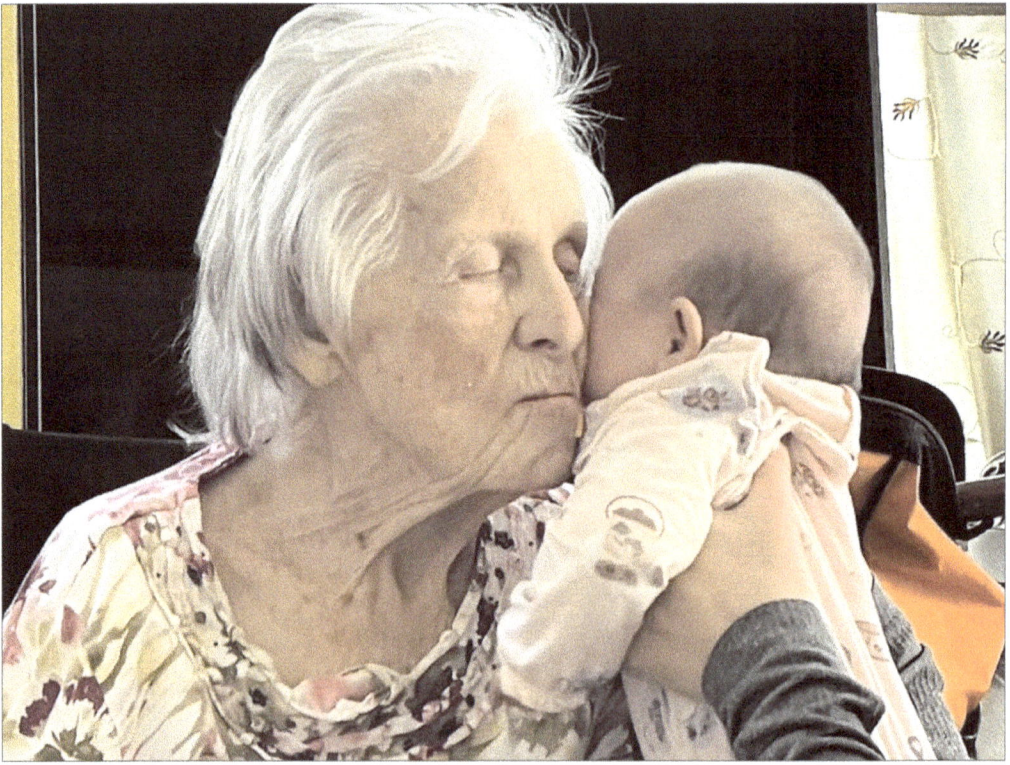

Great-Grammy Alzada, celebrating her 96th birthday, gives her new great-granddaughter, Juliette, a kiss in October of 2022.

Lasts & Firsts

We celebrated Mom's ninetieth birthday in 2016 by throwing a huge party in her honor. With more than 100 guests in attendance, we showed a special film produced by a close friend, filmmaker Eduardo Caraballo, a truly touching tribute, followed by lots of merrymaking and music. Everyone danced, especially Mom, and when it was time for cake, the happiness on her face shone brighter than her birthday candles.

We were lucky to celebrate six more of Mom's birthdays, and as her physical and mental health slowly declined, I came to a new understanding of what "quality time" meant for us. Shopping and salon trips were once my special way of spending time with her, but she no longer needed or wanted me to *do* things with her – she simply wanted me to *be* with her.

I had to learn how to be still, and I now cherish the time we spent just silently holding hands as much as any of our special moments together.

Mom began hospice care in early 2022, but she surprised us all with a sudden spark of improvement just in time to celebrate her ninety-sixth birthday at Steve's house. It was a beautiful gathering of "all six" children, all of Mom's grandchildren, and her seven great-grandchildren, including the newest addition to the family, baby Juliette, who Mom got to hold and kiss for the first time.

Not long after this joyous celebration, Mom stopped talking and eating, silently signaling that she would soon be leaving us. All six of us kept watch, with Pam and I taking turns snuggling up next to her as she slept.

A few days before she passed away, as Mom and I were dozing in her bed, she suddenly exclaimed – "Where's my pocketbook? I need my pocketbook! I have to find it. Dad's waiting outside on the motorcycle!"

She never spoke again after that, but it comforted me to experience the echoes of her wonderful life through her dreams of seeing Dad again.

Mom passed away in the early hours of November 7th (*L'chaim!* – as 11+7=18, you see). We had a bit more time to prepare for her funeral, and we all helped with the arrangements – and once again, we nominated Steve to deliver the eulogy, an excerpt of which follows.

"We love you Mom – forever. Our fond memories of you will be a comfort to us for the rest of our lives, and we will continue to be a strong family, sharing our stories with much laughter. Laughter was and still is the centerpiece of the affection we have for each other. At 2:40 a.m. this past Monday, Mom took her last breath. It was a surreal moment in our lives, and I will never forget Pam and Deborah lying in the bed with Mom after she passed. Pam and Deb were exhausted and had closed their eyes.

"Shortly after this, the funeral director arrived, and Brian and I were in the living room to greet her and her assistant. They expressed their condolences as Brian led them into the bedroom. Upon seeing Mom and my two sisters lying in the bed, my brother says to them – 'My mother is the one on the left.' I don't know if Brian was just trying to be helpful to the funeral director, or if he was reassuring us that humor was still alive and well in our family."

The humor certainly helped us get through the ensuing series of somber commemorations of "firsts" without Mom – first Thanksgiving, first Christmas, first Easter, first Mother's Day, and all the birthdays and anniversaries in between and afterwards. Thankfully, we have so many happy memories of "lasts" and holidays-past with both Mom and Dad, memories full of love and laughter.

Though I miss them both more and more each day, I know Mom and Dad are reunited, and their love and kindness will live on in all who loved them, and still on in the ones we love, and so on, until we all meet and laugh again.

Our love will live on in our children.

*Inscription on the headstone of
Mr. & Mrs. Wonderful*

PART VII

A Wonderful Legacy

1960s – present

Irving *married* Alzada
(1927-2008)   1950   (1926-2022)

- **Steve** → Sarah → Rylee
- **Deborah** → Jessica, Rebekah, Alexandra
  - Leila, Meriem
  - Luke, Noah, Madeline, Juliette
- **Pam** → Cody
- **Dave**
- **Brian** → Allan, Benjamin, Brian
- **Dana** → Dylan, Kayla

Cross Children Marriages
Steve & Marcia Lombardo, 1972
Deborah & Bob MacFarlane, 1975 *(divorced)*
Dana & Linda Urbowicz, 1985 *(divorced)*
Pamela & Mark Antaya, 1987
Brian & Eleana Serrano, 1987 *(divorced)*
David & Theresa Burns, 2001
Dana & Sawako Fukushima, 2010
Deborah & Clarel Antoine, 2010

Cross Grandchildren Marriages
Jessica & Abdessalam Hamdoun, 2000
Rebekah & Jeff Barney, 2014
Alexandra & JP Prettybull, 2019
Sarah & Matthew Lennon, 2019
Dylan & Julia Picha, 2024
Brian & Natalie Mendez, 2024

A Wonderful Legacy

I'M FOREVER GRATEFUL for all the time I had with Mom and Dad, and for being part of the wonderful legacy they created.

The Cross kids are all mostly retired now, each with our own assortment of age-related ailments or injuries – for me, it was shoulder surgery in 2022 and a torn hamstring in 2023.

Like our parents, we're incredibly fortunate to be living our lives to the fullest, seeing our adult children, nieces, and nephews flourishing in their careers and families, and watching our grandchildren begin to find their way in the world.

I'm blessed to be who I am today, having led such a full, fun life, and it all started with my parents and the values they instilled in me and my siblings. When we were growing up and figuring things out, Dad would advise us with the aspirational adage – *"Do something you love, and you'll never work a day in your life"* – and when Dad advises, you listen up!

While we all had the same wonderful upbringing and went to all the same public schools – including Joseph Case High School in Swansea (Go, Cardinals!) – after graduation, we each went on to live fulfilling lives in our own unique ways.

And yet, we've also managed to stay connected all this time – and not just at our mandatory annual Christmas celebrations! Over the years, the phone calls and letters between our trips and visits were gradually enhanced by emails, and then text messages – which now includes our family group chat, where we post our results from the daily *New York Times* Wordle and Connections puzzles (Brian the Brain is usually winning, but Jessica is always on his heels).

And, while we're not getting a Grammy award any time soon, we do make a fine singing group – and by fine, I mostly mean loud. When we all get together, there's nothing anyone can do to silence our spontaneous singalongs – except maybe Jessica, who stars in one of our funniest you-had-to-be-there family moments.

We siblings were downstairs playing cards, and Jessica was upstairs trying to get her twin baby girls down for the night. About as soon as they fell asleep, the singalong spirit suddenly moved us to shout and clap our way through several rounds of "John Jacob Jingleheimer Schmidt." But somehow, Jess was able to trample all over our tra-la-las by yelling a single word at us – "SERIOUSLY?!"

She was cross and we were sorry – just not as sorry as she was cross – and we so-called elders exploded in a brief burst of hysterical laughter, followed by a very rare silence.

Like comedy, music is all about timing, and in the rhythm of life, the Crazy Crosses have always marched to our own beat, a carefree cadence marked with enthusiasm and love. The same way a symphony is made up of different instruments – some bold and brassy, others subtle and steady, with so many tones and tenors in between – each of us brings something special to our family's unique composition.

And so, in the spirit of *"all for one and one for all,"* here goes one last Crossketeer curtain call!

At left, me dancing with Dad, and at right, me and Mom dancing at her 90th birthday party.

All six with Mom and Dad in the early 2000s – singing the theme song from "The Addams Family." In front are me, Mom, and Pam, and behind us are Brian, Dana, Dave, Steve, and Dad.

At left, Steve's senior photo. At right, a newspaper photo of Steve with Marcia, taken after he won a bronze medal for the decathlon at the 1972 National Police Olympics in Tulsa, Oklahoma.

Marcia and Steve on their wedding day in 1972 with Mom and Dad.

Steve the Storyteller

In Steve's senior high school yearbook, he listed his ambition as college – but by the time he graduated, he knew his heart was set on becoming a police officer, his dream since childhood.

The year 1971 was a big one for Steve: he joined the police force in Providence, and not long after he met a pretty brunette named Marcia Lombardo. According to Marcia, "It was love at first sight and we've been together ever since."

Sound familiar? And just like Dad and Mom, Steve and Marcia were married less than a year after they met. It was a big Italian wedding in Providence, and we were all there to celebrate. Dad sported a full beard and looked really cool, and Mom was stunning in her blond bouffant updo and pale blue dress. That beautiful day, the first Cross kid wedding, kicked off five decades of feasting and storytelling and laughing and loving – always with gusto – with our new extended Lombardo family.

Steve was with the Providence Police Department for twenty-five years, first as an officer and then as a detective, and then he embarked on another twenty-five-year career as a lead investigator with the Rhode Island Ethics Commission, from which he retired in 2021.

Towards the end of his five-decade career, Steve also had a five-year "side gig" giving joy and comfort to ailing children and worried parents with his yellow lab, Duke, a therapy dog that became well-known and loved throughout the Providence hospital system. It was my niece Sarah who originally adopted Duke, but after bonding with the pup while dog-sitting, Steve and Duke were inseparable, and together they completed therapy dog training and went to work.

Duke retired from being a therapy dog when he was eight, and his final visit to Hasbro Children's Hospital was documented by the Providence Journal in December of 2018.

When asked how he would sum up this wonderful dog's legacy, Steve said *"Duke did a simple but powerful thing – he offered himself as a calming soul to people in pain, and in doing, he gave them moments of joy."*

As the oldest Cross kid, Steve the Storyteller has always played his role with responsibility and determination. He is the designated party host and family speaker, and by far the best of all of us at spinning a yarn!

Steve and Marcia have been happily married for more than fifty years. Through their wonderful daughter, Sarah, and her husband, Matthew Lennon, they are the devoted grandparents of Rylee Rose, and when they aren't giving Rylee all their love and attention, they spend their free time taking cruises around the world – living life to the fullest!

At left, Grandpa with Sarah and Steve, and at right, Steve and Duke.

Sarah's wedding day in 2019. From left are Brian, Mom, Pam, Sarah, Steve, Joan, and Marcia.

At left, Great-Grammy Alzada with her great-granddaughter, Rylee Rose Lennon (also at right), and Steve.

At left, me at my high school graduation after winning the "Voice of Democracy" speech contest trophy, and at right, cutting the cake with Bob at our wedding in 1975.

Mom, me, and Dad on the day I graduated from Columbia University in 1991. Almost thirty years later, in 2020, I had the great honor of receiving Columbia University's Distinguished Alumni Award.

Deborah the Executive

In my high school yearbook, I also listed college as my ambition, but while Steve was still undecided when he graduated, EVERYONE knew I would go to college – well, everyone except my junior high guidance counselor. I'll never forget the day he sat me down with my parents for a meeting about my academic future, which he began by saying – "We do not think Deborah is college material."

It hurt, but it also fueled my determination. No matter what, I was going to prove him wrong – I was going to become an educator. No matter what, I would make my dreams come true. I also knew, no matter what, my parents would be proud of me.

I'll never forget the overjoyed expressions on their faces at my high school graduation ceremony when I was awarded a trophy for winning the "Voice of Democracy" speech contest. I saw the same joy when I received my bachelor's degree from Fitchburg State, my master's degree from Salve Regina University, and then, as a mother with three children, when I earned my Doctor of Education from Columbia University. They were also there the day I was awarded Salve Regina's Distinguished Alumni Award in 1992!

My professional path began as a twelfth-grade English teacher, a route which led me straight back to Case High School in Swansea, but it didn't take long for me to realize that I wanted to make a broader systemic impact – and to do that, I had to become a student again. Since then, it's been my life's work to help people by improving the quality of life in underserved communities, and now, after a decades-long career, I've had the honor of serving as an executive with six amazing nonprofit organizations, the first being the HOPE Program in New York City.

After HOPE came the South Bronx Overall Economic Development Corporation, then Per Scholas, followed by PBS Flagship Station Channel Thirteen, then New York Junior Tennis & Learning, and finally, the Women's Sports Foundation, founded by the iconic Billie Jean King.

I'm happy to report that all six of those nonprofits are still going strong, as are many of the treasured friendships I forged along the way with so many uniquely talented colleagues, including Olga Harvey, Jean Tatge, Jaclinn Tanney, Plinio Ayala, and Aleia Naylor. In addition to Billie Jean King, I've also been blessed over the years by the wisdom of some amazing mentors, especially John Stookey, Dr. Win Adkins, Paula Kerger, and Steve Simkin.

In 2020, I was honored to receive a Distinguished Alumni Award, from Columbia University, and in 2022, I temporarily retired from the professional world. When I founded HOPE in 1984, I couldn't have imagined I would be celebrating its fortieth anniversary in 2024 – and receiving HOPE's Lifetime Achievement Award in 2025! As I look back at my fulfilling and fascinating career, I feel lucky to be able to confirm Dad's sentiments about doing something you love.

Most recently, I launched my latest adventure, The Cross Collective, and I still proudly serve on several boards, including my recent appointment to the Mayor's Health Committee for the City of Yonkers, as well as a cause very close to my heart, Rx Compassion, which Clarel and I founded in 2009, dedicated to actively addressing inequities in maternal health care.

But let's briefly go back to the very beginning of my career. The year 1974 was a busy one for me: I graduated from college, started my first job, and met my first husband, Bob MacFarlane. We married in Fall River about a year after we met, and soon we were splitting our time between New York City and Newport, raising our daughters. When our marriage ended, I stayed in New York, and it was the beginning of a new chapter – and a new love!

By the mid-2000s, I was Senior VP of Channel Thirteen, and we often held special events for donors – and prospective donors – to mix and mingle with local dignitaries and cultural luminaries. It was because of one of these special events – its cancellation, actually – that I first spoke with Dr. Clarel Antoine, one of the nation's top OB-GYNs. I called to inform him about the event and offer my regrets, and as we talked, I learned that he loved tennis – and he quickly became a "prospect" of another sort.

The first time I brought Clarel to visit my parents, we took Dad in his wheelchair to the local public tennis courts by the baseball fields where all my brothers used to play. Dad watched from the sidelines as I won the match, and later, in a private aside, he asked me – "Couldn't you have let him win a few more points?"

My answer was "No!" – not then, not now. No free points! However, when the time was right, my answer for Clarel was "Yes!" – and then "I do!"

At left, Clarel and I with Mom on our wedding day in 2010, and at right, dancing at our reception.

Clarel with his siblings on our wedding day. From left to right are Yvon, Clarel, Bepty, and Allrich.

Me, Clarel, and Nathalie.

We were married in 2010, surrounded by loved ones, and with our marriage I've gained so many magnificent new family members, including Clarel's daughter, Nathalie, and his three siblings, brothers Allrich Antoine and Yvon Antoine, and his sister, the family matriarch, Bepty Laurençon.

Clarel and I have built a wonderful life together, and when he isn't out delivering babies, we're traveling the world, most recently to Ireland and Portugal, and usually with our true-blue friends of a lifetime, Gini Wright and Mike Gill. When we're home, you can usually find us socializing or on a tennis court with more of our wonderful friends – like Mona Swanson, Mary Denham, Dick Martin, Sanne Clark, Robin Good, Pattison Youngren, and Sharman and Bob McCoach – whom I've known for more than twenty-five years.

But our greatest joy comes from spending every moment we can with our big family, especially our six grandchildren – from volleyball games and ice hockey tournaments to theatre performances and dance recitals, to the pure simple sweetness of making my little loved ones laugh!

At left, Clarel and I, ready to hit the tennis court. At right, with our dear friends Gini and Mike.

Jessica, Ab, Leila, Meriem, and me – Zizza!

At left, Rebekah and Jeff with Noah, Madeline, Luke, and Juliette. At right, Jeff's wonderful parents, Janet and John Barney.

At left, almost all six of my grandkids together in 2024. At right, me with baby Noah in 2016.

At left, Allie and JP, and at right, Grammy with Allie on her and JP's wedding day in 2019.

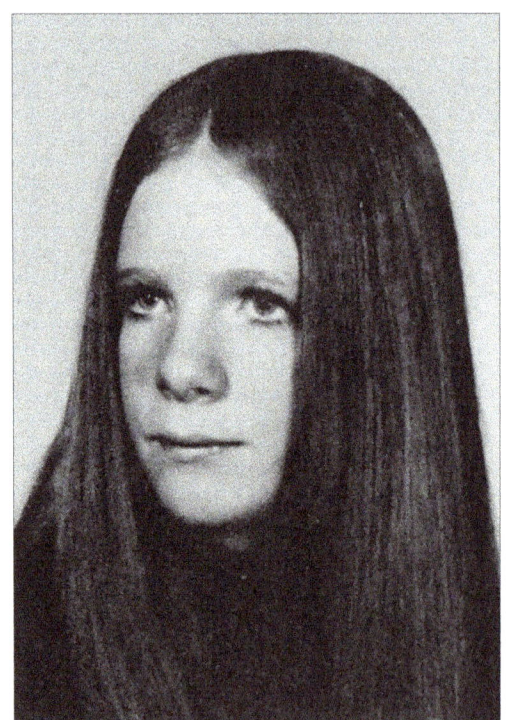 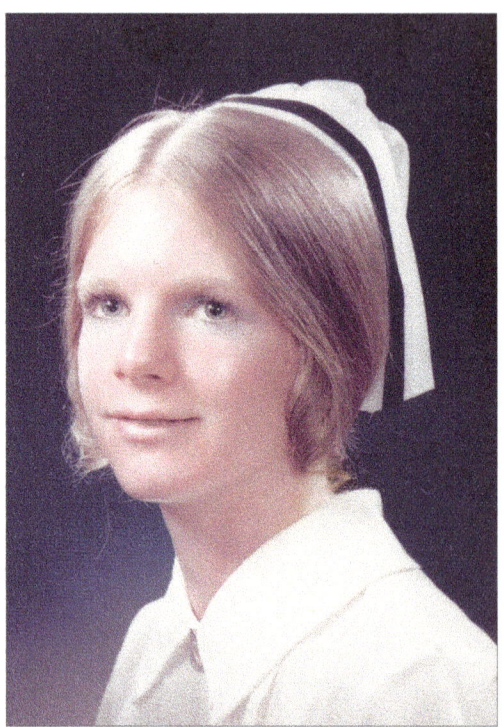

At left, Pam's senior yearbook photo, and at right, Pam in her nursing uniform.

Pam and Mark on their wedding day with Mom and Dad.

Pamela the Nurturer

Pam's senior yearbook clearly states her ambition to be a nurse, but that wasn't always her plan. She first considered being a teacher, but when she shared that idea with Mom, Pam got a gentle reminder that she didn't really enjoy speaking in front of large groups. Mom then suggested nursing, which turned out to be the perfect fit!

As Pam recalls, "Mom was the original nurturer. She always took care of us when we were sick – and when one of us got sick, we all got sick. She always thought I'd make a great nurse, and I always felt Mom would have been a great nurse."

Most of Pam's friends were planning to become teachers, but one girl was applying to nursing school and invited her along to go fill out an application.

"I got accepted," Pam recalled, "But I had never been in a hospital, never taken care of somebody that was sick. I really didn't know what I was getting into, but during the first few weeks, before we actually even started classes, we walked through the hospital and visited with patients, and I knew – I'm going to love this!"

And just like that, Pam began her decades-long career at St. Anne's Hospital in Fall River, where she became known for her dedication to her coworkers and the exceptional care she provided patients.

Pam met her husband Mark Antaya at a party in Swansea in 1980, and in 1987 they were married at our Bridlepath home in a beautiful ceremony and celebration with friends and family – which included a conga line around the swimming pool. A few years later, their wonderful son Cody arrived, bringing more joy into their lives.

Mark was an extraordinary son-in-law who lovingly cared – and cooked – for Mom and Dad, and he is also a fantastic brother-in-law, always making us laugh with his wildly wonderful sense of humor.

Pam retired from St. Anne's on July 9, 2023, exactly fifty years from the day she started, and she was honored with a special ceremony which was attended by the entire hospital nursing staff. As the guest of honor, she had written a short speech, but if you'll recall, Pam doesn't love talking in front of big groups – even a room full of people celebrating *her*.

This time, however, it was because Pam was so overcome with emotion that she couldn't speak, and she ended up handing her speech to the hospital CEO to read for her – and there wasn't a dry eye in the room.

"I will be forever grateful to my wonderful colleagues for the many opportunities, experiences, and friendships you have made possible," Pam wrote. *"You have brought meaning and joy to my life, and I cherish every moment. I have lovingly cared for my patients and their families, and they have loved me back, enriching my life with purpose and fulfillment."*

Though she is officially retired, "Nurse Pammy" remains our family nurturer, always ready to help with medical questions or concerns, always with compassion. All of us Cross siblings will forever be profoundly grateful for our sister Pam – for her naturally nurturing spirit, and for the way she cared for our parents with endless love and devotion.

At left, Mark holding newborn Cody (yes, that's a boat). At right, Cody with Grammy.

The Antayas – Mark, Pam, and Cody – at my and Clarel's wedding in 2010.

Uncle Dave with little Jessica.

Dave with Dad.

Dave the Musician

Dave somehow missed getting his senior photo into the yearbook, so allow me to paint a picture of this absolutely delightful, athletic, easy-going child, who, by high school, was an immensely talented musician, especially with percussion.

Our house was always filled with the steady rhythm of drumbeats when "Davey Boy" was around, and while our brother was always kind and respectful – and could have plenty of fun – he tended to be more withdrawn, at least compared to the rest of us.

As we would later realize, our sweet brother Dave was struggling with undiagnosed mental illness, and it made high school very difficult for him. But his talent shone through, and Dave was accepted into the prestigious Berklee College of Music in Boston.

Unfortunately, it was during his time in college that Dave got involved in a religious group that promised to help him conquer his mental illness. Mom became concerned when he started talking about "auditing" and "going clear," and then he explained that he was also working for twenty cents an hour and giving all his earnings back to the church.

Mom confided in Steve, who was a young police officer at the time, and when Steve, suspecting a scam, went to Boston to check on Dave, he quickly realized that it wasn't just a scam – it was a cult. Steve managed to get our brother away from it, but it took years before Dave actually quit of his own volition. He still gets mail from them.

Music will always be a big part of Dave's life. He still plays percussion and guitar, and while he's definitely the most musical of all six Cross kids, he's also an excellent photographer, as well as a gifted writer.

Dave was happily married to his wife Theresa for many years, until her passing in December of 2023. In a very happy twist, Dave now lives with and is lovingly cared for by the second-to-last Cross kid, our brainy brother Brian.

Above, Theresa and Dave, and below, Dave with Mom.

At top, Benjamin, Dave, Dad, Brian, and Allan doing karaoke. At bottom left, all six with Mom, and at bottom right, me, Dave, and our nephew Allan out boating.

At top left, Brian's senior photo, and at top right, Eleana and Brian on their wedding day. Below, Brian and Eleana's children, Allan, Benjamin, and Brian, with their cousin Cody at the very back.

Brian the Brain

Brian's yearbook ambitions were "college…and pinball" – and as a math club member for four years, it was no surprise that he even had the audacity to get perfect SAT scores!

Even as a small child, brainy Brian had an enormous gift for numbers, and Mom always loved telling the story of how, at a very young age, Brian critiqued a contestant's wager on the TV game show *Jeopardy!*, explaining to her that if the player had bet differently on the final question, he would have won.

Just like Mom, Brian has a razor-sharp wit and tremendous talent for trivia, puzzles, and games – but he would tell you he was a challenging kid, and as an adult, he now wonders if his frequently wandering focus was due to an attention deficit disorder.

One early instance – and also a charming family memory – comes from when Dad was managing Brian's local Pee Wee softball team. Brian, who was supposed to be playing center field, often lost interest in the game, and would instead chase after butterflies.

Brian did go to college – and play pinball – and after excelling at UMass Dartmouth in classes that he enjoyed, he decided to withdraw just a few credits shy of earning a bachelor's degree. It was unexpected, but no one worried, and Brian remains the undisputed math and technology whiz of the family! He can fix any hardware, learn any software, and, most impressively, can teach anyone how to do something for themselves – from Excel spreadsheet lessons and SAT prep to fixing a lawnmower. No matter what it is, just ask Brian – not only will he help you figure it out, you're sure to have fun doing it!

Brian met his wife, Eleana Serrano, while she was a nanny for our third daughter, Allie. Before we knew it, they were in love, and soon they were married in Steve and Marcia's Rhode Island home. With his marriage, Brian gained a wonderful son, Allan, and together Brian and Eleana had two more – Benjamin and Brian. Though they later divorced, we all love Eleana dearly, and she will always be a Crazy Cross!

Brian always had a very close relationship with Dad, but their bond grew even stronger when Brian became a father, as he could finally understand the stresses and worries of being a parent. Much like Dad, Brian also possesses a genuine enthusiasm for life and a boundless capacity for generosity, kindness, and humor.

He's even developed his own form of Dadisms, which I call Brianisms. I love his way of making a point by asking – *"Any comments, questions, or concerns?"* – and I find it very useful when sending an especially good tennis shot sailing past Clarel! But my favorite has to be Brian's gentle way of calling out selfish behavior by simply saying – *"You're better than that."*

Brian no doubt has the biggest brain of us Cross kids, but he also has one of the biggest hearts, and it's hard for my siblings and I to adequately describe our eternal gratitude for Brian, who so lovingly and selflessly cared for Mom in her final years, and who now gives the same loving care to our brother Dave.

 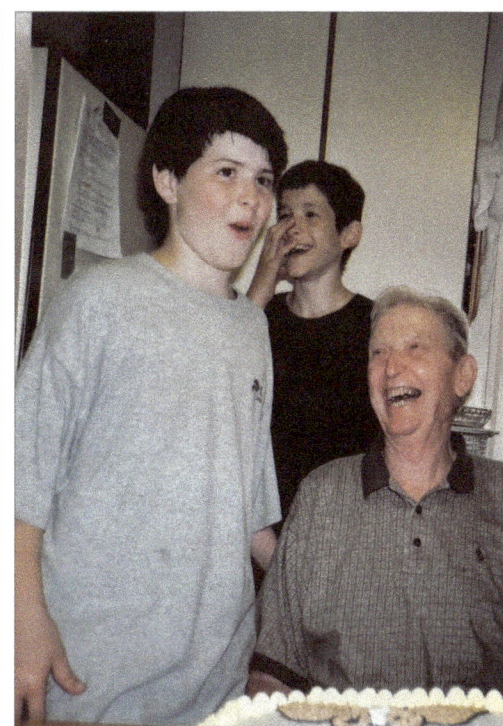

At left, Allan with Grandpa, and at right, Brian and Ben with Grandpa.

At left, Eleana, Brian, and Ben with Mom, and at right, Brian with his wife Natalie in 2024.

At left, four-year-old Dana, and at right, teenage Dana running cross country for Case High School.

Dana and Linda on their wedding day in 1985. From left to right are Brian, Steve, Marcia, Mark, Pam, Dave, Linda, Dana, Mom, Dad, Rebekah, me (pregnant with Allie), Jessica, and Bob.

Dana the Individualist

Dana didn't submit anything for his senior yearbook, but that's just Dana! He does his own thing and was never big on being in the spotlight, although he was co-captain of the cross country team. There are, however, some group photos in which Dana appears, and his National Honor Society and ski club photos suggest they caught him on the same day – same shirt, same smile. And, though he didn't list his ambitions, in the "Last Will and Testament" of the class, Dana says he *"leaves with 'high' hopes"* (which we can only assume is some kind of chairlift reference).

As the baby of the family, Dana knows he was "the favorite" – the one who, in Mom's eyes, could do no wrong, and who was therefore allowed to do pretty much anything – but I think it also allowed his extremely inquisitive and individualistic nature to flourish!

Dana's early and prolonged exposure to all things electrical and mechanical, combined with his natural aptitude for math and science, made a career in engineering a natural fit. After graduating from UMass Lowell, he quickly found a job, and since the 1990s he's enjoyed a long and successful career as an engineer with Raytheon.

Dana has two wonderful children, Dylan and Kayla, with his first wife Linda, whom he married in 1985, though they later divorced.

In 2010, Dana married Sawako Fukushima in a beautiful Japanese ceremony in Hawaii. Mom made the long trip, together with Steve, Brian and me, and we were all so happy to meet Sawako's mother and relatives from Japan. We also had some great island adventures! At first, Mom was worried she would slow us down or hinder our fun, but the boys weren't going to let that get in the way of a great day on Big Island Beach.

Cross cousins – Cody, Dylan, Benjamin, Brian, and Kayla.

Dylan and his wife Julia in 2024.

They rented a floating wheelchair with large, buoyant wheels made to move speedily over sand and safely enjoy the water, and though Mom was reluctant at first – "Oh, Brian!" – we got her cruising in no time.

Mom absolutely adored Sawako, who visited her almost every day, and we are so grateful for all the joy she brought to Mom in her golden years – as well as all of the spectacular family dinners she's prepared and hosted over the years, always with grace and a smile.

Dana, as a do-it-yourself guru, once bought a house that had been stripped to its bare bones and, in a phenomenal transformation, restored the whole thing all on his own. Electrician, mason, roofer, carpenter, landscaper, he also rebuilt his home on Little Neck Island – a home which happens to sit on the Lees River, giving our family 24/7 access to experiment any time we want with anything that floats!

In Hawaii for Dana and Sawako's wedding. Left to right are Sawako, Steve, Dana, me, Mom, and Brian.

All six in 2023.

The Ancestral Symphony

Many cultures sing the stories of their ancestors, preserving memories in the poetry of their people, and this memoir is a written celebration of Mr. and Mrs. Wonderful, composed with love.

With our parents gone, my siblings and I now hold the present responsibility of bridging past and future by preserving and passing down our family stories: by telling our true tales of resilience, kindness, humor, and love, and in doing so, connecting those who came before with those who followed, and with those yet to be born.

Each of us is a single string of notes in a much grander masterpiece stretching back generations, creating our own unique variations on the same miraculous melody, a continuous symphony of life. But, in the Crazy Cross cantata, there's no such thing as perfect pitch, and part of what makes my family so wonderful is how perfectly imperfect we are.

Let's play our notes fully, with intention and joy. It's not about delivering a perfect performance – the important thing is being together and raising our voices in celebration, whether with solemn remembrance or joyful clanking on the kitchen table with forks and spoons!

So, here's to keeping the music going – as Shakespeare wrote in the opening line of *Twelfth Night*:

"If music be the food of love, play on!"

Afterword

I never imagined that tracing my past would be such an exhilarating adventure. It feels like being a detective in my own historical mystery, piecing together clues and discovering "notes" in my own ancestral symphony I'd never even heard of.

Nowadays, uncovering the stories of our ancestors – which is so much more than just names and dates – has never been easier. I've been using Ancestry.com to compose my family tree, which currently has more than 5,000 people among its many roots and branches. Attached to these people are more than 31,000 records, which includes census data, city directory listings, military information, newspaper articles, photographs, and documentation for births, marriages, and deaths, along with countless research notes from the Ancestry.com community. These facts and figures are woven into the stories of this memoir, but are far too numerous to be included as footnotes, and curious readers are most welcome to go directly to my public "Cross / Weaver Family Tree" on Ancestry.com!

And then there's the modern-day "magic" of DNA technology, which, in addition to revealing your genealogical past, can connect you with living relatives in the present you didn't even know existed. I've been lucky to find several – Barbara Ashworth, Lynne Gifford, Carol Reed, Matthew Reed, Deborah Van Zee, and William Veselik – and getting closer to these distant cousins has enriched my life in the most wonderful ways.

Newspapers.com has been another valuable tool. I've uncovered everything from the tragic headlines of my Great-Grandmother Alzada's *"brutal outrage"* to the *"merry sailing"* trip that left my three-year-old Grandma Alice with a head injury. It's also where I discovered the *"spectral hand"* of my Spiritualist Great-Grandmother Angelina.

Many more resources await the eager researcher. You can browse online from the comfort of your home, or visit libraries, museums, and historical societies, which hold countless undigitized records, newspapers, and genealogical books.

A wonderful resource for me was the Swansea Free Public Library, and there's also the affiliated "Tuesday Club," which meets weekly to discuss the methods – and madness! – of researching family history. Many modern libraries are connected to the past in some way, from housing rooms full of records to hosting free genealogy seminars, like the ones I've benefited from through the New York Public Library.

Some places hold actual ancestral artifacts – it was in the Barracks Museum in Eastport, Maine, where I discovered postcards demonstrating Reverend Thomas the Great's wooing of the formidable Nettie Holmes!

What I absolutely cherished the most, however, was traveling to the places my ancestors lived. Walking in their footsteps put everything together for me in the most adventurous, enlightening, and emotional ways. The images and feelings that washed over me when I stood on the dock in Liverpool – where, over a century ago, Angelina and five of her children departed for America – linger with me still.

You don't need to be an expert historian – I'm certainly not – but over time, I've become a better detective, and I always feel rewarded by what I learn, even with the smallest of new details. And you can always team up with an expert if you need to – I definitely did!

I've had some wise help along the way, and I'm most grateful to memoir specialist Lilian Duval, who thought I had a story to share; my collaborator, fellow traveler, and Rishton historian, Pamela Edgar; Sandra Harwitt, a freelance journalist who kept me going during the pandemic; and my editor, Jane Disla, whose patience and wisdom flow in equal measure.

Of all the images, information, and insights contained within these pages, some of the most precious inclusions have come from my first cousins, to whom I'm so thankful: Susan Blackburn; Robert Weaver; Diane Blandin Napier, widow of Jack, who passed away in 2023; and my curious collaborator, Cathy (Pereira) Catudal.

I'm blessed and especially grateful for the many spoken stories and traditions we've preserved, all captured on film during visits and interviews I've had with my siblings, my Aunt Joan, and, most special of all, with Mom.

Several years before she passed away, I talked with Mom on video for hours, and her stories, laughter, tears, and beautiful singing are now priceless gifts our family will eternally treasure.

May your own future voyage into the past be just as meaningful. I wish you Godspeed on your journey.

– Deborah the Writer

Index

Accrington, England ... 290, 293, 300
Ainsworth, Margaret ... 282, 287, 291-92
American Civil War ... 259-60, 275, 276, 295-96
American Revolutionary War ... 244, 249, 256
Antaya, Cody ... 371, 390, 409, 422, 439-41, 446
Antaya, Mark ... 82, 422, 438-41
Antaya, Pamela (Cross) ... 12, 18, 21, 23, 26, 30-31, 36, 39-41, 46, 50, 74-75, 82-84, 87-89, 92, 370, 380, 386, 401-03, 405, 411, 415, 416-418, 422, 425, 429, 438-41, 445, 450, 454
Antoine, Clarel ... 9, 38, 82, 234, 331, 334, 349-50, 353, 355, 357, 411, 416, 422, 432-35, 448
Ashworth, Albert ... 189, 304
Ashworth, Barbara ... 304, 335-37, 457
Ashworth, Eliza (Cross) ... 182, 189-90, 219, 282, 304, 307-08, 312, 320, 322, 325-30, 360-61
Ashworth, Norman ... 282, 304
Ashworth, Russell ... 282, 304

Bahamas ... 376-77
Barney, Janet ... 436
Barney, Jeff ... 411, 422, 436
Barney, John ... 436
Barney, Juliette ... 411, 416-17, 422, 436
Barney, Luke ... 411, 422, 436-37
Barney, Madeline ... 72, 411, 422, 436-37
Barney, Noah ... 411, 422, 436-37

Barney, Rebekah (MacFarlane) ... 9, 162, 371-73, 375, 380, 383, 390, 396-497, 409, 411, 422, 436, 450
Beech Grove Cemetery ... 105, 226, 261, 358
Blackburn, Lancashire ... 283, 286-90, 291, 293, 295-96, 299-300, 307-308, 313-17
Blackburn, Susan (Weaver) ... 107, 120-121, 154, 459
Borden, Lizzie ... 267, 276
Boston, MA ... 57, 60, 90, 217, 229, 241, 244, 245, 252, 259, 276, 320, 323, 343, 353, 354, 355, 384, 443
Bristol, RI ... 109, 229, 247, 252-257, 260, 268
Burns, Theresa ... 422, 444

Cape of Good Hope Colony ... 299-300
Catudal, Cathy (Pereira) ... 58, 196, 199, 210, 212, 345, 347, 349, 370, 459
Christmas ... 26, 27, 54, 80, 82, 86-91, 98, 125, 174, 204, 206, 209, 211, 299, 315, 320, 354, 357, 372, 412, 418, 423
Coggeshall ... 240, 242, 243-246, 249
Connecticut ... 19-20, 50-51, 68, 81, 170, 205, 256
Cooke, Francis ... 230-33
County Armagh, Ireland ... 338-342
Cross, Alice (Gates) ... 19-20, 57-59, 83, 182-83, 187, 190-92, 194-202, 203, 208, 209, 211, 219, 221, 338-339, 370, 457

Cross, Allan . . . 38, 371, 390, 409, 422, 442, 445, 446-449
Cross, Angelina (Whittaker) . . . 182-83, 189, 192, 282-84, 287, 289-91, 293-95, 297, 301-02, 305-09, 310, 316, 318, 320-22, 323-28, 329, 331-334, 335-37, 339, 343, 354, 358-61, 457, 458
Cross, Benjamin . . . 371, 390, 409, 422, 445, 446-449
Cross, Brian . . . 12, 18, 22-23, 30-31, 37-38, 39-41, 42, 44, 48-49, 55, 58, 67, 84, 87, 91, 92, 149, 392, 412-413, 415, 416, 418, 422, 423, 425, 429, 444-45, 446-49, 450-52, 454
Cross, Brian Jr. . . . 371, 390, 409, 422, 446-449
Cross, Cecil . . . 57-59, 81, 182-84, 187-188, 189-93, 196-97, 208-11, 218, 219-21, 282, 284, 307, 322, 342, 346, 353
Cross, Dana . . . 12, 18, 22-23, 31, 32-34, 38, 39, 42, 44, 92, 220, 268, 378, 384, 392, 411, 415, 422, 425, 445, 450-53, 454
Cross, David . . . 12, 18, 22-23, 30-31, 32, 39-41, 42, 44, 48, 50, 52, 67-69, 72, 84, 86, 91, 92, 370, 392, 415, 422, 425, 442-45, 448, 450, 454
Cross, Dylan . . . 371, 390, 409, 422, 451-53
Cross, Ivy . . . 182, 189-90, 219, 307, 312, 320, 346, 360-61
Cross, Kayla . . . 371, 390, 409, 422, 451-52
Cross, Marcia (Lombardo) . . . 82, 92, 370, 385, 422, 426-29, 448, 450
Cross, Mary (Bonsall) . . . 182, 282, 287, 299-300
Cross, Natalie (Mendez) . . . 422, 449

Cross, Nettie (Holmes) . . . 190, 283-84, 348-53, 355-57, 359, 458
Cross, Steven . . . 12, 13, 18-21, 29, 31, 35, 36, 38, 39-41, 43-44, 50, 52-55, 61-62, 64, 67, 71-72, 73, 79-80, 82, 84, 86-90, 92, 120, 122, 124-126, 207, 370, 384-85, 387-88, 392, 403, 405-08, 412, 415-18, 425, 426-29, 431, 443, 448, 450, 451, 453, 454
Cross, Thomas (the Elder) . . . 182, 282, 299-301, 307-308, 343
Cross, Thomas (the Great) . . . 182, 187-188, 189-90, 282-83, 284-85, 287, 297, 299-301, 302-05, 306-310, 313-18, 319-24, 325-30, 329, 335-37, 339, 342, 343-47, 348-54, 356, 360, 458
Cross, Thomas Jr. . . . 182, 190, 282, 307, 320-21, 344, 346

Dadisms . . . 63-66, 217, 367, 397, 406, 408, 423, 448
Dartmouth, MA . . . 229, 252-53, 256, 259, 261, 268, 447
Darwen, Lancashire . . . 291, 293
Durfee High School . . . 45, 119, 163, 164-167, 171, 205, 209, 391
Dyer . . . 246

Easter . . . 18, 26, 32, 52, 121, 348, 350, 356, 372, 418
Eastport, ME . . . 190, 345, 349-50, 353, 355-57, 359, 458
Edgar, Pamela . . . 307, 335-37
English Civil War . . . 239, 288
Estes . . . 261, 268

Index

Fall River, MA ... 7, 15, 17, 19-20, 23, 26, 39-41, 53-54, 58, 62, 71, 97, 99-101, 103-05, 108-13, 119-20, 123-25, 129, 132, 137, 141, 171-173, 179, 186-92, 195, 199-201, 209-10, 215, 219, 221, 251, 252, 257, 259-60, 261, 267-69, 272-277, 284, 319-24, 325-30, 342, 343-45, 354, 358-59, 371, 384, 391, 432, 439
Fish ... 224, 230, 256, 258, 260, 270
Florida ... 175, 205, 377, 412, 415
Foxwoods Casino ... 68-69, 384, 388-89
Freeborn ... 241-244, 245-47, 250
Freetown, MA 126, 229, 251, 251-53, 256
Frew, Rand ... 397-99
Fukushima, Sawako ... 411, 422, 451-53

Gates, Agnes ... 220-21
Gates, Eliza ... 221
Gates, Irving (Uncle Red) ... 182, 219-21
Gates, James ... 182, 195, 200-01, 221, 338-42
Gates, Jane (Stratton) ... 182, 195, 221, 338-42
Gates, John ... 182, 195, 221, 338-42
Gates, Lottie (Jones) ... 182, 195-96, 200-01, 339, 359
Gifford, Alzada Estes ... 96-97, 102-03, 105, 114, 117, 141, 161-62, 224-226, 230, 238, 258-60, 259-60, 261-62, 263-66, 267-70, 271-73, 275-79, 334, 358-59, 457
Gifford, Eli ... 96, 102, 224, 230, 238-40, 258-60, 261, 271-72, 358
Gifford, Frank Bradford ... 96, 102-03, 105, 114, 117, 136-43, 226, 267-270, 273, 278

Gifford, Helen (Hale) ... 102, 105, 136-42
Gifford, Lynne ... 231, 457
Gifford, Susan (Pettey) ... 96, 102, 224, 230, 256, 258-60, 261, 270, 271, 358
Gifford, William ... 230, 238-40, 256
Great Harwood Cemetery ... 292-93, 307
Greece ... 378, 380-81

Halloween ... 26, 329-30, 372-73, 407
Hamdoun, Abdessalam ... 82, 393, 396, 399, 422, 436
Hamdoun, Leila ... 8, 56, 78, 399, 403-04, 413, 436-37
Hamdoun, Meriem ... 8, 56, 78, 399, 403-04, 413, 436-37
Hart, Minnie (Cross) ... 182, 189-90, 219, 307, 318, 320, 322
Haworth, Ivy ... 282, 321, 343-44, 354
Haworth, John Drudy ... 189, 343, 354
Haworth, Lillian (Cross) ... 142, 182, 189, 192, 304, 307-08, 312, 320-321, 323, 326, 329, 337, 343-44, 354, 358-61
Holmes, Marie ... 355
Horseneck Beach ... 38, 120, 173
Hutchinson, Anne ... 243, 245, 247

Ireland ... 285, 287, 299, 321, 338-42, 435
Italy ... 138-39, 216

Jones, Hannah (Hinchcliffe) ... 182, 195
Jones, John ... 182, 195
Joseph Case High School ... 76, 423, 426, 438, 446, 450

Kancamagus Highway ... 34
King Philip's War ... 250, 253-55

Lake ... 224, 230, 256
Lancashire, England ... 63, 283, 285-86, 287-90, 291-93, 294-97, 299-301, 309-12, 313-18, 319, 335-337, 339, 343, 361
Lees River ... 37-38, 452
Lennon, Matthew ... 411, 422, 428
Lennon, Rylee ... 411, 422, 428-29
Lennon, Sarah (Cross) ... 371, 390, 409, 411, 422, 426-29
Lincoln, Abraham ... 236, 295, 313
Little Neck Island ... 13, 18-23, 37, 61, 65, 208, 253, 452
Liverpool, England ... 195, 286, 289, 296, 297, 299, 320, 335-37, 340, 342, 458

MacFarlane, Alexandra ... 82, 236, 371-373, 375, 390, 396-97, 409, 411, 413, 422, 437, 450
MacFarlane, Jessica ... 26-27, 62, 82, 369, 370-73, 375-77, 380, 390, 393, 396, 399, 403, 409, 413, 422, 423-424, 436, 442, 450
MacFarlane, Robert ... 43-44, 85, 92, 370-71, 376-77, 380, 388, 396-397, 422, 430, 432
Manchester, England ... 286, 295-96, 299, 310
Massachusetts Bay Colony ... 229, 239-240, 241-44, 249, 252-53
Massasoit ... 236, 253
Mayflower ... 96, 225, 230- 235, 239
Metacomet ... 254-55
Middleborough, MA ... 229, 251

Middletown, RI ... 244, 245
Mount Hope ... 229, 252, 254
Mount Hope Cemetery ... 9, 277, 408-09

Napier, Diane ... 459
Napier, George ... 50, 81-85, 203-07, 213, 218, 370
Napier, Irene (Cross) ... 26, 50, 70, 81-84, 182, 185, 187, 192, 203, 204-207, 209-211, 213, 216, 370
Napier, Jack ... 84-85, 203, 205-06, 459
Napier, Michael ... 85, 203, 205-06
New Hampshire ... 32, 43, 210
New Jersey ... 20, 79, 110
New York ... 139, 146, 152-54, 169-70, 172, 174, 195, 313, 320, 355, 374-375, 388, 394-99, 403, 415, 431-433, 458
New York City, NY ... 146, 152-154, 169-170, 172, 174, 331, 335, 375, 394-398, 431-33
Newport, RI ... 120, 129, 187, 192, 205, 209, 229, 244, 245-47, 249, 252, 373, 383, 388, 397, 432
North Carolina ... 210, 228, 396-97

Oak Grove Cemetery ... 58, 141, 167, 173, 324, 354
Orleans, MA ... 190, 353
Ormerod, Caroline (Gifford) ... 102-03, 105, 114, 135, 137, 140-43, 175, 262, 270
Ormerod, William ... 102, 141, 270

Pease ... 248-51
Pendle Hill, Lancashire ... 286, 288
Pereira, Ed (uncle) ... 81, 203, 210-213
Pereira, Eddie (cousin) ... 203, 210-12

Pereira, Joan (Cross) ... 19, 58, 81-85, 192, 196, 199, 203, 207, 208-13, 345, 370, 429, 459
Pettey, Elusana (Fish) ... 224, 230, 254, 258, 260, 270
Picha, Julia ... 422, 453
Plymouth Colony ... 228-29, 231-33, 235-37, 239, 245, 250-51, 253-54
Pokanoket ... 236, 253-54
Ponca ... 236-37
Portsmouth, RI ... 129, 229, 241, 243-44, 245-47, 249, 252
Preston, Lancashire ... 286, 289, 291, 299
Prettybull, JP ... 236, 422, 437
Providence, RI ... 58, 68, 81, 85, 196, 199, 205, 210, 229, 239, 241, 243, 245, 252, 346, 387, 427-28

Quakers (Society of Friends) ... 227, 239-40, 243, 245, 249, 310

Raytheon ... 45-46, 451
Recipe, Nana's Doughnuts ... 54
Recipe, Pam's Cheese Dip ... 88
Reed, Anne ... 138, 140
Reed, Bradford ... 138, 140
Reed, Carol ... 138, 140-42, 457
Reed, Holly ... 138, 140
Reed, Janice ... 138, 140
Reed, Jonathan ... 138, 140
Reed, Loren ... 102, 139-141, 216
Reed, Matthew ... 138, 140-41, 457
Reed, Patricia (Gifford) ... 102, 105, 136-142, 216
Reynolds ... 224, 248-50
Rhode Island Colony ... 229, 239, 241-244, 245-47, 249, 252-55

Rishton, England ... 189, 286, 289, 292, 297, 298-99, 300-01, 303-05, 307-11, 312, 313-18, 319, 335-337, 343, 361, 458
Roanoke Colony ... 228
Roderick, Jennifer (Pereira) ... 83, 203, 210
Rothwell, Cynthia (Weaver) ... 52, 61, 117, 121, 154, 173-74

Salem Witch Trials ... 250-51
Salem, MA ... 239, 241, 250-51
Scotland ... 124, 299, 340, 356
Serrano, Eleana ... 422, 446-49
Soule, George ... 230-33, 235
Spiritualism ... 310, 313-20, 324, 325-330, 331-34, 360, 457
Sturbridge, MA ... 144-45
Swansea, MA ... 9, 13, 18-23, 35, 48-49, 53, 65, 67, 77, 90, 109, 198, 208, 221, 229, 247, 251, 252-57, 262, 263, 277, 359, 371, 375, 391, 409, 411-12, 415, 423, 431, 439, 458
Switzerland ... 377-78, 382

Taunton, MA ... 229, 252-53
Thanksgiving ... 81-85, 87, 235-37, 254, 370, 418
Tiverton, RI ... 229, 252, 256, 257, 261

Urbowicz, Linda ... 422, 450-51

Valentine's Day ... 103, 271
Van Zee, Deborah ... 457
Veselik, William ... 258-59, 457
Virginia ... 228-29, 277
Virginia Colony ... 228-29

Wales ... 229, 249, 285, 299
Wampanoag ... 235-236, 241, 243, 253-54
Washington, D.C. ... 259, 377, 397
Weaver II, Parker ... 96, 108-109, 113, 246-47, 248, 253, 277
Weaver, Betty (Wise) ... 17, 23, 61, 107, 117, 118, 120, 127, 155, 171-73, 175, 177, 178-79
Weaver, Emma (Brailey) ... 108-09, 113, 224, 247, 248-49, 253, 276-77, 359
Weaver, Frank ... 17, 23, 61, 96, 98, 99, 102, 105-06, 113-17, 118-121, 123, 127, 155, 158, 166, 172-73, 176, 273
Weaver, Joan ... 23, 117, 122, 124, 126
Weaver, Johanna (Kelly) ... 23, 117, 122, 124-26
Weaver, Louis Crandall ... 23, 58, 96-98, 105-06, 108-15, 117, 119, 123, 127-28, 129-30, 137, 144-47, 166-67, 224, 244, 248, 253, 276-77
Weaver, Lydia (Manchester) ... 224, 245-247
Weaver, Robert ... 23, 117, 122, 124, 126, 459
Weaver, Susan (Gifford) ... 19-21, 52-56, 57-58, 87, 96-98, 99-100, 102, 103-108, 110-115, 117, 119-120, 123-24, 127, 129, 133-135, 137-138, 141-142, 146, 153, 155, 157-158, 161-162, 166, 169-170, 171-172, 174, 175-177, 224, 226, 253, 262, 270, 271-73, 275-278
Weaver, William "Joe" ... 23, 96, 98, 99, 105-06, 114-117, 119, 122-126, 130, 144-45, 166, 172, 174, 175-177, 179

Wesley, John ... 303-04, 340
Westport, MA ... 105, 161, 226, 229, 252, 256, 259-60, 261, 272, 358-59
Weymouth, MA ... 229, 244
Whittaker, Seth ... 282, 287, 291-92, 293, 295, 297
Williams, Roger ... 241, 243, 245
World War I ... 100, 109, 155, 189, 277, 401
World War II ... 62, 71, 109, 124, 154, 156-57, 165-66, 172, 175, 179, 214-218
Wright 230, 256, 339
Wright, Sarah (Soule) ... 230

Zizza ... 56, 399, 413, 436

www.ingramcontent.com/pod-product-compliance
Lightning Source LLC
Chambersburg PA
CBHW041035050426
42337CB00060B/5123